Marcel Alexande [redacted]

Mr Boyd Room 138

McGraw-Hill Ryerson

SCIENCE LINKS 10

Authors

Jonathan Bocknek
B.A.
Science Writer

Jenna Dunlop
Ph.D., M.B.A.
Science Writer

Lois Edwards
Ph.D.
Science Writer

Beth Lisser
B.Sc. (Hons.), B.Ed., M.Ed.
Peel District School Board

Barbara Nixon-Ewing
B.Sc. (Hons.), B.Ed.
Ontario Institute for Studies in Education
Seconded from Toronto District School Board

Sandy Searle
B.Sc. (Hons.), M.B.A.
Calgary Board of Education
Calgary, Alberta

Christine Weber
B.Sc.
Science Writer

Contributing Authors

J. Randy Attwood
B.Sc.
Science Writer

Andrew Borkowski
B.A.
Professional Writer

Eric Brown
B.A.Sc., M.Sc.T(P)
Peel District Board of Education (retired)

Glen Hutton
B.Sc., B.Ed., M.Ed.
Science Writer

Natasha Marko
B.Sc., M.Sc., M.A.
Science Writer

Program Consultant

Beth Lisser
B.Sc. (Hons.), B.Ed., M.Ed.
Peel District School Board
Brampton, Ontario

Curriculum and Pedagogical Consultants

Tigist Amdemichael
B.Sc., B.A., B.Ed., M.Ed.
Toronto District School Board
Toronto, Ontario

Stephanie Grant
B.Sc., B.Ed.
Dufferin-Peel Catholic District School Board
Mississauga, Ontario

Assessment Consultant

Katy Farrow
B.Sc., B.Ed., M.Ed.
Thames Valley District School Board
London, Ontario

Literacy Consultants

Steve Bibla
B.Sc., B.Ed.
Toronto District School Board

Beth Lisser
B.Sc. (Hons.), B.Ed., M.Ed.
Peel District School Board
Brampton, Ontario

Differentiated Instruction Consultant

Nadine Morrison
B.Sc., B.A., B.Ed., French & I.B. Cert.
Hamilton Wentworth District School Board
Hamilton, Ontario

ELL Consultants

Wendy Campbell
B.A., B.Ed.
Waterloo Region District School Board

Maureen Innes
B.A.
Nipissing University

Al Tordjman
B.A., B.Ed.
Waterloo Region District School Board

Advisors

Patricia Gaspar
B.Sc. (Hons.), B.Ed.
Head of Science, King City Secondary School
York Region District School Board

Keith Gibbons
B.Sc., B.Ed.
London District Catholic School Board
London, Ontario

John Hallett
B.Sc., B.Ed.
Peel District School Board
Caledon, Ontario

Kay Moreland-Stephen
B.Sc., B.Ed.
Ottawa Carleton Catholic School Board
Ottawa, Ontario

Mirella Sanwalka
B.Sc., B.Ed.
York Region District School Board
Newmarket, Ontario

McGraw-Hill Ryerson

Toronto Montréal Boston Burr Ridge, IL Dubuque, IA Madison, WI New York San Francisco
St. Louis Bangkok Bogotá Caracas Kuala Lumpur Lisbon London Madrid Mexico City
Milan New Delhi Santiago Seoul Singapore Sydney Taipei

The McGraw·Hill Companies

McGraw-Hill Ryerson

Copies of this book may be obtained by contacting:

McGraw-Hill Ryerson Ltd.

Web site:

http://www.mcgrawhill.ca

Toll-free fax:

1-800-463-5885

Toll-free call:

1-800-565-5758

or by mailing your order to:

McGraw-Hill Ryerson
Order Department
300 Water Street
Whitby, ON L1N 9B6

Please quote the ISBN and title when placing your order.

Student Text ISBN:

978-0-07-072221-7

Science Links 10

ISBN-13:978-0-07-072221-7
ISBN-10: 0-07-072221-8

http://www.mcgrawhill.ca

1 2 3 4 5 6 7 8 9 0 TCP 8 7 6 5 4 3 2 1 0

Printed and bound in Canada

Care has been taken to trace ownership of copyright material contained in this text. The publishers will gladly accept any information that will enable them to rectify any reference or credit in subsequent printings.

PUBLISHER: Diane Wyman
PROJECT MANAGER: Susan Girvan
DEVELOPMENTAL EDITORS: Jon Bocknek, Lois Edwards, Julie Karner, Rita Vandenheuvel, Christine Weber
MANAGING EDITOR: Crystal Shortt
SUPERVISING EDITOR: Janie Deneau
COPY EDITOR: Paula Pettitt-Townsend
PROOFREADERS: Andrew Borkowski, James Gladstone
PHOTO RESEARCH/PERMISSIONS: Linda Tanaka
ART BUYING: Pronk&Associates
REVIEW COORDINATOR: Alexandra Savage-Ferr
EDITORIAL ASSISTANT: Michelle Malda
MANAGER, PRODUCTION SERVICES: Yolanda Pigden
PRODUCTION COORDINATOR: Lena Keating
COVER DESIGN: Pronk&Associates
ELECTRONIC PAGE MAKE-UP: Pronk&Associates
COVER IMAGES:
Top right image ©PHOTOTAKE Inc./Alamy
Top middle image ©Matthias Kulka/zefa/Corbis
Top left image ©Andrew Syred/Photo Researchers, Inc.
Bottom right image ©MITSUTOSHI KIMURA/amanaimages/Corbis
Bottom left image ©Paul Souders/Corbis

The pages within this book were printed on paper containing 30% Post-Consumer Fiber.

Acknowledgements

Pedagogical Reviewers

Elizabeth Frawley
Durham Catholic
District School Board
Whitby, Ontario

Keith Gibbons
London District Catholic School Board
London, Ontario

Mari Hakim
Greater Essex County
District School Board
Windsor, Ontario

Stephen Jacobs
Dufferin-Peel Catholic
District School Board
Mississauga, Ontario

Christopher Meyer
Toronto District School Board
North York, Ontario

Frank Mustoe
Former Science Coordinator
University of Toronto Schools

Annette Nelson-Szpak
Greater Essex County
District School Board
Windsor, Ontario

Stephen Park
Durham District School Board
Oshawa, Ontario

Jason Pavelich
Peel District School Board
Mississauga, Ontario

Jim Raso
Niagara Catholic District School Board
Welland, Ontario

Mary-Ann Rupcich
Dufferin-Peel Catholic
District School Board
Mississauga, Ontario

Philip Snider
Lambton-Kent District School Board
Chatham, Ontario

Patricia Thomas
Ottawa-Carleton District School Board
Ottawa, Ontario

Frank Villella
Hamilton Wentworth Catholic
District School Board
Hamilton, Ontario

Accuracy Reviewers

Robert Noble (Unit 1)
B.Sc., M.Sc., B.Ed.
Toronto Catholic District School Board
Toronto, Ontario

John F. Eix (Unit 2)
B.Sc. (Hons.), B.Ed., M.Ed.
Upper Canada College (retired)
Toronto, Ontario

Harvey Shear (Unit 3)
Ph.D.
Professor, Department of Geography
University of Toronto
Mississauga, Ontario

T. J. Elgin Wolfe (Unit 4)
M.Ed.
Professor, Ontario Institute for
Studies in Education
University of Toronto
Toronto, Ontario

Bias and Equity Reviewer

Nancy Christoffer
Scarborough, Ontario

Lab Testers

Leesa Blake
Toronto District School Board
Toronto, Ontario

Clyde Ramlochan
Toronto District School Board
North York, Ontario

Sharon Ramlochan
Toronto District School Board
North York, Ontario

Safety Reviewer

Jim Agban
Past Chair, STAO Safety Committee
Mississauga, Ontario

Aboriginal Content Reviewer

Francis McDermott
Shabot Obaadjiwan Algonquin First Nation
Shawville, Quebec

Contents

Exploring *Science Links 10* x

Safety in Your Science Classroom xii

Unit 1 Tissues, Organs, and Systems 2

Unit 1 At A Glance 4

Get Ready for Unit 1 6

Topic 1.1 Why are cells important? 8

Topic 1.2 Why do animal cells divide and what happens when they do? 20

Investigation 1A: Observing the Cell Cycle in Animal Cells 32

Topic 1.3 How do cells work together in the human body? 38

Investigation 1B: Viewing Specialized Human Cells 50

Strange Tales of Science: Stomach for Science 52

Topic 1.4 How do systems work together in the human body? 56

Investigation 1C: The Effect of Exercise on Breathing Rate and Heart Rate 68

Investigation 1D: Frog Dissection 70

Making a Difference: April Dutheil 74

Topic 1.5 How do technology, substances, and environmental factors affect human health? 76

Investigation 1E: Advances in Medical Technology 86

Investigation 1F: How Much Exposure is Too Much? 88

Case Study Investigation: What's the Price of Peak Performance? 90

Making a Difference: Kristopher Knowles and Prashanthi Baskaran 92

Science at Work Radiological Technologist 94

Unit 1 Summary 96

Unit 1 Projects: **Inquiry Investigation:** How Disease Affects Organs 98

An Issue to Analyze: Encouraging Healthy Lifestyles 99

Unit 1 Review 100

Unit 1 Literacy Test Prep 103

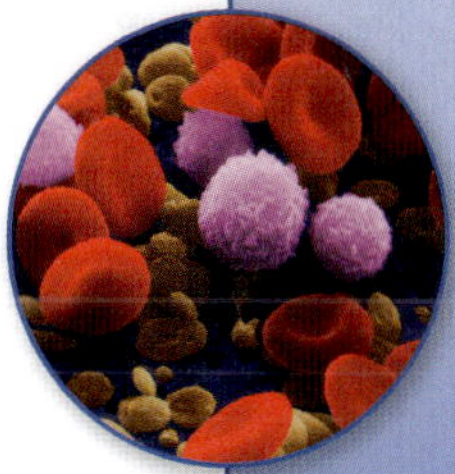

Unit 2 Chemical Reactions and Their Practical Applications

Unit 2 Chemical Reactions and Their Practical Applications 104

Unit 2 At a Glance 106

Get Ready for Unit 2 108

Topic 2.1 How do chemical reactions affect your daily life? 110

Topic 2.2 How can we understand, describe, and name chemical compounds? 118

Investigation 2A: Ionic or Molecular? 138

Topic 2.3 What happens during a chemical reaction, and how can it be described? 140

Investigation 2B: The Law of Conservation of Mass 153

Strange Tales of Science: Crime Scene Chemistry 154

Making a Difference: Simon Pickup, Sergio Morales, and Andrew Hanna 156

Topic 2.4 What are acids and bases, and how do they react? 158

Case Study Investigation: Acid Rain—Still an Ongoing Concern 168

Investigation 2C: Acid-Base Neutralization Reactions 172

Investigation 2D: The Effectiveness of Antacids 173

Science at Work Glass Artist 176

Unit 2 Summary 178

Unit 2 Projects **Inquiry Investigation:** The pH of your "Pop" 180

An Issue to Analyze: Mining Gold from e-Waste 181

Unit 2 Review 182

Unit 2 Literacy Test Prep 185

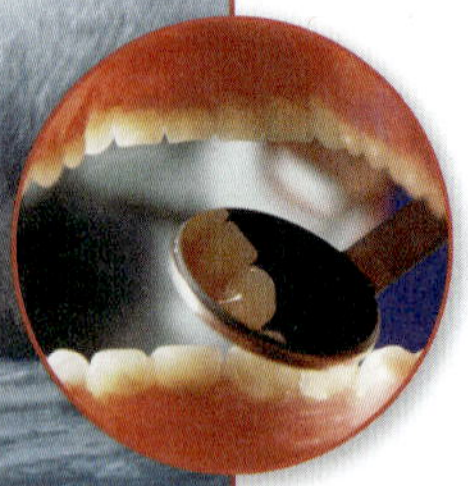

Unit 3 Earth's Dynamic Climate

Unit 3 Earth's Dynamic Climate 186
Unit 3 At a Glance 188
Get Ready for Unit 3 190

Topic 3.1 What is climate, and how has it changed during Earth's history? 192
Strange Tales of Science: Snowball Earth 200

Topic 3.2 Where are the effects of climate change felt, and what is their impact? 202

Topic 3.3 What natural factors affect climate, and how do they affect it? . . 212
Investigation 3A: Solar Radiation and Earth's Surface 226
Investigation 3B: Modelling the Greenhouse Effect 227

Topic 3.4 How do human activities affect the natural greenhouse effect? . . 230
Investigation 3C: Cross-Country Climate Change 236
Case Study Investigation: Can Biofuel Solve the Problem of Climate Change? 238

Topic 3.5 How can we assess present climate change and reduce our impact? 242
Investigation 3D: Transportation Choices and Your Carbon Footprint 256
Making a Difference: Asha Suppiah and Colin Carter 258

Science at Work Green Roofer 260

Unit 3 Summary 262

Unit 3 Projects: **Inquiry Investigation:** Reflecting on Land Use 264
An Issue to Analyze: Dealing with Climate Change 265

Unit 3 Review 266

Unit 3 Literacy Test Prep 269

Unit 4 Light and Applications of Optics 270

Unit 4 At a Glance 272

Get Ready for Unit 4 274

Topic 4.1 What is light and how is it produced? 276

Making a Difference: Charlie Sobcov, Pénélope Robinson, and Maude Briand-Lemay 284

Topic 4.2 How does light interact with objects to give them colour? 286

Topic 4.3 How can you mix colours to make different colours?........... 294

Topic 4.4 What is the law of reflection and how do mirrors form images?. . 304

Investigation 4A: Exploring Images with a Concave Mirror 326

Case Study Investigation: How Can Mirrors Help Keep You Safe? 328

Strange Tales of Science: Not Seeing is Believing 330

Topic 4.5 What is refraction and how can it be used? 332

Topic 4.6 What are lenses and what are some of their applications? 344

Investigation 4B: Investigating Converging Lenses........... 353

Investigation 4C: Options for an Optical Device 355

Science at Work Laserist 356

Unit 4 Summary 358

Unit 4 Projects: **Inquiry Investigation:** Design a Light Tunnel 360

An Issue to Analyze: LEDs Brighten Up the Darkness. . . 361

Unit 4 Review 362

Unit 4 Literacy Test Prep.. 365

Guide to the Skills Toolkits

Guide to the Skills Toolkits 366

SCIENCE SKILLS TOOLKITS

Science Skills Toolkit 1: Analyzing Issues—Science, Technology, Society, and the Environment 367
Science Skills Toolkit 2: Scientific Inquiry 371
Science Skills Toolkit 3: Measuring 376
Science Skills Toolkit 4: Using a Microscope 380
Science Skills Toolkit 5: Scientific Drawing 382
Science Skills Toolkit 6: Using Models and Analogies in Science 384
Science Skills Toolkit 7: How to Do a Research-Based Project 386
Science Skills Toolkit 8: Creating Data Tables 390

NUMERACY SKILLS TOOLKITS

Numeracy Skills Toolkit 1: Significant Digits and Rounding 391
Numeracy Skills Toolkit 2: Organizing and Communicating Scientific Results with Graphs 392
Numeracy Skills Toolkit 3: The GRASP Problem-Solving Method 398

LITERACY SKILLS TOOLKITS

Literacy Skills Toolkit 1: Preparing for Reading 399
Literacy Skills Toolkit 2: Reading Effectively 403
Literacy Skills Toolkit 3: Reading Graphic Text 407
Literacy Skills Toolkit 4: Word Study 410
Literacy Skills Toolkit 5: Organizing Your Learning: Using Graphic rganizers 412

Glossary 418

Index 442

Credits 447

Chemistry References 449

Periodic Table 450

Exploring *Science Links 10*

Answer the Questions, Reveal a Quote

In your notebook, answer the questions on these two pages as you explore *Science Links 10*. Use the numbered letters in each answer to find the missing words in the quote.

Ontario-born in 1849, Sir William Osler studied medicine at the University of Toronto (1868) and McGill University (1872), and did post-graduate studies in London, Vienna, and Berlin. Osler was one of the first to appreciate the interaction between body systems. He was also the first to bring medical students into hospitals for hands-on medical training.

1 2 3 4 5 6 7 , 8 9 10 11 12 13 , 14 15 16 17 18 19 20 21 ,

22 23 24 25 26 27 28 29 30 31 32 . 33 34 35 36 37 38 39 40 41 42 43

44 45 46 47 48 49 .

Learn to see, learn to hear, learn to feel, learn to smell, and know that by practice alone you can become expert.

—Sir William Osler

Sir William Osler published over 1,500 scientific articles detailing his research and medical innovations and published a textbook "The Principles and Practice of Medicine," that was the standard medical text for over 30 years.

Introducing *Science Links 10*

You will study four units in *Science Links 10*. What are they?

Unit 1: ____ (17) __, Organs, and ______ (3)

Unit 2: ____ (28) ___ Reactions and Their _ (5) ________ __________ (11) __

Unit 3: _ (15) ___'_ _______ ___ (24) ___

Unit 4: _ (41) ___ and __________ (37) __ of ____ (10) _

The material at the beginning of each unit helps you prepare for study. The Big Ideas summarize the information in the unit. They are found on the page that begins each unit.

What's the second Big Idea in Unit 3?

______ (4) ______ ___ (43) ___ __ (42) ___ _____ (49) and ___ (26) ___ ____ (9) __ in a variety of ways.

Which feature at the beginning of the unit shows you what the unit is all about in a graphic format?

33 22

The information in each unit is organized into topics. Each topic asks a question. What question does Topic 2.4 ask?

7 2 8 ?

Doing Science

What safety hazard does this icon represent? 

34 16

Each investigation features a Skill Check that tells you which science skills will be featured in the investigation. What are these skills?

31 and 46

12 and 29

19 and

48 14

20

Checking Your Learning

What feature gives you a chance to check your understanding as you read through a topic?

39 21

At the end of each topic, what are you asked to do?

6 36

45

It's important that you understand scientific terms and know how to use the words correctly. Where would you look in the textbook if you wanted to review a definition?

1

Finding Science in Unexpected Places

Each unit features a Canadian working in a career that uses scientific knowledge. What is this feature called?

27

Each unit features Canadian students who are using their scientific knowledge to do something in their community. What is this feature called?

30 40

Every unit tells you a "Strange Tale" about science. What is the tale in Unit 1?

25 44

Tools for Success

At the back of this textbook, there are three groups of toolkits that explain and demonstrate skills that will help you in all your learning, both in and outside of school. What are these toolkits?

47, 38 and

18 Skills

Numeracy Toolkit 3 is called The GRASP Problem Solving Method. What does GRASP stand for?

32, 13,

, 23, and

35

Safety in Your Science Classroom

Become familiar with the following safety rules and procedures. It is up to you to use them and your teacher's instructions to make your activities and investigations in *Science Links 10* safe and enjoyable. Your teacher will give you specific information about any other special safety rules that need to be used in your school.

1. Working with your teacher ...

- Listen carefully to any instructions your teacher gives you.
- Inform your teacher if you have any allergies, medical conditions, or other physical problems that could affect your work in the science classroom. Tell your teacher if you wear contact lenses or a hearing aid.
- Obtain your teacher's approval before beginning any activity you have designed for yourself.
- Know the location and proper use of the nearest fire extinguisher, fire blanket, first-aid kit, and fire alarm.

2. Starting an activity or investigation ...

- Before starting an activity or investigation, read all of it. If you do not understand how to do a step, ask your teacher for help.
- Be sure you have checked the safety icons and have read and understood the safety precautions.
- Begin an activity or investigation only after your teacher tells you to start.

3. Wearing protective clothing ...

- When you are directed to do so, wear protective clothing, such as a lab apron and safety goggles. Always wear protective clothing when you are using materials that could pose a safety problem, such as unidentified substances, or when you are heating anything.
- Tie back long hair, and avoid wearing scarves, ties, or long necklaces.

4. Acting responsibly ...

- Work carefully with a partner and make sure your work area is clear.
- Handle equipment and materials carefully.
- Make sure stools and chairs are resting securely on the floor.
- If other students are doing something that you consider dangerous, report it to your teacher.

5. Handling edible substances ...

- Do not chew gum, eat, or drink in your science classroom.
- Do not taste any substances or draw any material into a tube with your mouth.

6. **Working in a science classroom ...**
   - Make sure you understand all safety labels on school materials or those you bring from home. Familiarize yourself, as well, with the WHMIS symbols and the special safety symbols used in this book, found on page xv.
   - When carrying equipment for an activity or investigation, hold it carefully. Carry only one object or container at a time.
   - Be aware of others during activities and investigations. Make room for students who may be carrying equipment to their work stations.

7. **Working with sharp objects ...**
   - Always cut away from yourself and others when using a knife or razor blade.
   - Always keep the pointed end of scissors or any pointed object facing away from yourself and others if you have to walk with such objects.
   - If you notice sharp or jagged edges on any equipment, take special care with it and report it to your teacher.
   - Dispose of broken glass as your teacher directs.

8. **Working with electrical equipment ...**
   - Make sure your hands are dry when touching electrical cords, plugs, or sockets.
   - Pull the plug, not the cord, when unplugging electrical equipment.
   - Report damaged equipment or frayed cords to your teacher.
   - Place electrical cords where people will not trip over them.

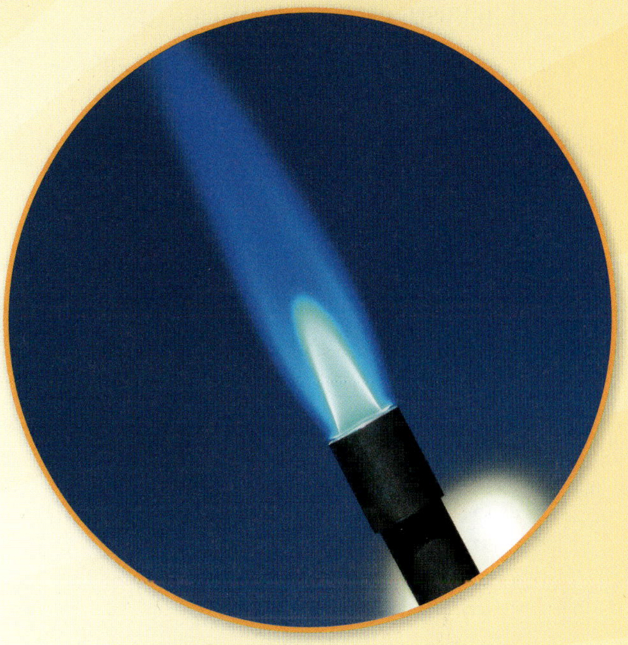

9. **Working with heat ...**
   - When heating an item, wear safety goggles and any other safety equipment that the text or your teacher advises.
   - Always use heatproof containers.
   - Point the open end of a container that is being heated away from yourself and others.
   - Do not allow a container to boil dry.
   - Handle hot objects carefully. Be especially careful with a hot plate that looks as though it has cooled down.
   - If you use a Bunsen burner, make sure you understand fully how to light and use it safely.
   - If you do receive a burn, inform you teacher, and apply cold water to the burned area immediately.

10. Working with various chemicals ...

- If any part of your body comes in contact with a substance, wash the area immediately and thoroughly with water. If you get anything in your eyes, do not touch them. Wash them immediately and continuously for 15 minutes, and inform your teacher.
- Always handle substances carefully. If you are asked to smell a substance, never smell it directly. Hold the container slightly in front of and beneath your nose, and waft the fumes toward your nostrils.
- Hold containers away from your face when pouring liquids.

11. Working with living things ...

On a field trip:

- Try not to disturb the area any more than is absolutely necessary.
- If you move something, do it carefully, and always replace it carefully.
- If you are asked to remove plant material, remove it gently, and take as little as possible.

In the classroom:

- Make sure that living creatures receive humane treatment while they are in your care.
- If possible, return living creatures to their natural environment when your work is complete.

12. Cleaning up in the science classroom ...

- Clean up any spills, according to your teacher's instructions.
- Clean equipment before you put it away.
- Wash your hands thoroughly after doing an activity or an investigation.
- Dispose of materials as directed by your teacher. Never discard materials in the sink unless your teacher requests it.

13. Designing and building ...

- Use tools safely to cut, join, and shape objects.
- Handle modelling clay correctly. Wash your hands after using modelling clay.
- Follow proper procedures when using mechanical systems and studying their operations.
- Use special care when observing and working with objects in motion.
- Do not use power equipment such as drills, sanders, saws, and lathes unless you have specialized training in handling such tools.

Safety Symbols

Science Links 10 Safety Symbols

The following safety symbols are used in *Science Links 10* to alert you to possible dangers. Be sure you understand each symbol used in an activity or investigation before you begin.

Disposal Alert
This symbol appears when care must be taken to dispose of materials properly.

Thermal Safety
This symbol appears as a reminder to use caution when handling hot objects.

Sharp Object Safety
This symbol appears when a danger of cuts or punctures caused by the use of sharp objects exists.

Electrical Safety
This symbol appears when care should be taken when using electrical equipment.

Skin Protection Safety
This symbol appears when use of caustic chemicals might irritate the skin or when contact with micro-organisms might transmit infection.

Clothing Protection Safety
A lab apron should be worn when this symbol appears.

Fire Safety
This symbol appears when care should be taken around open flames.

Eye Safety
This symbol appears when a danger to the eyes exists. Safety goggles should be worn when this symbol appears.

Fume Safety
This symbol appears when chemicals or chemical reactions could cause dangerous fumes.

Chemical Safety
This symbol appears when chemicals used can cause burns or are poisonous if absorbed through the skin.

Instant Practice—Safety Symbols

Find four of the *Science Links 10* safety symbols in activities or investigations in this textbook. For each symbol, identify the possible dangers in the activity or investigation that the symbol refers to.

WHMIS Symbols

Look carefully at the WHMIS (Workplace Hazardous Materials Information System) safety symbols shown here. The WHMIS symbols are used throughout Canada to identify dangerous materials. Make certain you understand what these symbols mean. When you see these symbols on containers, use safety precautions.

Compressed Gas

Flammable and Combustible Material

Oxidizing Material

Corrosive Material

Poisonous and Infectious Material Causing Immediate and Serious Toxic Effects

Poisonous and Infectious Material Causing Other Toxic Effects

Biohazardous Infectious Material

Dangerously Reactive Material

Instant Practice—Safety Symbols

Hydrogen gas is stored in containers under pressure. This gas is highly flammable.

1. What two symbols would you expect to see on a label for hydrogen gas?
2. Describe the following.
   a) the risks illustrated by the two symbols
   b) precautions someone would need to take when working with the gas
   c) where it could be safely stored
   d) first aid or emergency treatment
3. If you did not know the answer to part d), where would you find this information?

Unit 1 Tissues, Organs, and Systems

Big Ideas

- All animals are made of specialized cells, tissues, and organs that are organized into systems.
- Although technology and chemicals can be used to improve human health, they can also constitute a health hazard.

The venomous bite of a radioactive spider triggers change at the cellular level and transforms nerdy Peter Parker into wall-crawling, web-spinning Spider-Man.

Expert in nuclear physics, Otto Octavius, suffers an accident that fuses a harness with octopus-like tentacles to his body and initiates cellular changes that enable him to control the apparatus with the merest thought.

Cellular change, whether through spider bites, radiation, or inherited mutation, is a common means for transforming ordinary people into extraordinary heroes and villains—the stuff of great stories for comics, movies, and video games.

Do cellular changes really happen, or is that just in the movies? How are your own cells organized into the tissues, organs, and systems that give you your own unique abilities? What can impair their health and, therefore, yours?

Unit 1 At a Glance

In this unit you will learn how tissues, organs, and systems work together in the human body. You will also learn about the function of the basic unit of life, the cell, and how human health is affected by technology and environmental factors.

***Think** about answers to each question as you work through the topic.*

Tissues, Organs, and Systems

Topic 1.1: Why are cells important?

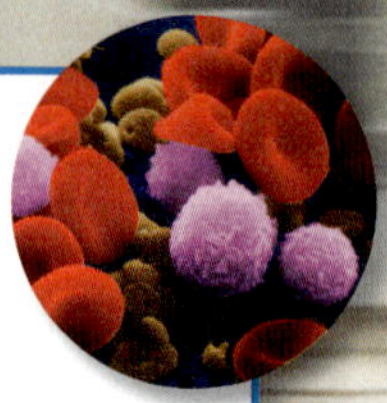

Key Concepts

- Studying cells helps us understand how organisms function.
- Cellular organelles work together to carry out life functions.
- Cellular processes enable organisms to meet their basic needs.

Topic 1.5: How do technology, substances, and environmental factors affect human health?

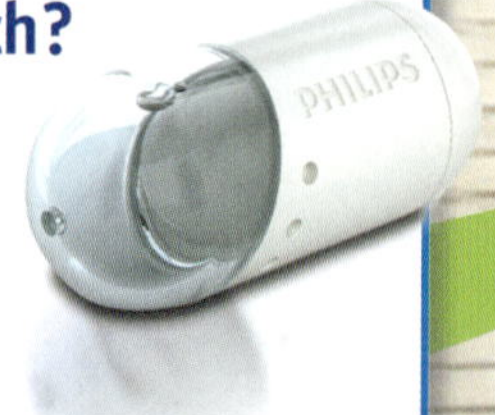

Key Concepts

- Medical imaging technologies are used to explore, diagnose, and treat the human body.
- Exposure to various technologies, substances, and environmental factors can impair health.
- Technology will affect human health in new ways in the future.

Topic 1.4: How do systems work together in the human body?

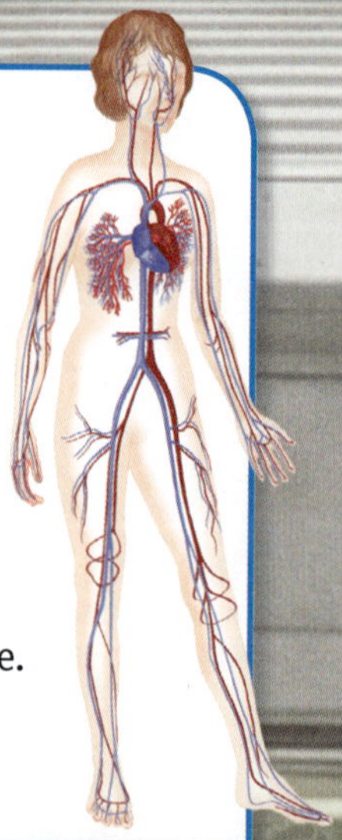

Key Concepts

- The respiratory system carries oxygen to and removes carbon dioxide from the blood.
- The circulatory system transports dissolved gases and nutrients through the body.
- The digestive system breaks down food, absorbs nutrients, and eliminates solid waste.
- Organ systems working together carry out important tasks in the body.

Topic 1.2: Why do animal cells divide and what happens when they do?

Key Concepts

- Cells must divide for an organism to survive.
- Hereditary material is passed on during cell division.
- Animal cells have a life cycle that includes both growth and division.
- New animal cells are created during the cell cycle.
- Uncontrolled, rapid division of animal cells can be cancer.

Topic 1.3: How do cells work together in the human body?

Key Concepts

- All cells begin alike and differentiate into specialized cells.
- Specialized cells have different structures that allow them to perform unique functions.
- Groups of cells working together form tissues.
- Groups of tissues working together form organs, which work together in systems.

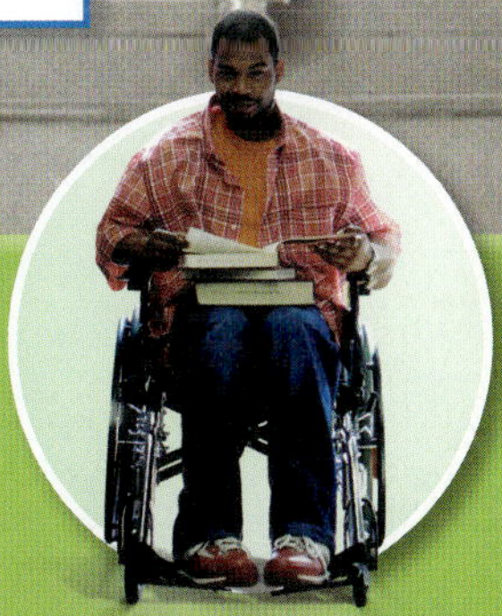

Looking Ahead to the Unit 1 Projects

At the end of this unit you will have the opportunity to apply what you have learned. In your unit projects, you will research how one disease affects human tissues, organs, and organ systems, and you will try to define society's responsibility for the health of its citizens.

Get Ready for Unit 1

Concept Check

1. Decide whether each statement about the cell theory is true or false. If a statement is false, explain why.
   - **a)** The cell is the basic unit of life.
   - **b)** All cells come from pre-existing cells.
   - **c)** All living things are made up of many cells.

2. **a)** Select one of the plants shown in the illustration below, and draw what you think one of its cells looks like.
   - **b)** Select one of the animals in the diagram, and draw what you think one of its cells looks like.
   - **c)** Draw what you think a skin cell from your own body looks like.
   - **d)** Draw what you think a muscle cell from your own body looks like.

3. In your notebook, write the number that matches each part of the microscope listed below.
   - **a)** light source
   - **b)** stage
   - **c)** eyepiece
   - **d)** objective lens

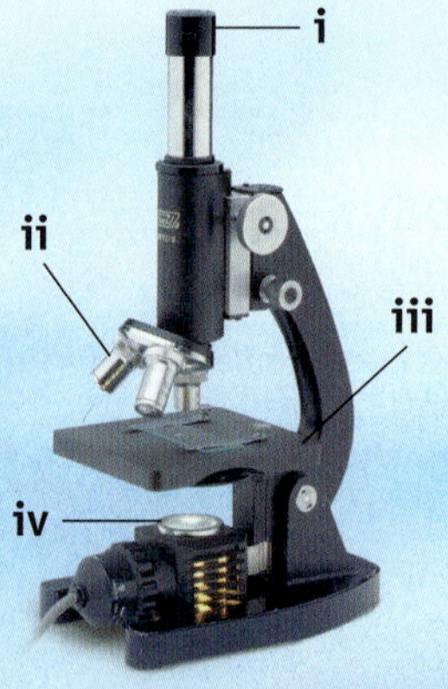

4. When you start to view a specimen with a microscope, which objective lens do you use first?
   - **a)** high magnification
   - **b)** low magnification
   - **c)** medium magnification
   - **d)** whichever one is already in place

5. When you are using the high magnification lens, how can you bring the object you are viewing into sharper focus?
   - **a)** use the coarse adjustment knob
   - **b)** adjust the eyepiece
   - **c)** adjust the stage clips
   - **d)** use the fine adjustment knob

6. The correct way to hold a microscope is
   - **a)** with one hand on the arm
   - **b)** with one hand on the arm and the other hand on the base
   - **c)** with one hand on the arm and the other hand on the stage
   - **d)** with one hand supporting the base

Inquiry Check

7. Brainstorm In your notebook, use a t-chart to list as many characteristics of single-celled and many-celled organisms as you can. Compare your list with a partner's list.

8. Evaluate The photo below shows a tea bag that has been sitting in boiled water for several minutes. Before the tea bag was placed in the water, the water was clear and colourless. Now the water is dark brown. Your partner says that the process responsible for the change in the appearance of the water is diffusion. Explain why your partner is or is not correct.

Numeracy and Literacy Check

9. Graph Bacterial cells replicate by splitting into two cells. When conditions are favourable (for example, when there is space and a food source), bacteria can divide every 20 min. Draw a graph of the data with time on the horizontal axis and number of bacteria on the vertical axis.

Growth of Bacteria Cells

Time (min)	Number of Bacteria
0	1
20	2
40	4
60	8
80	16

10. Write Use the words below to explain how many-celled organisms are structured.

cells	tissues
organs	organ systems

Topic 1.1

Why are cells important?

Key Concepts

- Studying cells helps us understand how organisms function.
- Cellular organelles work together to carry out life functions.
- Cellular processes enable organisms to meet their basic needs.

Key Skills

- Inquiry
- Literacy

Key Terms

organelle
diffusion
concentration
osmosis

In our high tech world, one of the hottest areas of development is nanotechnology—the science and the technology of the very, very small. A group of researchers in Europe has taken on the mind-boggling challenge of creating an artificial cell that can replicate on its own and even evolve under certain conditions. In other words, their goal is to create the world's first robotic cell. To achieve their goal, these researchers will have to create artificial components that mimic the components found in a real cell. Only by studying real cells will they be able to create the perfect fake!

Starting Point Activity

1. The large picture here shows how an artist imagines robotic cells mingling with real cells in a body. The disk-shaped cells are red blood cells. You may have learned about them in an earlier grade. What do you know or recall about the function of red blood cells in the body?
2. Write down as many details about cell components as you can recall from your study of cells in earlier grades.

This photo shows real red blood cells, as well as other cells that are part of blood: white blood cells, which help fight infection, and platelets, which help heal over wounds.

Studying cells helps us understand how organisms function.

Much of this unit focuses on how cells function, divide, and work together. But before you read any further, take a moment to think about one very important question:

Why should we learn about cells?

The answer is that studying cells helps us understand how organisms, including humans, function. After all, our bodies are made up of trillions of cells. By learning about cells, we come to understand how we can

- protect cells to prevent infection and other harmful effects
- observe cells to diagnose disease
- treat cells to heal illnesses
- stop harming cells through our choices and actions

Consider the medical advances shown in the four pictures on these two pages. None of these advances would have been possible without an understanding of how different cells work.

Malaria is a deadly disease. It is transmitted by mosquitoes in tropical parts of the world. Scientists have recently developed a vaccine that can protect human cells from malaria infection. To develop this vaccine, scientists needed to learn about cells in both humans and mosquitoes. They also needed to understand the single-celled organism that causes malaria.

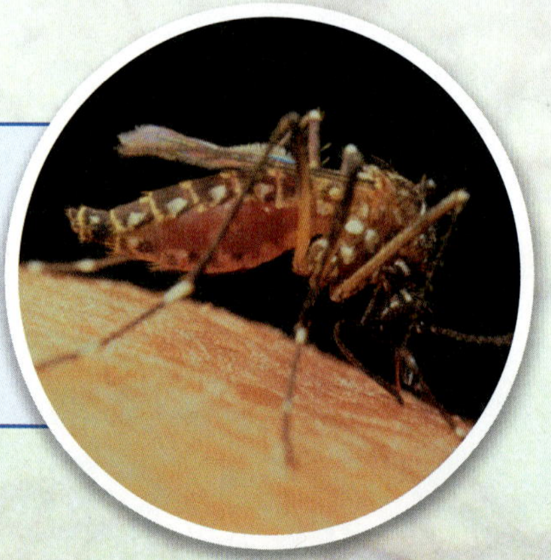

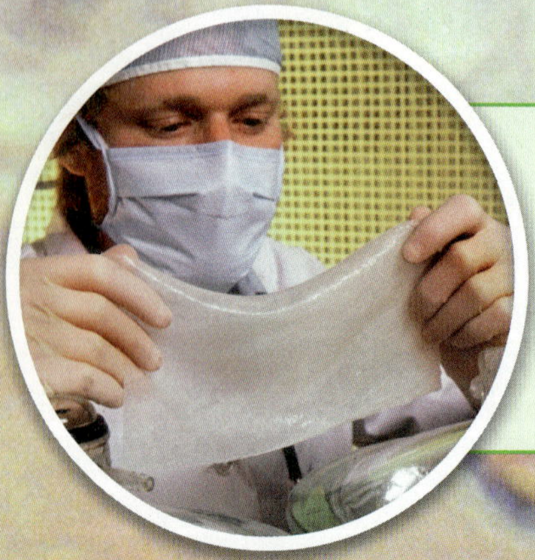

A person with severe burns is often treated with skin grafts taken from another region of their body. However, sometimes there is little healthy skin left on the body. In such cases, doctors place an artificial skin substitute over the burns. This nylon-based material contains a substance that works with the blood to heal the wound. Knowledge of how both skin and blood cells function has made this technology possible.

Literacy Focus

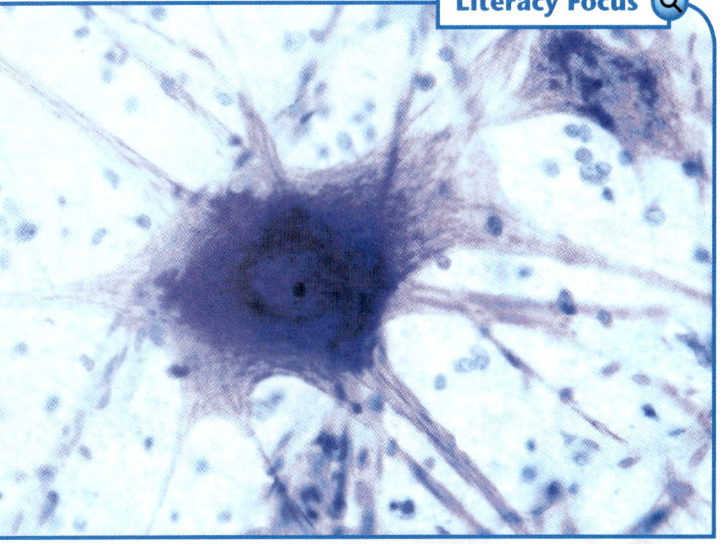

Activity 1.1

WHY STUDY CELLS?

1. Look through the resources provided by your teacher to find an article about a new medical breakthrough, discovery, or technology.
2. Describe the breakthrough in your own words.
3. Explain how this research relates to cells.
4. Explain how this research helps you, your family, or society.

LEARNING CHECK

1. Why bother learning about cells?
2. What types of cells would you have to study to develop a malaria vaccine?
3. How would knowledge of cells help doctors create an artificial skin substitute?
4. What type of technology might an understanding of nerve cell function help researchers create?

Medical doctors have discovered that reducing body temperature can help a person survive a heart attack. Cold temperatures reduce the harm to heart and brain cells after a heart attack. By studying cells, doctors have been able to develop this new life-saving treatment.

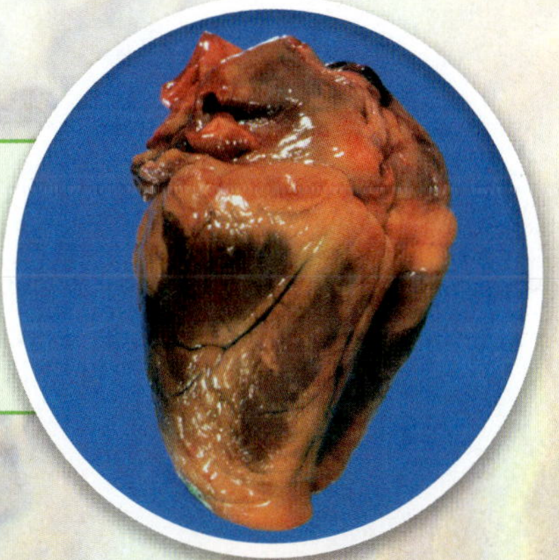

A human heart

Did you know that artificial sweeteners can make us gain weight? Scientists have discovered that consuming artificially sweetened foods and beverages "disappoints" brain cells that were expecting sugar, based on the taste. As a result, our brain tells us to keep eating, hoping to get the sugar it was promised. Such knowledge about cells can help us make healthier choices in the foods and beverages we consume.

Cellular organelles work together to carry out life functions.

The flies on this page have a lot in common with the Venus's-flytrap. As well as providing the Venus's-flytrap with nutrients, the flies are composed of the same basic units of life that make up the plant—cells. Plants, flies, people, and all other living things are made up of one or more cells. Each cell, in turn, is made up of smaller components. These smaller components are called organelles.

organelle: a structure within a cell that carries out specific functions to support the life of the cell

An **organelle** is a structure within a cell. Organelles work together to carry out specific functions that support the life of the cell. These functions include

- bringing in nutrients
- removing wastes
- generating and releasing energy for the cell to use
- making substances that the cell needs
- reproducing

Inquiry Focus

Activity 1.2

ORGANELLES ON STRIKE

This activity is designed to help you determine what you remember about cells and cell parts from earlier grades. If you need any reminders, you can turn to the next page, where this information is reviewed.

The organelles and cell parts that are involved with the following functions have gone on strike:

- transporting substances such as water and salt into the cell
- transporting waste substances such as carbon dioxide out of the cell
- reproducing to make two identical copies of the cell

Use what you know or remember to identify the organelles that are important for each of these functions.

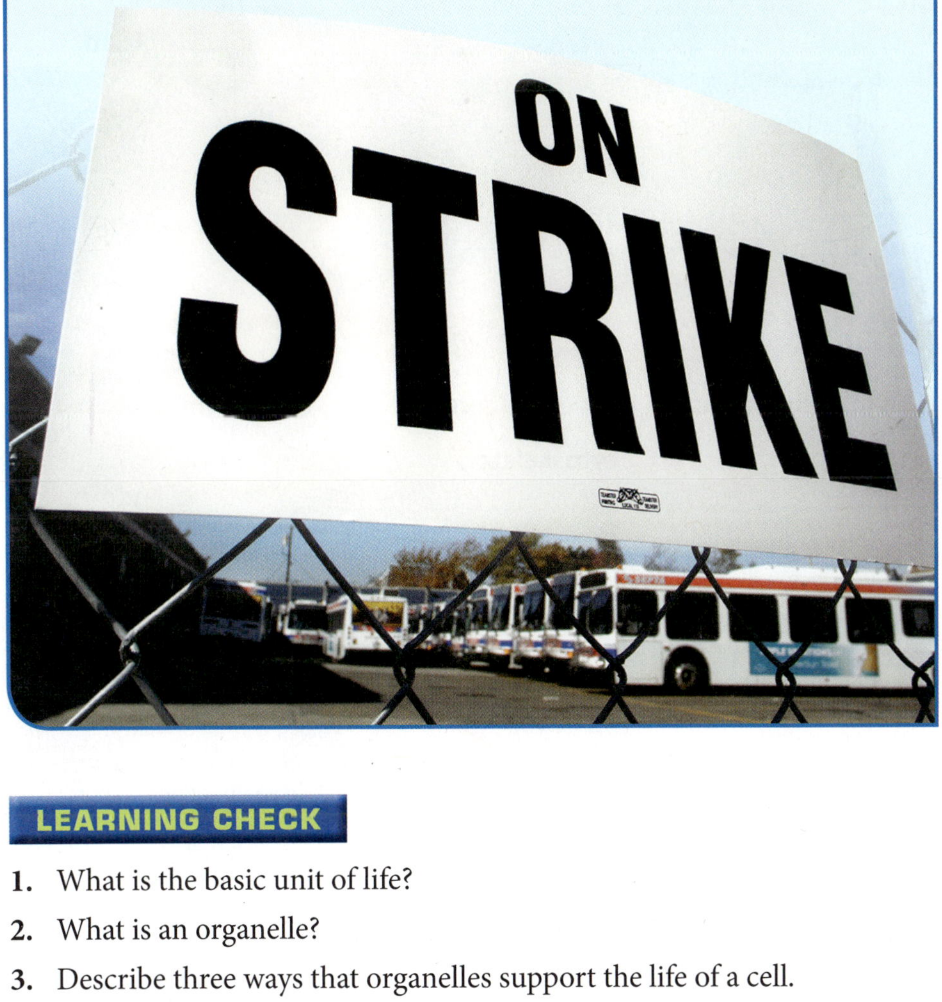

LEARNING CHECK

1. What is the basic unit of life?
2. What is an organelle?
3. Describe three ways that organelles support the life of a cell.
4. What would happen to the cells of your body if they didn't have organelles to control the materials entering and leaving the cells?

continued on the next page...

... continued from previous page

Organelles and other structures in cells have different tasks.

Go to **scienceontario** to find out more

Each organelle and cell part has a specific role within a cell. This role is important to the proper functioning of both the cell and the organism. Some cells have more of one type of organelle and less of another. This is because different cells also perform different roles in an organism. For example, a muscle cell requires a lot of energy. As a result, it may have many organelles that make energy available to the cell. These organelles are called mitochondria. **Figures 1.1** and **1.2** show the organelles that are found in a typical animal cell and a typical plant cell.

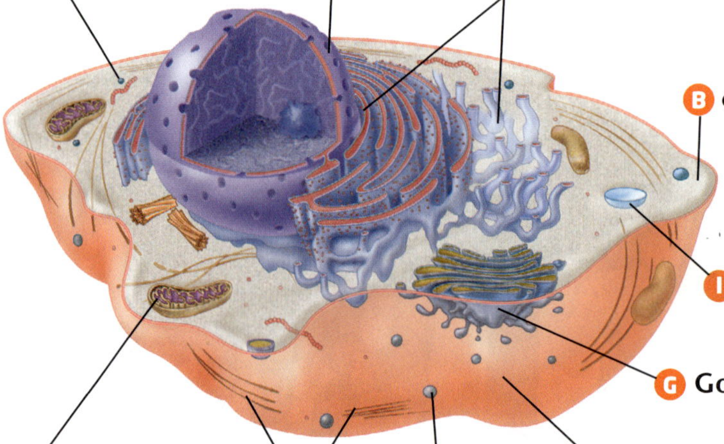

▶ **Figure 1.1** This diagram shows a typical animal cell. As you will learn on the next few pages, animal cells vary greatly within an organism. The organelles they contain also vary according to the role of each cell.

- **A cell membrane** separates the inside of the cell from the external environment; controls the flow of materials into and out of the cell
- **B cytoplasm** includes the organelles, and other life-supporting materials, such as sugar and water, all contained by the cell membrane
- **C mitochondria** (singular: mitochondrion) where energy is released from glucose to fuel cell activities
- **D ribosomes** help to produce proteins, which make up much of a cell's structure and are required for activities necessary for the cell's survival; some ribosomes float in the cytoplasm, and others are attached to the endoplasmic reticulum
- **E endoplasmic reticulum** a network of membrane-covered channels that transport materials made in the cell; is connected to the nucleus
- **F vesicles** membrane-covered sacs that transport and/or store materials inside the cell and sometimes help these materials cross the cell membrane to enter or exit the cell
- **G Golgi body** sorts and packages proteins and other molecules for transport out of the cell
- **H nucleus** controls all cell activities

Literacy Focus

Activity 1.3

ORGANELLE BINGO

Create a game that will help other students learn about cellular organelles and their functions. Develop rules for organelle bingo, cell function Jeopardy!, or another game of your choice.

LEARNING CHECK

1. Why do some cells have more of one type of organelle?
2. Identify three differences between an animal cell and a plant cell.
3. Muscle cells have a lot of mitochondria. What do you think might happen if a person got a disease that destroyed all the mitochondria in muscle cells?

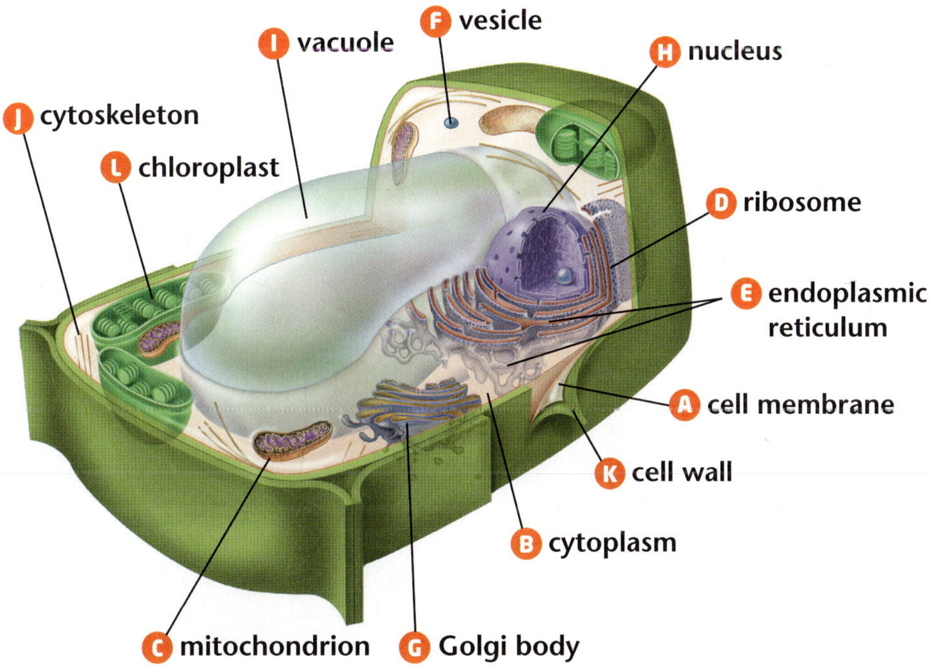

◂ **Figure 1.2** This diagram shows a typical plant cell. Like animal cells, plant cells vary according to their role.

- I **vacuoles** contain water and other materials and are used to store or transport small molecules; plant cells tend to have one large vacuole; animal cells may have several smaller vacuoles
- J **cytoskeleton** filaments and tubules that provide a framework for the cell, helping it maintain its structure and providing "tracks" along which vesicles and organelles can move
- K **cell wall** a tough, rigid structure lying just outside a plant cell's membrane; provides support for the cell; not found in animal cells
- L **chloroplasts** found only in plant cells; trap energy from the Sun to make glucose, which is broken down in the mitochondria to power cell activities (animals must get glucose from the food they eat)

Cellular processes enable organisms to meet their basic needs.

diffusion: the movement of molecules (or other particles) from an area of high concentration to an area of low concentration until they are evenly distributed

concentration: the number of molecules of a substance in a given volume

Cellular processes are the activities that organelles perform to carry out the cell's life functions. Two of the most important cellular processes are diffusion and osmosis.

How Diffusion Works

Figure 1.3 shows ink particles spreading through water. The ink particles move from an area where there is a lot of ink to an area where there is little or no ink. This process is called diffusion. **Diffusion** is the movement of particles of a substance from an area of high **concentration** to an area of low concentration until all the particles are evenly distributed.

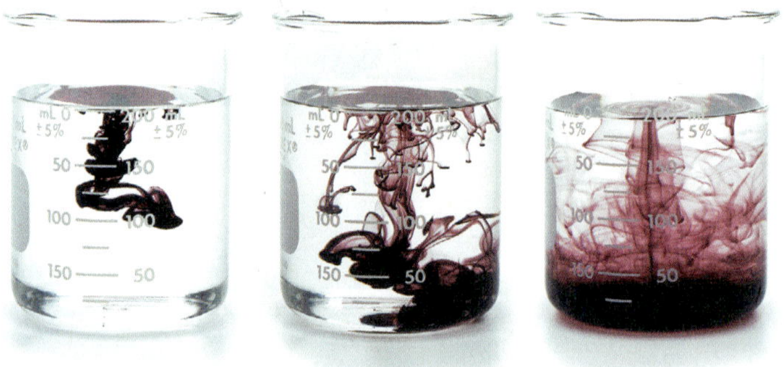

▶ **Figure 1.3** As ink diffuses in water, the ink particles spread through the water from where there is lots of ink (high concentration) to where there is little or no ink (low concentration).

Diffusion is an essential cellular process. Without it, life as we know it would not be possible. Diffusion occurs:

- within a cell

Example: Substances that are produced by one organelle may travel to another organelle or the cell membrane by diffusing through the cytoplasm.

- across the cell membrane

Example: Each time you breathe in, your blood picks up oxygen. Your blood then transports this oxygen to your cells. The concentration of oxygen molecules is at first greater outside the cell than inside the cell. As a result, the oxygen molecules pass through the cell membrane into the cytoplasm. They continue to do so until there is an equal concentration of oxygen inside and outside the cell.

- outside a cell in body fluids

Example: Nerve cells release chemicals to communicate with each other. These chemicals diffuse through the fluid in the space between nerve cells.

How Osmosis Works

After a fast-paced game of Ultimate Frisbee, the first thing you probably want is a big glass of cold water. Because your body loses nutrients such as sodium and potassium when you sweat, some people might recommend a glass of a sports drink, which has these nutrients in it. It's important that nutrients and other dissolved substances in your body stay in balance. But why? One answer involves a cellular process called **osmosis**.

Osmosis involves the diffusion of water through a *semi-permeable membrane*. A semi-permeable membrane lets water and some molecules diffuse across it but keeps molecules of other substances from penetrating it. You have read that cell membranes control the movement of substances into and out of cells. Cell membranes are semi-permeable. Water can penetrate the membrane, but molecules of many substances cannot. **Figure 1.4** shows what would happen to a cell if it was placed in pure water.

osmosis: the movement of water molecules across a membrane in response to concentration differences

▼ **Figure 1.4** When a substance cannot penetrate a membrane, it cannot diffuse from an area of higher concentration to an area of lower concentration. Therefore, by osmosis, more water diffuses across the membrane to make up for the difference in concentration.

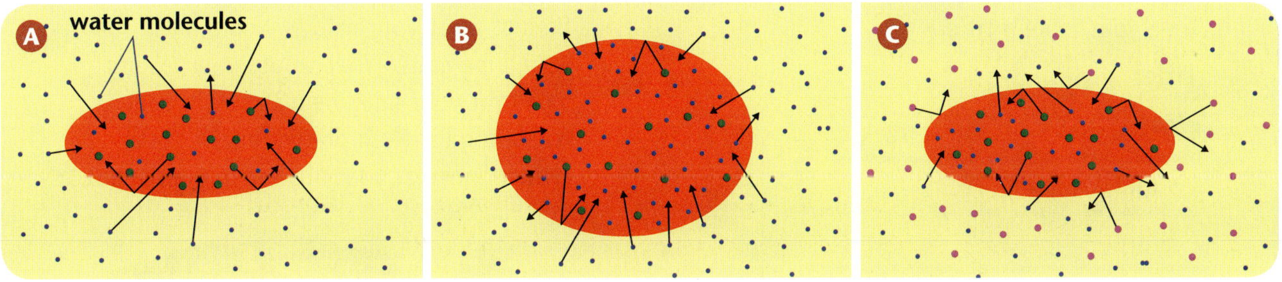

If you placed this cell in pure water, the concentration of green molecules would be zero outside the cell but high inside the cell. However, the green molecules cannot diffuse to the lower concentration, because they cannot penetrate the membrane. So, by osmosis, more water molecules diffuse into the cell to equalize the concentrations of water molecules inside and outside the cell.

Although some water molecules diffuse out of the cell, more water molecules will continue to diffuse in. But the concentration of the green molecules will never be equal on the two sides of the membrane. As a result, so much water will keep diffusing into the cell that it will eventually burst.

Fortunately, your body has many mechanisms to ensure that the concentrations of molecules are balanced on the two sides of cell membranes. Here, for instance, you see purple molecules outside the cell and green molecules inside the cell. Water diffuses in because of the green molecules, and water diffuses out because of the purple molecules. The diffusion of water is balanced.

LEARNING CHECK

1. Use a Venn diagram to compare osmosis and diffusion.
2. Explain why your life would not be possible without the cellular process, diffusion.

ACTIVITY LINK

Activity 1.4, on page 18

Inquiry Focus

Activity 1.4

DIFFUSION IN ACTION

Observe and measure how long it takes for food colouring to diffuse through water.

Safety

- Do not use your mouth with the pipette.

What You Need

- 25 mL graduated cylinder
- warm tap water
- long pipette
- pipette filler
- undiluted blue or red food colouring
- watch or stopwatch
- graph paper

What To Do

1. Copy the table below into your notebook. Give your table a title.

   Title: ____________________

Volume	Time
5 mL	
10 mL	
15 mL	
20 mL	

2. Fill the graduated cylinder with tap water. Gently tap the side of the cylinder to eliminate any air bubbles in the water.
3. Use a pipette to take a 1 mL sample of food colouring. Rinse the outside of the pipette with water. Carefully insert the pipette into the graduated cylinder until the tip reaches just above the bottom of the cylinder. Slowly release the food colouring into the water.
4. Time how long it takes for the colour to move up to the 5 mL mark on the cylinder.

   Continue timing to find out how long it takes for the colour to move to the 10 mL, 15 mL, and 20 mL mark on the cylinder.
5. Record your observations.
6. Graph your results. Place time on the *x*-axis and volume on the *y*-axis of your graph.

What Did You Find Out?

1. Identify the dependent variable and the independent variable.
2. Describe the results that are shown on your graph.
3. What conclusion can you make about the speed of diffusion and the distance that a substance diffuses?
4. Predict what your results would mean for very large cells. What would your results mean for very small cells? Explain your reasoning for each prediction.
   (**Hint:** Consider your answer to question 3.)

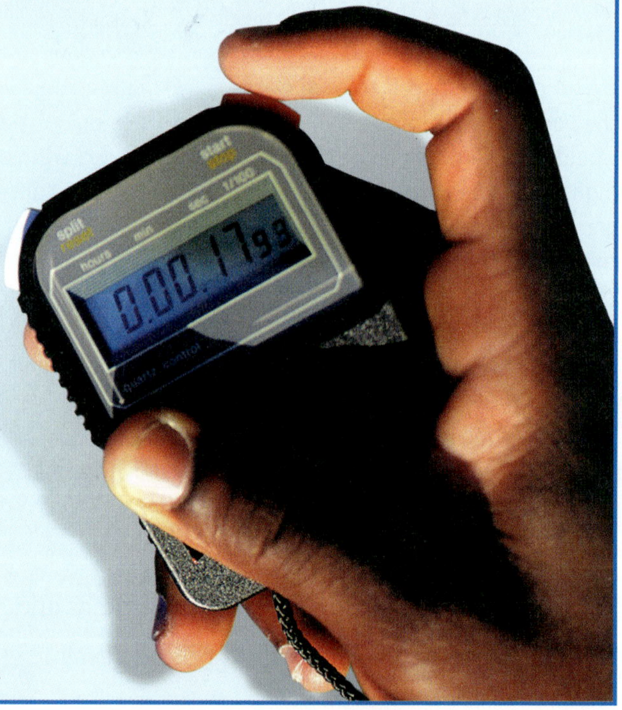

Topic 1.1 Review

Key Concept Summary

- Studying cells helps us understand how organisms function.
- Cellular components work together to carry out life functions.
- Cellular processes enable organisms to meet their basic needs.

Review the Key Concepts

1. K/U Answer the question that is the title of this topic. Copy and complete the graphic organizer below in your notebook. Fill in four examples from the topic using key terms as well as your own words.

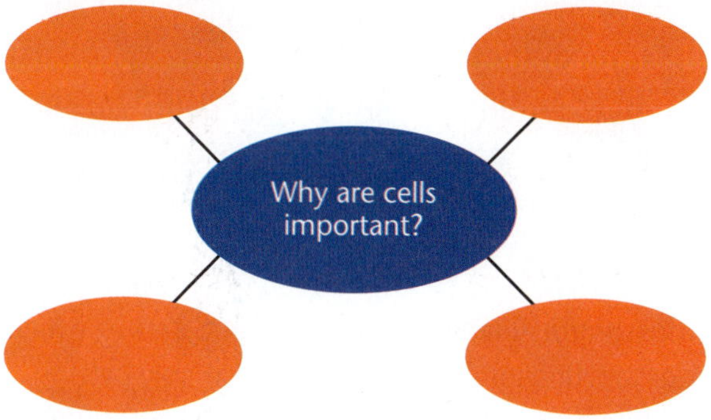

2. K/U Describe three benefits that result from studying cells.
3. K/U Why is the cell considered the basic unit of life?
4. K/U Identify the function of each of the following cellular components.

Organelle or Cell Part	Function
a) mitochondria	
b) cell membrane	
c) nucleus	
d) vacuole	

5. A After painting your room and putting your brush into some clean water, you notice that the water is turning green. Explain why using scientific terminology.
6. A This squid is releasing ink from its body. The ink quickly diffuses in the water, enabling the animal to escape from a predator. Provide two other examples of diffusion in nature or in your own life.

7. C Organelles are structures within a cell that carry out specific roles. Create a rap, rhyme, or song that includes at least three organelles. Your lyrics must explain the role each organelle plays in carrying out one of the cell's life functions.

Topic 1.2

Why do animal cells divide and what happens when they do?

Key Concepts

- Cells must divide for an organism to survive.
- Hereditary material is passed on during cell division.
- Animal cells have a life cycle that includes both growth and division.
- New animal cells are created during the cell cycle.
- Uncontrolled, rapid division of animal cells can be cancer.

Key Skills

Inquiry
Literacy
Numeracy

Key Terms

cell cycle
interphase
mitosis
cytokinesis
regeneration
prophase
metaphase
anaphase
telophase

In the world of science fiction movies, a creature may lose its head—literally—and then grow it right back again. Of course, nothing like that happens in real life—unless you happen to look in a pond! If a pond-dwelling planarian flatworm loses its head or tail to one of its many predators, it can grow an entirely new one. It can even regenerate an entirely new body from just a small fragment of tissue. Other organisms such as starfish and earthworms have a similar ability. They can re-grow a missing limb or tail. Scientists are studying cell division in these organisms in an attempt to understand how such complex healing is possible. If this knowledge could be applied to cell division in the human body, medical breakthroughs such as regenerating an amputated limb could become a reality for humans.

Starting Point Activity

1. As a class, brainstorm as many situations as you can in which the following organisms might need to produce new cells: starfish, snake, human.
2. With your classmates, try to explain why a planarian flatworm can grow a new head but you cannot.

A HORROR HORDE OF CRAWL-AND-CRUSH GIANTS
CLAWING OUT OF THE EARTH
FROM MILE-DEEP
CATACOMBS!
"THEM"
"This city is under martial law until we annihilate THEM!"
Kill one and two take its place!
THE AMAZING NEW WARNER BROS. SENSATION!

Cells must divide for an organism to survive.

Cells divide because there is a limit to how large they can grow. For a cell to survive, it must take in a constant supply of materials such as nutrients, oxygen, and water. It must get rid of waste products it produces. And materials must travel within the cell's cytoplasm to reach the cell membrane and other organelles. If a cell grows too large, it cannot carry out these processes efficiently. Read the information below to find out why.

Cell size is limited because the amount of material in a cell increases faster than the cell membrane grows.

The only way for nutrients and wastes to get in and out of a cell is to pass through the cell membrane. As a cell gets larger, the amount of material inside the cell increases more than the cell membrane can grow to contain it. After a while, nutrients and wastes can no longer pass through the cell membrane in the amounts required. As a result, the cell dies.

Cell size is limited because the amount of material in a cell increases, but the speed of diffusion does not.

As the cell grows, the amount of material inside it increases. As a result, it takes longer for nutrients and wastes to diffuse between the cell membrane and all parts of the cell. Use **Figure 1.5** to help you understand this idea. To keep this model cell alive, you need to swim from the edge of the pool to the centre carrying a pool noodle. Then you must swim back to the edge carrying a beach ball. If the pool is small, you can keep up with moving these materials in and out. As the pool gets bigger, however, it takes longer to make these trips. Over time, you can't supply nutrients or remove wastes from all parts of the cell fast enough to meet its needs. Eventually, it will either starve to death or be poisoned from a build-up of waste products.

▶ **Figure 1.5** A pool can be used to model a cell. As the size of the pool increases, it takes longer to transport pool noodles and beach balls between the edge of the pool and the centre. Similarly, as the size of a cell increases, it takes longer to transport nutrients and wastes between the cell membrane and the rest of the cell.

Numeracy Focus

Activity 1.5

CELL NUMBER CRUNCH

The *cell surface* is the area of the cell over which all nutrients must enter and all wastes must leave. The *cell volume* determines how much the cell holds. It also determines how far nutrients and waste must diffuse to be used or removed.

If a cell has a larger surface, it means that more nutrients can get in and more wastes can get out. But when the cell surface increases, the volume increases even more. Refer to the table below to see why this is the case. A larger volume means that the amounts of nutrients that must travel in or out of the cell increase even more. As well, the distance that nutrients must diffuse also gets longer. In the case of a growing cell, there will be a point at which the surface area is not large enough to meet the demands of the cell's volume.

1. If Cube B, with sides that are 2 mm, grows to have sides that are 3 mm
   - **a)** what is the new surface area?
   - **b)** what is the new volume?
2. **a)** Which has increased more: surface area or volume?
   - **b)** Why would this be a problem if the cube were a cell?

Cube	Side Length	Surface Area (length × width × number of sides)	Volume (length × width × height)
A 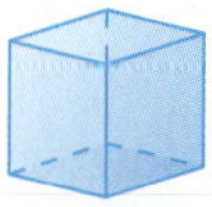	1 mm	1 mm × 1 mm × 6 = 6 mm^2	1 mm × 1 mm × 1 mm = 1 mm^3
B 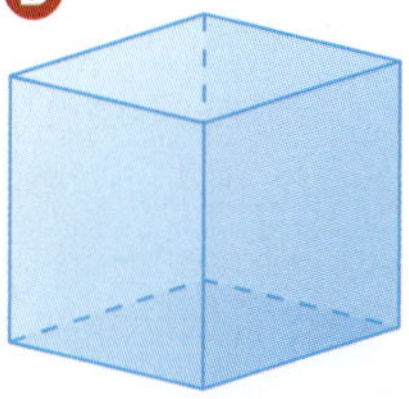	2 mm The length of any side on Cube B is two times larger than on Cube A.	2 mm × 2 mm × 6 = 24 mm^2 The surface area of Cube B is four times larger than the surface area of Cube A.	2 mm × 2 mm × 2 mm = 8 mm^3 The volume of Cube B is eight times larger than the volume of Cube A.

LEARNING CHECK

1. Why do cells divide instead of simply growing larger and larger?
2. Use **Figure 1.5** to explain why a cell may die if it becomes too large.
3. As a cell grows, which increases in size faster: the cell membrane or the cell contents?

Hereditary material is passed on during cell division.

When a cell divides, two new cells are created. Each new cell is identical to the original cell. Each new cell inherits a set of instructions from the original cell. These instructions determine all the details of the organism's life. They determine its characteristics, its functions, and even how long it will live. These instructions are found in the nucleus of the cell. They are stored in a unique molecule called DNA. DNA is short for **d**eoxyribo**n**ucleic **a**cid.

DNA: The Cell's Hereditary Material

The nucleus of almost every cell in an organism carries all the DNA needed to create an identical twin of itself. How does so much information fit into the nucleus of each cell? DNA molecules are shaped like long strands of a very thin, twisted ladder (**Figure 1.6**). To fit into a small space, they coil and compact to form threads called *chromatin* (**Figure 1.7**). The chromatin are packed together tightly within the nucleus. If you were to uncoil the DNA in one of your cells, it would be 2 m long—taller than most grade 10 students. Amazingly, the diameter of a nucleus is only about 5 μm (0.000 005 m). (In comparison, imagine stuffing a piece of string that is 100 km long into a lunch box, as in **Figure 1.8**.)

When a cell divides, the DNA is packed together even more tightly. A super-condensed form of chromatin called *chromosomes* is formed at this time. Because chromosomes are so compact, they are a convenient way to pass on hereditary information when a cell divides.

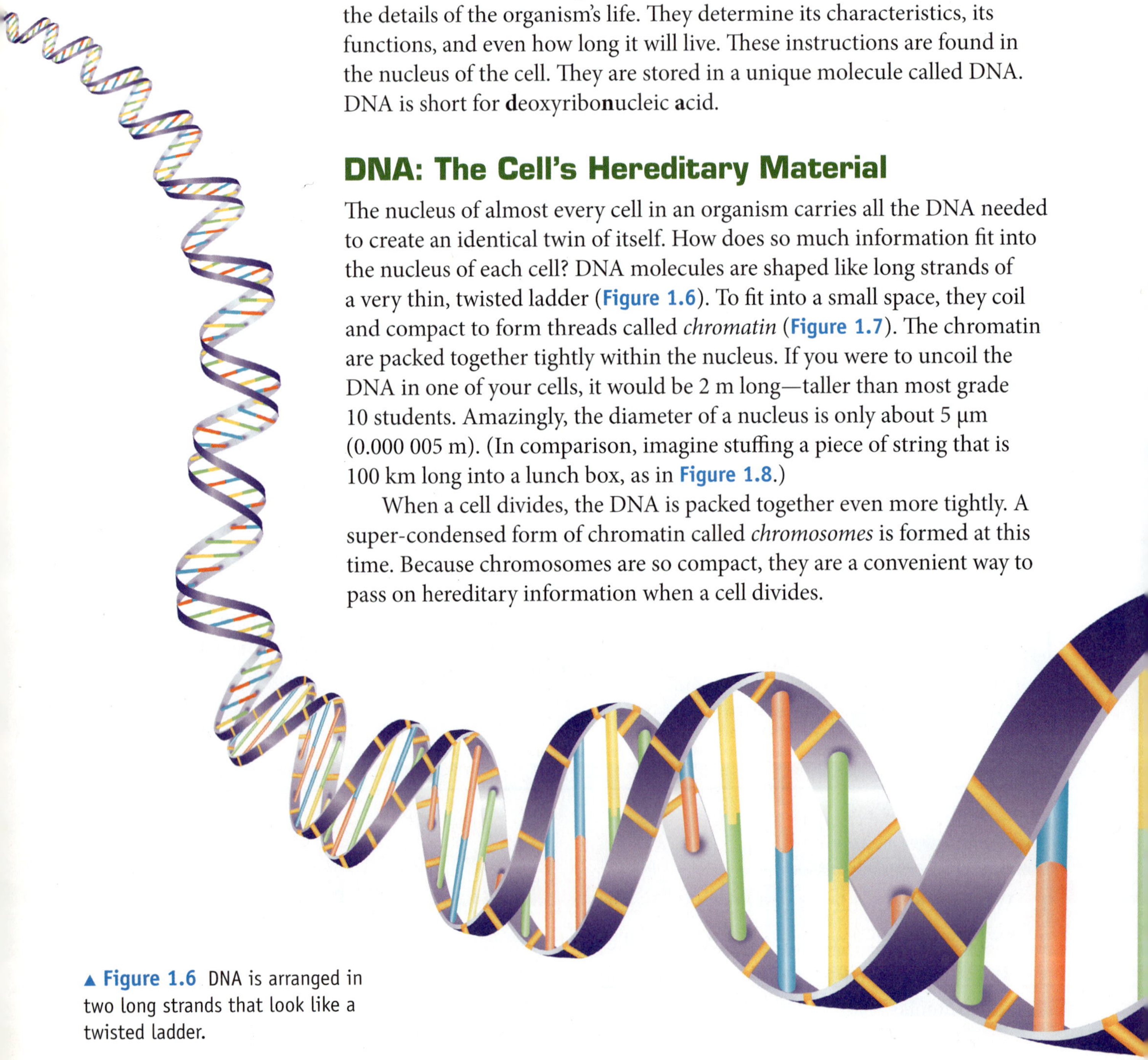

▲ **Figure 1.6** DNA is arranged in two long strands that look like a twisted ladder.

Inquiry Focus

Activity 1.6

MODELLING THE COILING AND CONDENSING OF DNA

To get an idea of how much DNA is packed into a nucleus, see how much string you can stuff into a small box such as the box from a deck of cards. *Much* more DNA fits into the nucleus than string fits into a small box.

◀ **Figure 1.7** DNA is further condensed into coiled threads called chromatin.

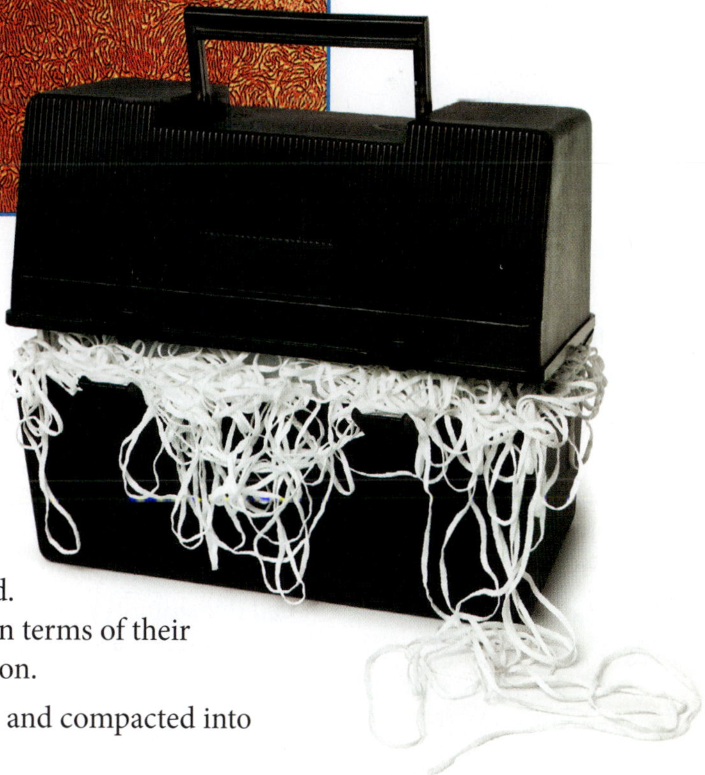

▶ **Figure 1.8** About 2 m of DNA are coiled and condensed to fit into the nucleus. This is like stuffing 100 km of string into a lunch box.

LEARNING CHECK

1. When a cell divides, two new cells are created. Compare these new cells to the original cell in terms of their appearance, their organelles, and their function.
2. What is the benefit of DNA being condensed and compacted into coiled threads of chromatin?
3. Why do you think DNA is packed together even more tightly into chromosomes when a cell divides?

Animal cells have a life cycle that includes both growth and division.

cell cycle: the continuous series of events in the life of a cell in which it is born, grows, reproduces, and dies

All organisms must be able to produce new cells. Many-celled organisms have a special set of cells, called stem cells, that can divide to produce new cells. The series of events that occur when they are dividing is called the **cell cycle**.

Stages of the Cell Cycle

As shown in **Figure 1.9**, the cell cycle is made up of two main stages: a growth stage called interphase and a division stage that consists of mitosis and cytokinesis. Each of these stages includes a series of distinct events.

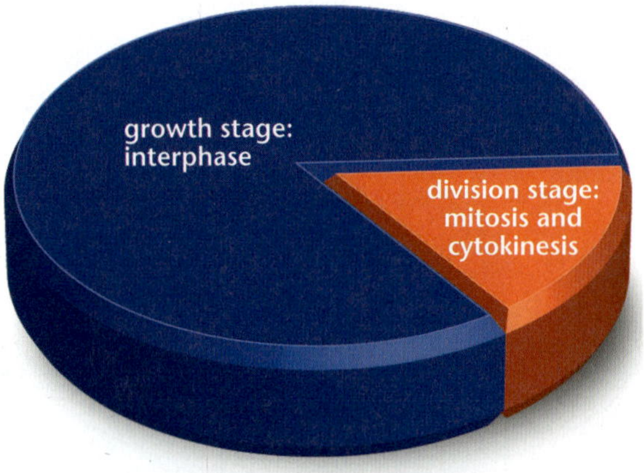

▶ **Figure 1.9** The cell cycle is divided into a growth stage and a division stage.

interphase: the stage in the cell cycle when a cell grows and carries out its usual functions, as well as making a copy of its DNA and organelles to prepare for cell division

mitosis: the stage in the cell cycle when the contents of the nucleus separate into two identical copies

cytokinesis: the stage in the cell cycle when the cytoplasm and organelles divide into two identical, separate cells

The Growth Stage: Interphase

Most of a cell's life cycle is spent in a growth stage called **interphase**. During interphase, the cell grows and carries out its usual functions. The cell also makes a copy of its organelles and the DNA in its nucleus to prepare for division. The majority of cells spend most of their lives in interphase. Interphase ends when a cell begins its division stage.

The Division Stage: Mitosis and Cytokinesis

Cell division is a process in which one cell produces two new cells that are exact copies of the original cell. There are two main phases of cell division:

1. **Mitosis**: During mitosis, the contents of the nucleus separate into two identical copies.
2. **Cytokinesis**: During cytokinesis, the cytoplasm and organelles divide into two identical, separate cells. Each of these cells will now go on to complete its own cell cycle.

Inquiry Focus

Activity 1.7

HOW IS DNA REPLICATION LIKE A GAME OF "TELEPHONE?"

Imagine how many times DNA replicates during a person's life. How likely do you think it is that mistakes are made during replication?

Form a group of at least eight students. Whisper a message to your neighbour. Pass the message from one person to the next. Has the message changed by the time it reaches the last person? How do the results of this game affect your answer to the question in the introduction? How might errors in DNA replication affect the human body?

Why Cell Division Is Important

Cell division enables organisms to carry out three important functions:

- **Growth**: Cell division enables organisms to grow from a single cell into a multi-celled organism that can contain trillions of cells.
- **Maintenance**: Cell division produces new cells to replace worn-out or dead cells.
- **Repair**: Cell division regenerates damaged tissues. **Regeneration** is the ability to grow new cells to replace damaged or lost body components. If you cut your finger, skin cells reproduce so that skin is regenerated over the injured area. Some organisms, such as the starfish in the topic opener, can even regenerate entire body parts.

regeneration: the ability to grow new cells to replace damaged or lost body components

LEARNING CHECK

1. State two reasons why cells reproduce.
2. Make a flowchart to outline what happens during cell division.
3. Do you think cell division occurs more often in a 4-year-old or a 40-year-old? Explain your thinking.

ACTIVITY LINK

Activity 1.10, on page 34

New animal cells are created during the cell cycle.

prophase: the first phase of mitosis when the nucleus and nuclear membrane disappear and chromosomes form

metaphase: the second phase of mitosis when the chromosomes align in the centre of the cell

anaphase: the third phase of mitosis when the chromosomes separate and move to opposite ends of the cell

telophase: the fourth phase of mitosis when the membrane surrounding the nucleus re-forms, creating two new nuclei

In the cell cycle of dividing cells, a precise sequence of events leads to the creation of new cells. Those events are:

- **interphase**;
- the four phases of mitosis (**prophase**, **metaphase**, **anaphase**, and **telophase**);
- **cytokinesis**.

Figure 1.10 shows and describes these events of the cell cycle.

Literacy Focus

Activity 1.8

CELL CYCLE MNEMONICS

You can use a mnemonic (a memory aid) to help you remember the order of events of the cell cycle. For example, look at this statement:

"**I** **P**refer **M**ice **A**nd **T**alking **C**ats."

See that each word starts with the same letter as an event from the cell cycle: **I**nterphase, **P**rophase, **M**etaphase, **A**naphase, **T**elophase, **C**ytokinesis.

Make up your own mnemonic for the events in the cell cycle.

LEARNING CHECK

1. Name the three main events in the life cycle of a cell.
2. Use a main idea web to summarize the phases of mitosis.
3. Describe how Figure 1.10 on page 29 and Figure 1.9 on page 26 are related.
4. Explain what you think could happen if a cell makes an error copying its DNA during interphase.

INVESTIGATION LINK

Investigation 1A, on page 32

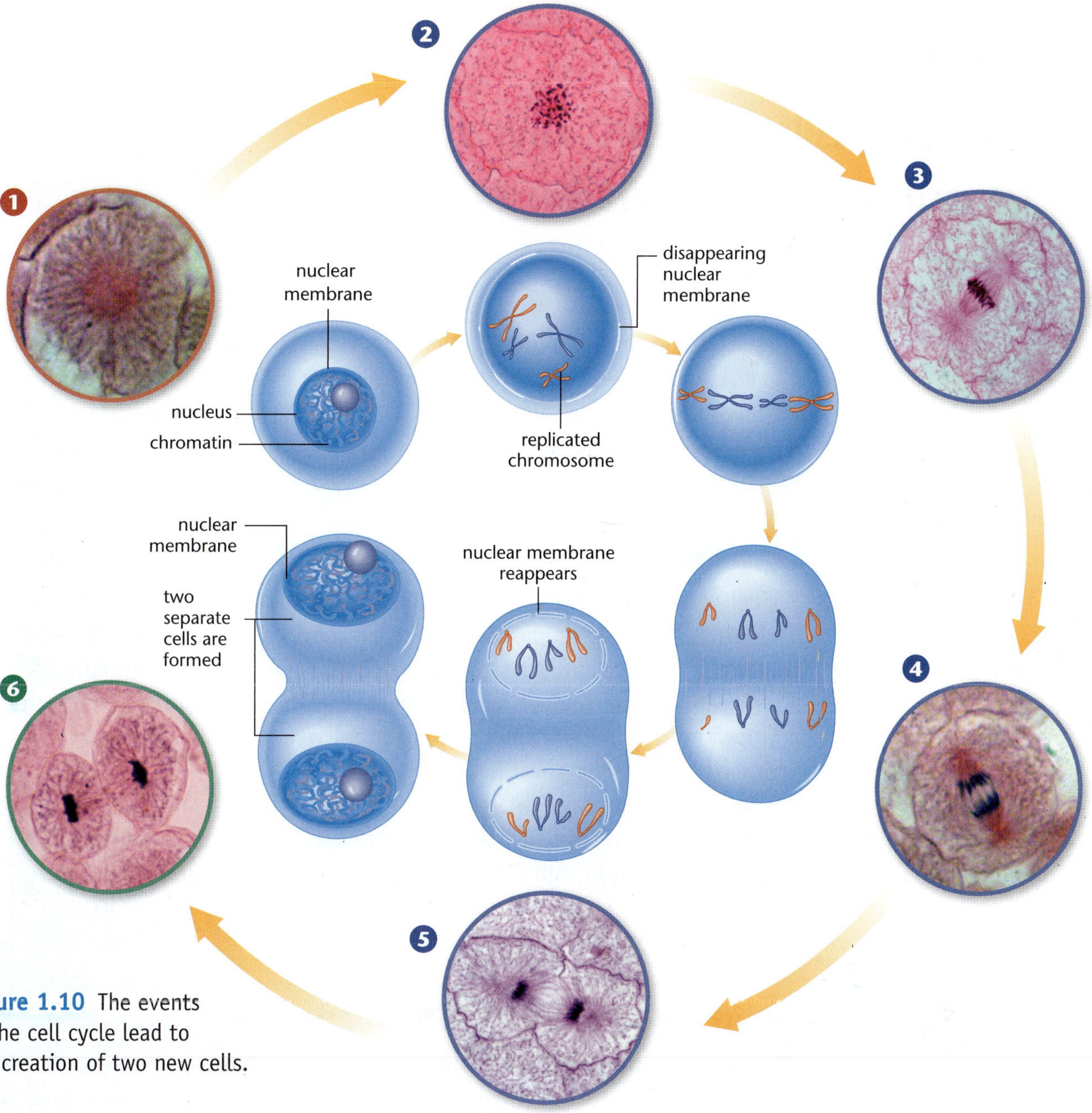

Figure 1.10 The events in the cell cycle lead to the creation of two new cells.

1. Interphase
- The cell grows to nearly twice its original size.
- The number of organelles in the cytoplasm increases.
- The DNA in the nucleus duplicates into two identical copies.

2. Prophase (Mitosis Phase 1)
- The nuclear membrane begins to disappear.
- The duplicated DNA condenses into chromosomes that are visible under the microscope. Each chromosome is made up of two identical copies of DNA that are joined at one point.

3. Metaphase (Mitosis Phase 2)
- Fibres in the cytoplasm push the chromosomes together, lining them up in the middle of the cell.

4. Anaphase (Mitosis Phase 3)
- The points where the two copies of DNA were attached in each chromosome split apart, separating the identical copies of DNA. Each part is now called a chromosome.
- The new chromosomes are pulled apart and drawn to each end of the cell.

5. Telophase (Mitosis Phase 4)
- Membranes begin to form around the two new nuclei. Each nucleus has a complete set of chromosomes that contain a complete copy of the cell's DNA.
- The chromosomes begin to uncoil.

6. Cytokinesis
- The elongated cell begins to pinch apart at the centre, dividing the cytoplasm into two parts.
- Cytokinesis ends when there are two identical, separate cells.

Uncontrolled, rapid division of animal cells can be cancer.

What determines when a cell starts and stops dividing? The cell cycle is controlled by a communication system that involves chemical signals. Consider a cell that is dividing to heal a wound. At a certain point, it receives a chemical signal that the wound has healed and it adjusts its rate of division accordingly.

Unchecked Cell Growth Results in Tumours

Go to **scienceontario** to find out more

If a cell ignores a signal to stop dividing, unchecked cell growth can result. Over time, the newly divided cells form a mass called a *tumour*. Why do some cells ignore signals to stop dividing? The answer lies in mutations. A *mutation* is a permanent change in a cell's DNA. All tumours start with a mutation that affects a cell's response to division signals. This mutation is passed on to other cells during mitosis.

Some mutations are inherited. Some simply occur randomly. And others result from exposure to environmental factors. Environmental factors that result in mutations include ultraviolet light and radiation. Many chemicals, such as those in cigarettes, alcohol, and other drugs, also cause mutations.

Some Tumours are Cancerous

Different mutations can result in different types of tumours. Some mutations can cause benign tumours, while others cause cancerous tumours. Several factors distinguish cancer from a benign tumour, as shown in **Table 1.1.**

Table 1.1 Comparing Cancer and Benign Tumours

Tumour	Characteristics
Benign	• Cell division is unchecked and proceeds at a moderate rate. • Does not invade surrounding cells, but may push nearby cells out of the way. • Does not spread to other parts of the body • Relatively harmless unless found in a part of the body, such as the brain, where it may press on other cells
Cancer (malignant tumour)	• Cell division is unchecked and occurs very quickly. Cells spend little time in interphase. • Damages and destroys surrounding cells by invading them • Can spread to other parts of the body • May interfere with the function of other cells, sometimes resulting in death if the tumour is not destroyed or removed

Literacy Focus

Activity 1.9

COMPARING CELLS

Benign tumour cells tend to look normal. It can be hard to distinguish them from the cells they originated from. Cancer cells, however, look much more "unusual." The image below shows normal cells and and a cancer cell.

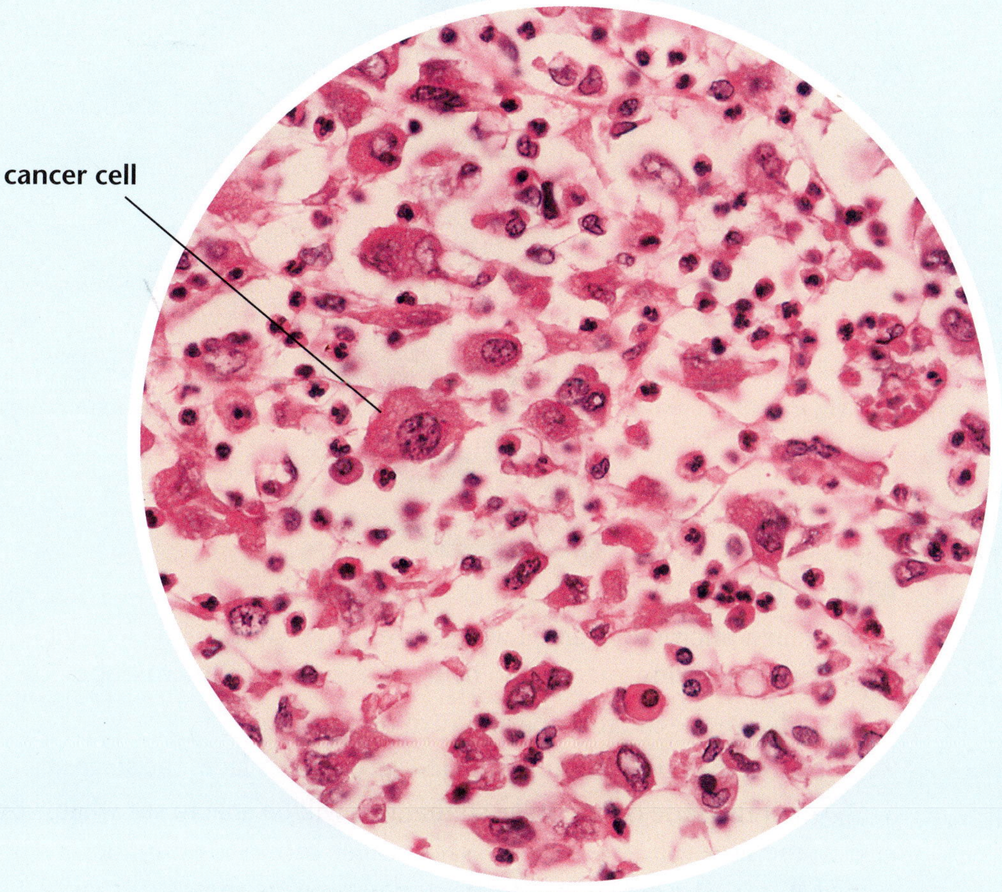

1. Use a graphic organizer to record the similarities and differences you see between the normal cells and cancer cells shown in this photo.
2. Compare organizers with another student. Add any similarities and differences you may have missed.

Hint: Note how cancer cells differ from normal cells in shape, size, and content.

LEARNING CHECK

1. How is the cell cycle regulated?
2. What is cancer?
3. Is cancer (a malignant tumour) always more life threatening than a benign tumour? Explain.

ACTIVITY LINK

Activity 1.11, on page 35, and Activity 1.12, on page 36

Investigation 1A

Observing the Cell Cycle in Animal Cells

Observe and compare the stages of the cell cycle using prepared slides of whitefish embryo cells. Whitefish embryos are in a period of rapid growth.

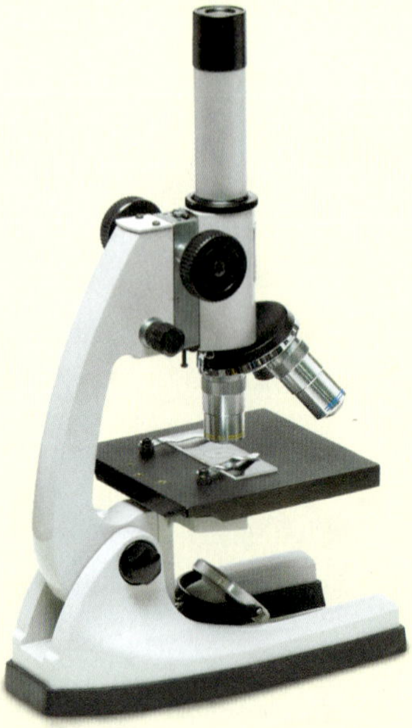

Skill Check

initiating and planning

✓ **performing and recording**

✓ **analyzing and interpreting**

✓ **communicating**

Safety

- Microscope slides are made of glass. If they break, put them in the container for broken glass.
- Make sure that the microscope is turned off and your hands are dry when you plug or unplug the cord.
- To unplug a microscope, pull on the plug not the cord.

What You Need

- microscope
- prepared slides of whitefish embryo cells

What To Do

1. Obtain a microscope and a whitefish embryo slide.
   Use the following checklist to help you set up your microscope:
   - ☑ Plug in the microscope and turn on the light.
   - ☑ Turn the nosepiece until the low-power lens faces the stage.
   - ☑ Put the slide on the stage so that you will be able to see what is on the slide.
   - ☑ Secure the slide using the stage clips.
   - ☑ Looking from the side of the microscope, use the coarse-adjustment knob to bring the lens as close as it will go to the stage.
   - ☑ Look in the eyepiece. Slowly turn the coarse-adjustment knob to get the slide in focus.
   - ☑ Find an area of dividing cells. Make sure that the cells you want to observe are in the centre of the circle.
   - ☑ Turn the fine-adjustment knob to get the best possible focus.
   - ☑ Looking from the side of the microscope, turn the nosepiece until the medium-power lens faces the stage. Look through the eyepiece again. Focus using only the fine-adjustment knob.
   - ☑ Looking from the side of the microscope, turn the nosepiece until the high-power lens faces the stage. Look through the eyepiece again. Focus using only the fine-adjustment knob.
   - ☑ Determine the stage of the cell cycle you are viewing.

2. Identify one cell in each of the following stages of cell division.
   - interphase
   - prophase
   - metaphase
   - anaphase
   - telophase
   - cytokinesis

   Draw each cell. Use **Figure 1.10** on page 29 to help you label as many parts as you can. Refer to the Science Skills Toolkit for instructions for drawing scientific diagrams.
3. Look again for an area of dividing cells on your slide. Move the slide until you are viewing about 100 cells. Record how many cells are dividing and how many are not dividing within your field of view.

What Did You Find Out?

1. Explain how you determined whether or not a cell was dividing.
2. What were the easiest parts of the cell to identify and label?
3. Were most of the cells you examined in step 3 dividing or not dividing? Explain your result.
4. Would you expect most of the cells on a slide of an adult whitefish bone to be dividing or not dividing? Explain your thinking.

Inquire Further

Repeat this investigation using prepared slides of human skin cells. Would you expect to see as many cells dividing? Use your prediction to create a hypothesis.

Stages of the cell cycle in whitefish embryo cells.

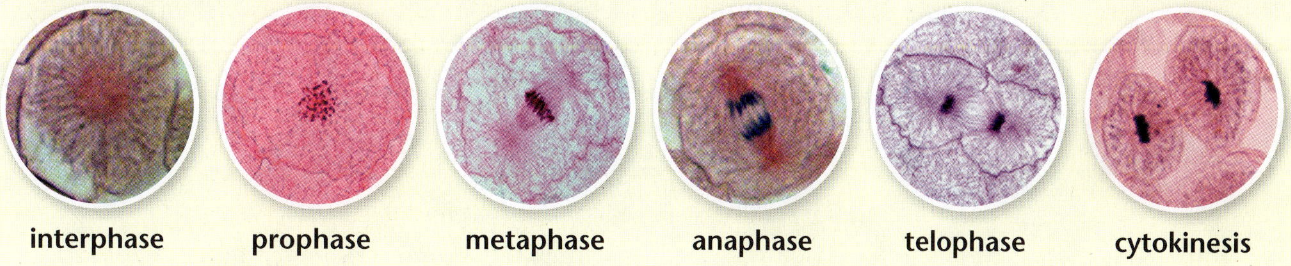

Numeracy Focus

Activity 1.10

HOW MANY TIMES HAVE YOU SHED YOUR SKIN?

Unlike a snake, which sheds all its skin at once, you are always shedding cells from the outer layer of your skin. This happens because older cells are constantly being pushed to the surface by new cells that are growing below. In fact, your entire outer layer of skin is replaced by new cells every 28 days.

What You Need

- calendar
- calculator

What To Do

1. Determine the number of times you have changed your skin in your lifetime. Use a calendar and the hints below to complete the following equation:

$$\text{Number of times you have changed your skin} = \frac{\text{your age} \times 365 + \text{number of days since your last birthday}}{28}$$

(365: number of days in a year)

(28: number of days your skin takes to replace itself completely)

What Did You Find Out?

1. How many times in your lifetime have you changed your skin?
2. Do you think this number is exact? Explain why or why not.

A snake sheds all its skin at once. But you are always shedding cells from the outer layer of your skin.

Research Focus

Activity 1-11

CELLS CYCLING OUT OF CONTROL

Mutations can occur in all types of cells. Some mutations cause a cell to ignore a signal to stop dividing. Such a mutation can result in out-of-control cell division unless the mutated cell dies. In this activity, you will explore how such a mutation affects cell division in cancerous and non-cancerous cells.

What To Do

1. Examine illustrations A and B. Both illustrations begin with a normal cell in the process of dividing.
2. Use the Internet to find and view animations of cell division in normal cells and cancerous cells. Write a paragraph that compares the division of both types of cells.

What Did You Find Out?

1. At what stage of the cell cycle are the cells in A and B?
2. Explain what happens during normal cell division when a cell mutation causes the cell to ignore a signal to stop dividing.

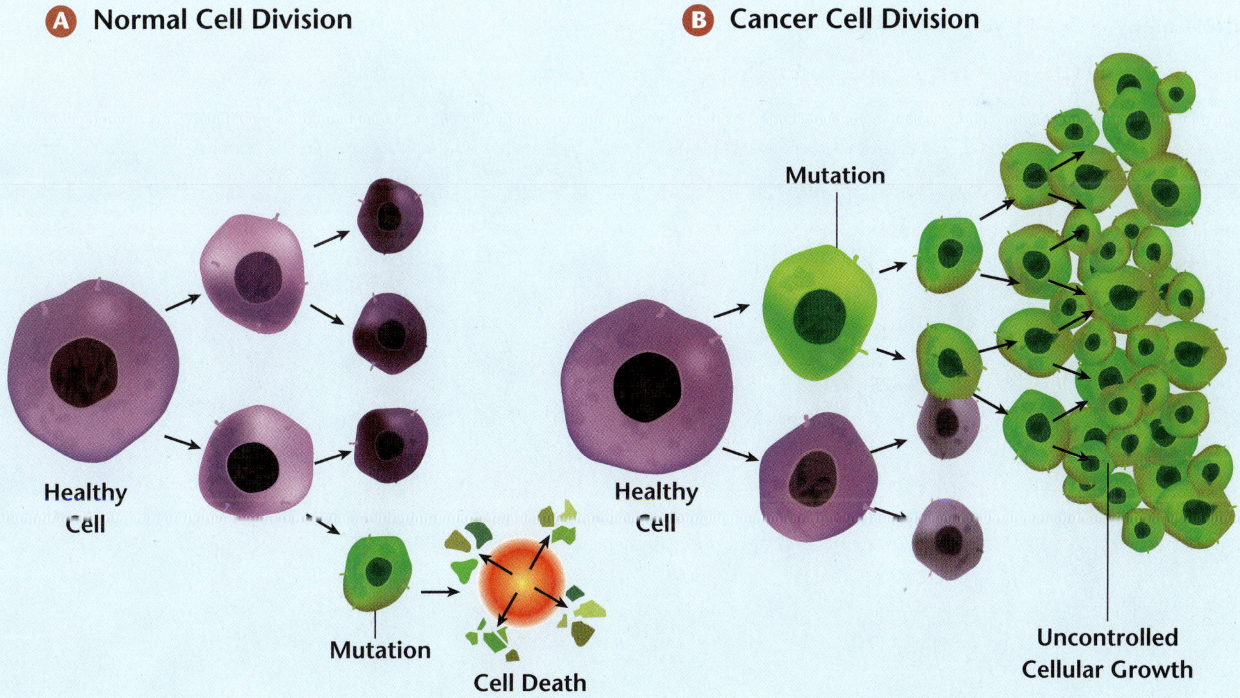

Inquiry Focus

Activity 1.12

ELEPHANTS AND CELLS RUN AMOK

What could elephants and cancer cells possibly have in common? Imagine what would happen if the birth rate of elephants skyrocketed and their death rate decreased to zero. The elephant population would grow unchecked. The elephants would devastate the environment, knocking down trees and trampling over fields and cities. They would eat all the food so nothing else could survive. Eventually the elephants would destroy life on Earth!

What To Do

1. Create a graphic organizer that compares the effects of unchecked elephant population growth with cancer cell division.

What Did You Find Out?

1. a) How would the growth of the elephant population affect other animals and plants on Earth?
   b) How is this similar to how cancer affects cells around it?
2. Describe two other ways in which the uncontrolled growth of an elephant population is similar to the uncontrolled growth of cancer cells.
3. The idea of out-of-control elephant population growth is an analogy, which is a comparison that helps us understand the effects of cancer better. With a partner or as a class, come up with another analogy to help explain the effects of cancer to someone who is not in your class.

Topic 1.2 Review

Key Concept Summary

- Cells must divide for an organism to survive.
- Hereditary material is passed on during cell division.
- Animal cells have a life cycle that includes both growth and division.
- New animal cells are created during the cell cycle.
- Uncontrolled, rapid division of animal cells can be cancer.

Review the Key Concepts

1. K/U Answer the question that is the title of this topic. Copy and complete the graphic organizer below in your notebook. Fill in four examples from the topic using key terms as well as your own words.

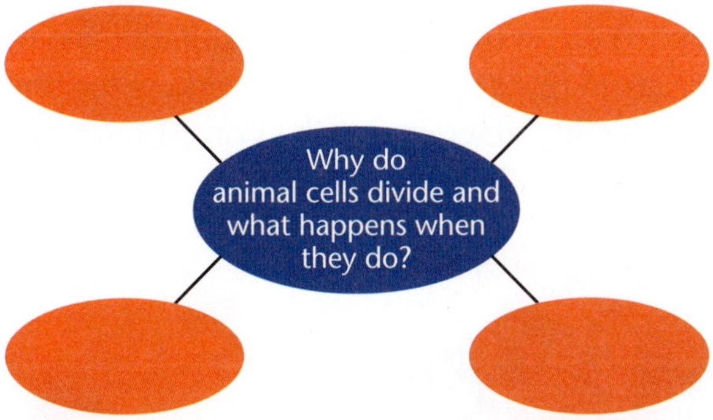

2. A After you are fully grown, why do your cells continue to divide?
3. A Imagine you are made of one giant cell instead of billions of small ones. Describe two problems you would encounter. Explain why you would have these problems.
4. K/U Explain the role DNA plays in cell division.
5. K/U In which stage of the cell cycle is DNA replicated?
6. K/U Describe what happens during the following phases of mitosis: prophase, metaphase, anaphase, and telophase.
7. T/I A What evidence do you have that some cells in your body are dividing?
8. T/I The dark spot on this photo turns out to be skin cancer. What might have been the cause? How was cell division involved?

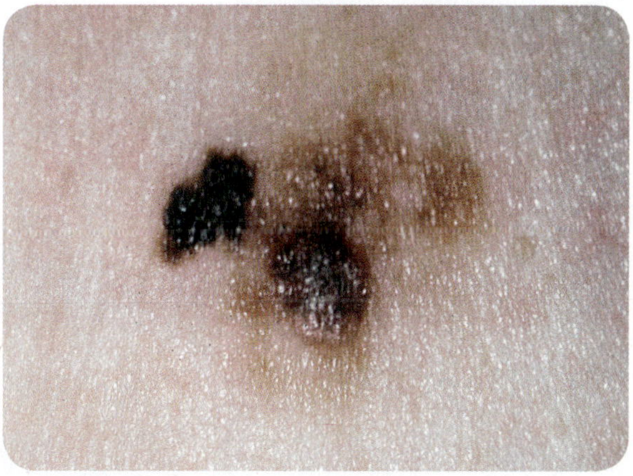

9. C Cigarettes are known to cause cell mutations. Write a letter to the editor of the school paper that explains mutations and why it is important to avoid smoking and limit exposure to cigarette smoke.

Topic 1.3

How do cells work together in the human body?

Key Concepts

- All cells begin alike and differentiate into specialized cells.
- Specialized cells have different structures that allow them to perform unique functions.
- Groups of cells working together form tissues.
- Groups of tissues working together form organs, which work together in systems.

Key Skills

Inquiry
Literacy
Numeracy

Key Terms

cell specialization
cell differentiation
tissue
organ
organ system

Life comes in an enormous range of sizes. It can be as small as a bacterium, which is invisible to the unaided eye. Or it can be large enough to fit half a dozen humans in its jaws alone, such as the school-bus-sized, prehistoric Megalodon shark. Scientists can only observe Megalodon through the fossils it left behind. Due to its huge size, however, it was made up of hundreds of trillions of cells.

A single-celled organism relies on the organelles within its one cell to carry out its life functions. A multi-celled organism requires a greater degree of organization to survive. Most of the cells in a multi-celled organism have different structures and abilities that help them carry out specific functions. But even these specialized cells are limited in what they can do on their own. As a result, the survival of a multi-celled organism relies on teamwork. Working together, specialized cells carry out life functions, such as digestion, breathing, and circulation. Such organization is key to developing complex life forms such as Megalodon and you.

Starting Point Activity

By working together, specialized cells can accomplish tasks they cannot do alone. In this activity, each of your team members will be a specialized cell. Each "cell" will have some abilities but not others. As a result, your team can only complete a given task through teamwork.

1. Assign one student the role of Cell 1 and another student the role of Cell 2. The remaining team members are Cell 3.
   - Cell 1: can move but not talk
   - Cell 2: can talk but not move
   - Cell 3: cannot move or talk other than to tell other cells its birth date
2. Complete the task of lining up all Cell 3 team members in the order of their birth dates, from earliest to latest in the year.
3. Explain how working together as you did enabled you to accomplish a task that each member of your team could not have done alone.

All cells begin alike and differentiate into specialized cells.

Imagine that you are building a shelving unit. You cut the wood, join the shelves together, and mount the unit on the wall. Now imagine that you have only one tool, such as a hammer, to work with. Will you have a harder time completing the job? After all a hammer is great for pounding nails but is inefficient for cutting wood. To build a shelving unit successfully, you need tools that are specialized for the different tasks you must complete.

As the construction task becomes more complex, such as building a shed, the tools you need become more specialized. In this sense, organisms have a lot in common with construction jobs—as they become more complex, more specialized tools (or cells) are required to perform different functions. **Figures 1.11** and **1.12** help illustrate the difference between organisms made of one or many cells in terms of performing life functions.

▼ **Figure 1.11** Like all single-celled organisms, this amoeba relies on the organelles in just one cell to perform all its life functions.

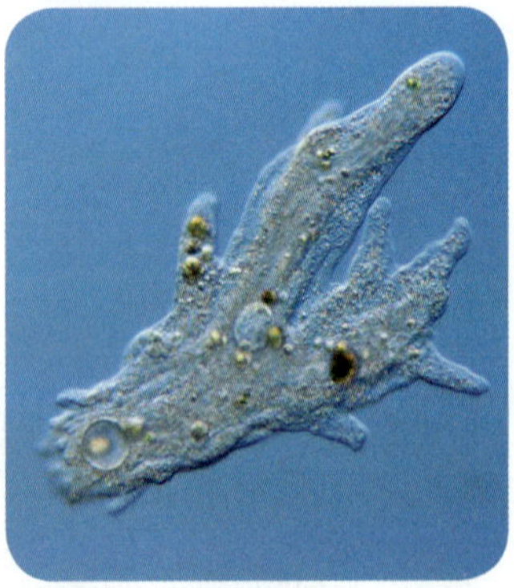

▲ **Figure 1.12** The transparent glass frog is found in Venezuela. It is made up of many specialized cells that have different functions. They form different parts of this organism, which are easy to see through its "glass" skin.

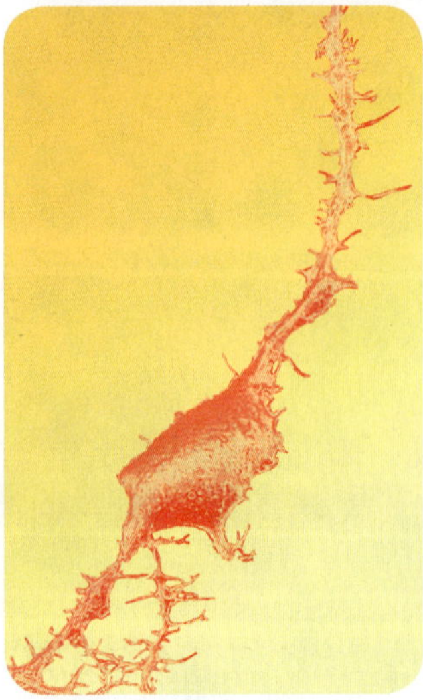

▲ **Figure 1.13** This cell is specialized to transmit messages to the brain.

Cell Specialization and Differentiation

We talk about specialized cells and tools, but what does it mean to become specialized? If you are a mechanic who specializes in Harley Davidson motorcycles, you have to learn a lot about these motorcycles and how to fix them. You have to gain the knowledge you need to work on the motorcycles, as well as obtain the tools. Similarly, a cell that transmits messages to your brain, such as the one shown in **Figure 1.13**, has to have both the structures and the ability to perform this task.

[illegible] refers to the fact that different types of cells have different structures and abilities to perform their functions efficiently. All cells start their lives as identical cells called stem cells. Each stem cell has the potential to become a specialized cell, such as a muscle cell or nerve cell, as it matures. During this process, the cell becomes altered to suit its specific functions. The series of events through which stem cells develop into specialized cells is called **cell differentiation**. Scientists are very interested in studying how stem cells differentiate. These cells offer the potential for treating many diseases if scientists can trigger them to develop into cells that can repair damaged tissues.

cell specialization: refers to the fact that different types of cells have different structures and abilities that enable them to perform their functions efficiently

cell differentiation: the series of events through which stem cells develop into specialized cells

Inquiry Focus

Activity 1.13

MODEL SPECIALIZED CELLS

Design and build two specialized cells. Each cell will carry out one of these functions:

- move limbs by lengthening and shortening
- provide a protective barrier between the inside and outside of the organism

What You Need

- a variety of craft materials

What To Do

1. Working in a small group:
   - List the ideal features of the two specialized cells you want to model.
   - List the organelles you will need to include to support the cells in their function.
2. Sketch each specialized cell and its organelles. Label the organelles and other features that make the cell specialized.
3. Determine the materials you will use to create each specialized cell.
4. Collect the materials and build your cells. Label the features that make each cell specialized.

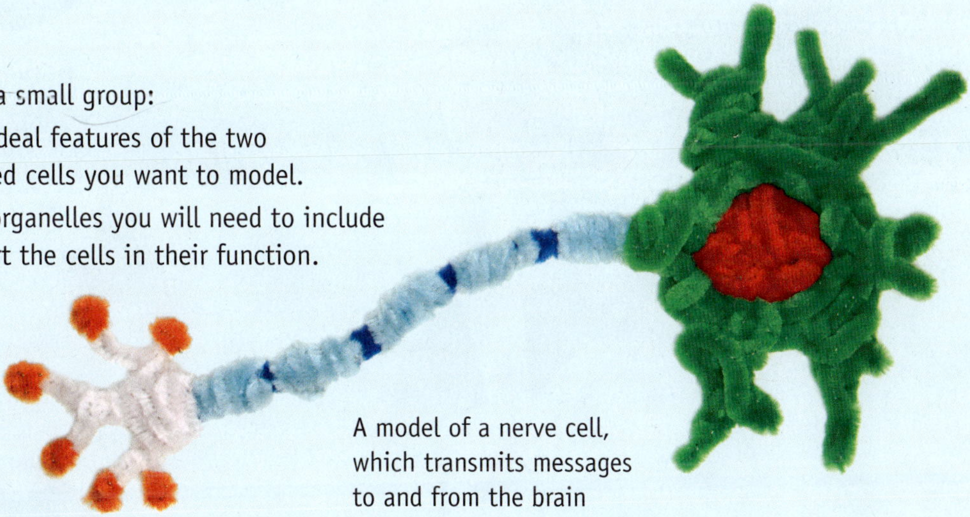

A model of a nerve cell, which transmits messages to and from the brain

LEARNING CHECK

1. Explain why a multi-celled organism such as the glass frog in Figure 1.12 has specialized cells.
2. Use a t-chart to compare cell specialization and cell differentiation.

INVESTIGATION LINK
Investigation 1B, on page 50

Specialized cells have different structures that allow them to perform unique functions.

▲ **Figure 1.14.** This funnel has a lot in common with a specialized cell.

Pouring a liquid into a bottle can be messy if you do not have a funnel such as the one shown in **Figure 1.14**. A funnel is small on one end to fit into the neck of a bottle and wide on the other end. It is specialized so that you can transfer liquid into a bottle without spilling. Similarly, the structure of each specialized cell is adapted for the task that it performs. **Figure 1.15** shows a variety of specialized human cells. **Table 1.2** describes how the structure of each cell influences its function.

▶ **Figure 1.15** In total, there are over 200 different types of cells in the human body! Muscle, nerve, bone, blood, and skin cells are shown here.

Table 1.2 Specialized Cells and Their Functions in the Human Body

Specialized Cells	How Structure Influences Function
Muscle cells	• Long and thin structure allows the cells to change size drastically when they contract. • Some have a branching pattern that increases muscle strength. • High concentration of mitochondria supply the energy required to change shape.
Nerve cells (called *neurons*)	• Long, threadlike branches enable the cells to receive and transmit signals from other cells throughout the body.
Red blood cells	• Doughnut-like shape with a depression in the centre provides a large surface area to carry oxygen.
Bone cells	• Framework of hard material, which contains minerals that provide strength and support, hold the cells together.
Skin cells	• Thin, flat, and layered cells form a gap-free barrier to keep out potential invaders and keep in moisture.

Inquiry Focus

Activity 1.14

DIFFERENT CELLS, DIFFERENT JOBS, DIFFERENT YOU!

Choose one of the specialized cells shown in **Table 1.2**. Consider what would happen to you if you did not have this type of cell in your body. Imagine that you are looking in a mirror. Would you look like yourself, or like a completely alien life form? Do you think you could survive without this type of cell? Explain your thinking.

▶ What would you look like if your body were covered with a totally different kind of covering instead of skin cells?

LEARNING CHECK

1. Why do different specialized cells have different structures?
2. Refer to **Table 1.2** to explain how neurons are specialized to carry out their function.
3. Do you think a fish would have the same types of specialized cells as a bird? Explain your thinking.

ACTIVITY LINK

Activity 1.16, on page 48

Groups of cells working together form tissues.

tissue: specialized cells working together to perform a function

Cells are the basic unit of life. But even specialized cells can only accomplish so much on their own. This is where teamwork becomes important, as you discovered in the topic opener. When specialized cells work together to perform a specific function, they are known as a **tissue**. There are four basic types of tissues: muscle, epithelial, connective, and nervous tissue. Many different tissues may be classified into these four groups, as shown in **Table 1.3**.

Table 1.3 Tissues in the Human Body

Tissue	Function	Example
Muscle	• Enables body parts to move, exert force, or change shape	Muscle cells in an arm 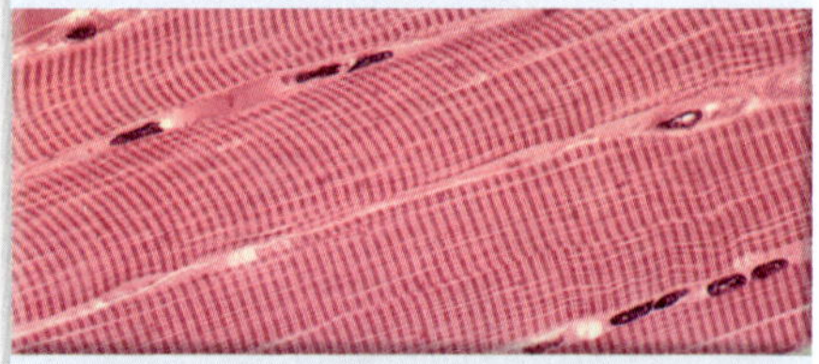 Muscle cells in the stomach 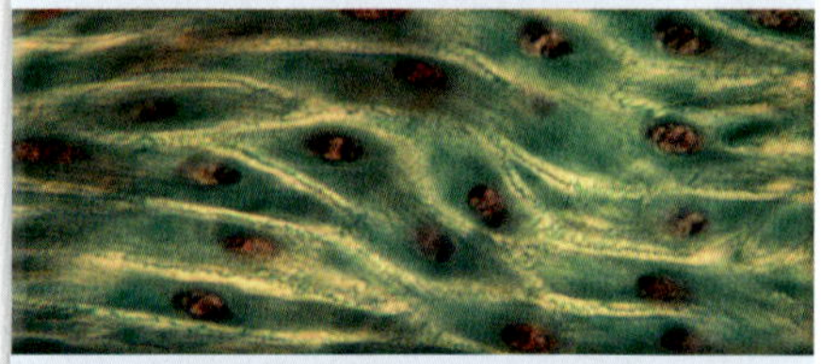 Muscle cells in the heart 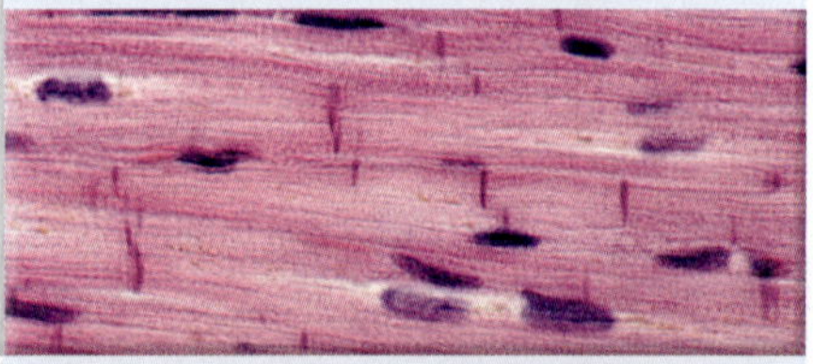
Epithelial	• Covers the external and internal body surfaces	Epithelial cells in skin 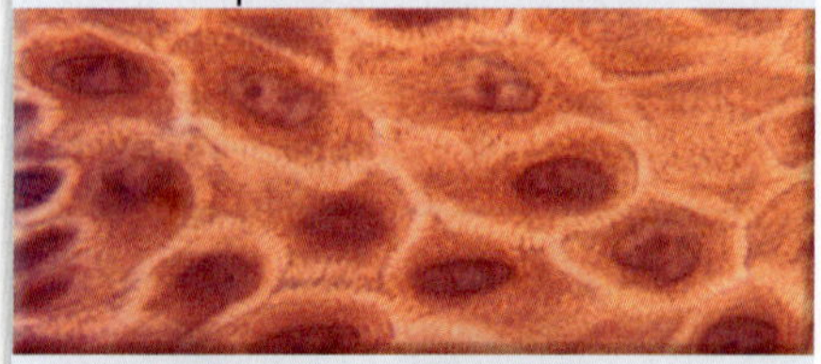 Epithelial cells in the small intestine 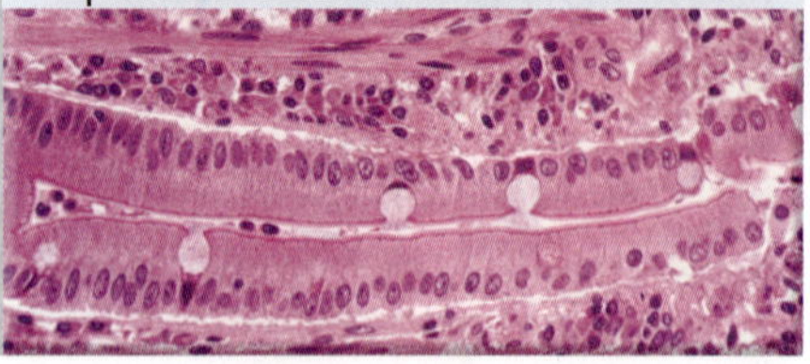

Tissue	Function	Example
Connective	• Strengthens, supports, or connects cells and tissues	Bone connective tissue 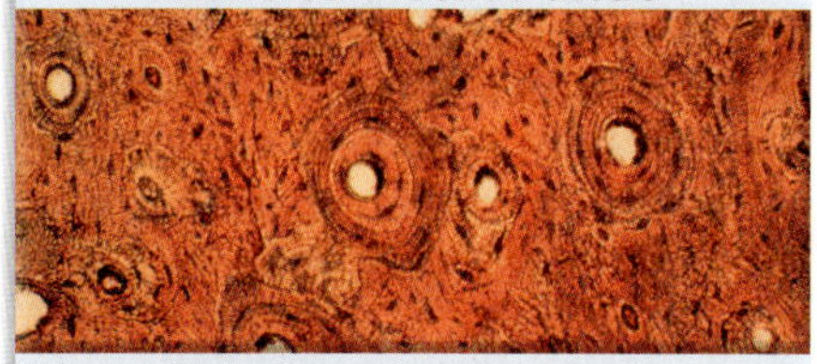 Blood connective tissue 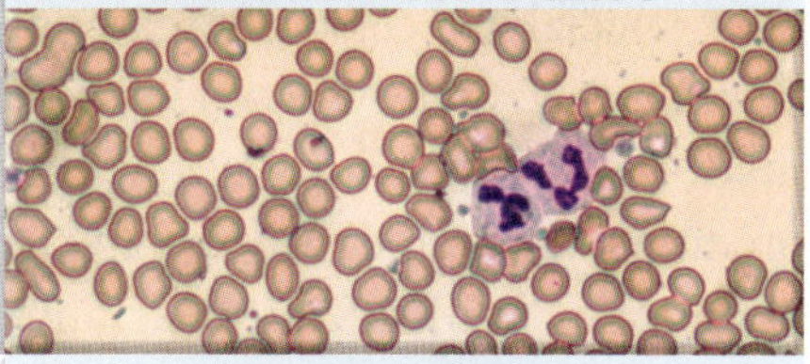
Nervous	• Senses, conducts, and transmits information	Nervous tissue 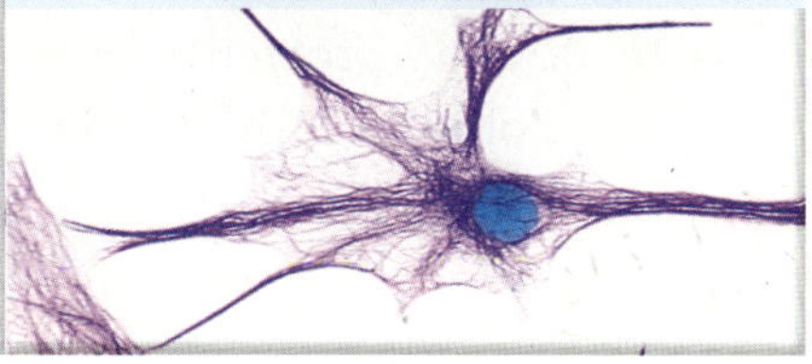

Literacy Focus

Activity 1.15

TISSUE MODELS

Your class is entering a contest in which the participants model complex materials with everyday items. Your class has chosen to model the four basic human body tissues. The everyday items you can use are a rubber band, a piece of plastic wrap, some electrical wire, and some modelling clay.

1. Refer to the information about tissues in **Table 1.3** and decide which item best models each type of tissue.
2. Choose four other items you could use to model the same four types of tissues. Explain why you chose each item.
3. In what ways were the items that you chose limited in their ability to represent the tissues they were modelling?

LEARNING CHECK

1. What are tissues?
2. List the four basic types of tissues.
3. There are four basic types of tissues, but many more types of specialized cells. Why might this be?

Groups of tissues working together form organs, which work together in systems.

organ: different tissues working together to perform a specific task

Go to **scienceontario** to find out more

Different tissues perform unique, individual functions. However, like specialized cells, they can only do so much on their own. Tissues working together overcome this limitation to form organs. An **organ** is made up of different tissues working together to perform a specific task. An organ contains at least two different types of tissues. For example, your heart is an organ. Within your heart, muscle tissue contracts and relaxes to pump blood through valves made of connective tissue. The heart also contains nerve tissue and a protective layer of epithelial tissue. **Figure 1.16** shows some of the other organs found in your body along with their functions.

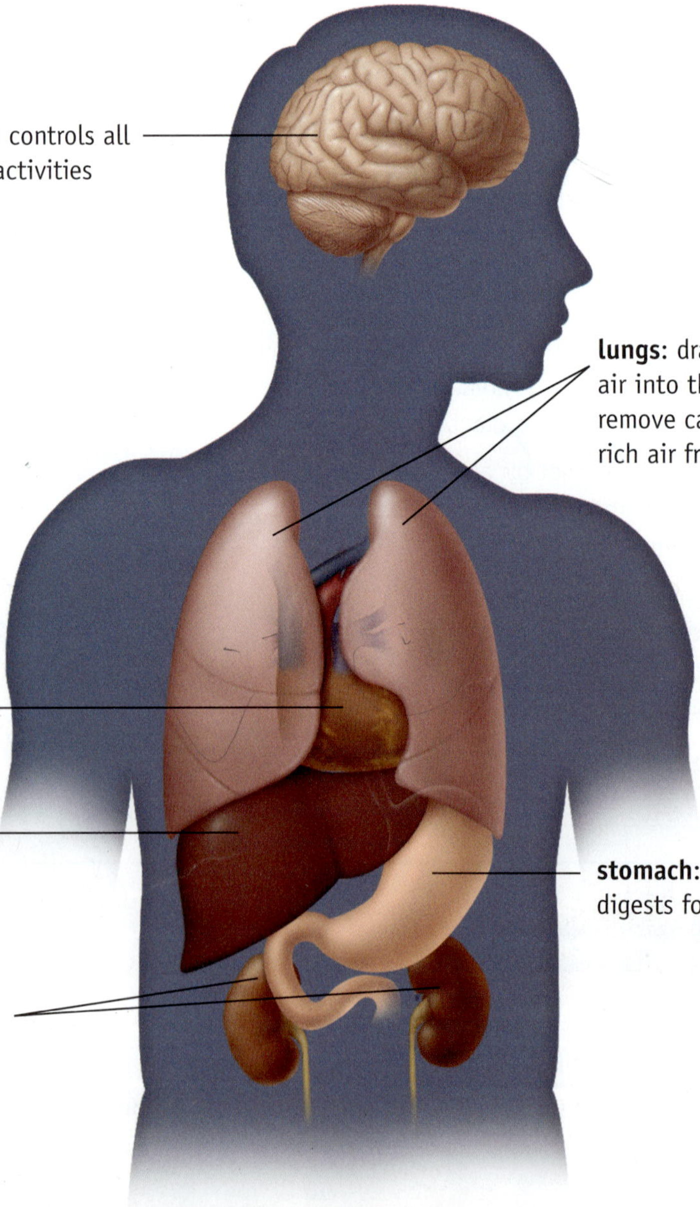

▶ **Figure 1.16** Some of the major human organs

Organs Working Together Form Systems

Just as tissues working together form organs, organs working together form **organ systems**. The organs in an organ system interact with each other to perform a common task. **Figure 1.17** shows the different organ systems in the human body and their basic functions.

organ system: a group of organs that interact with each other to perform a common task

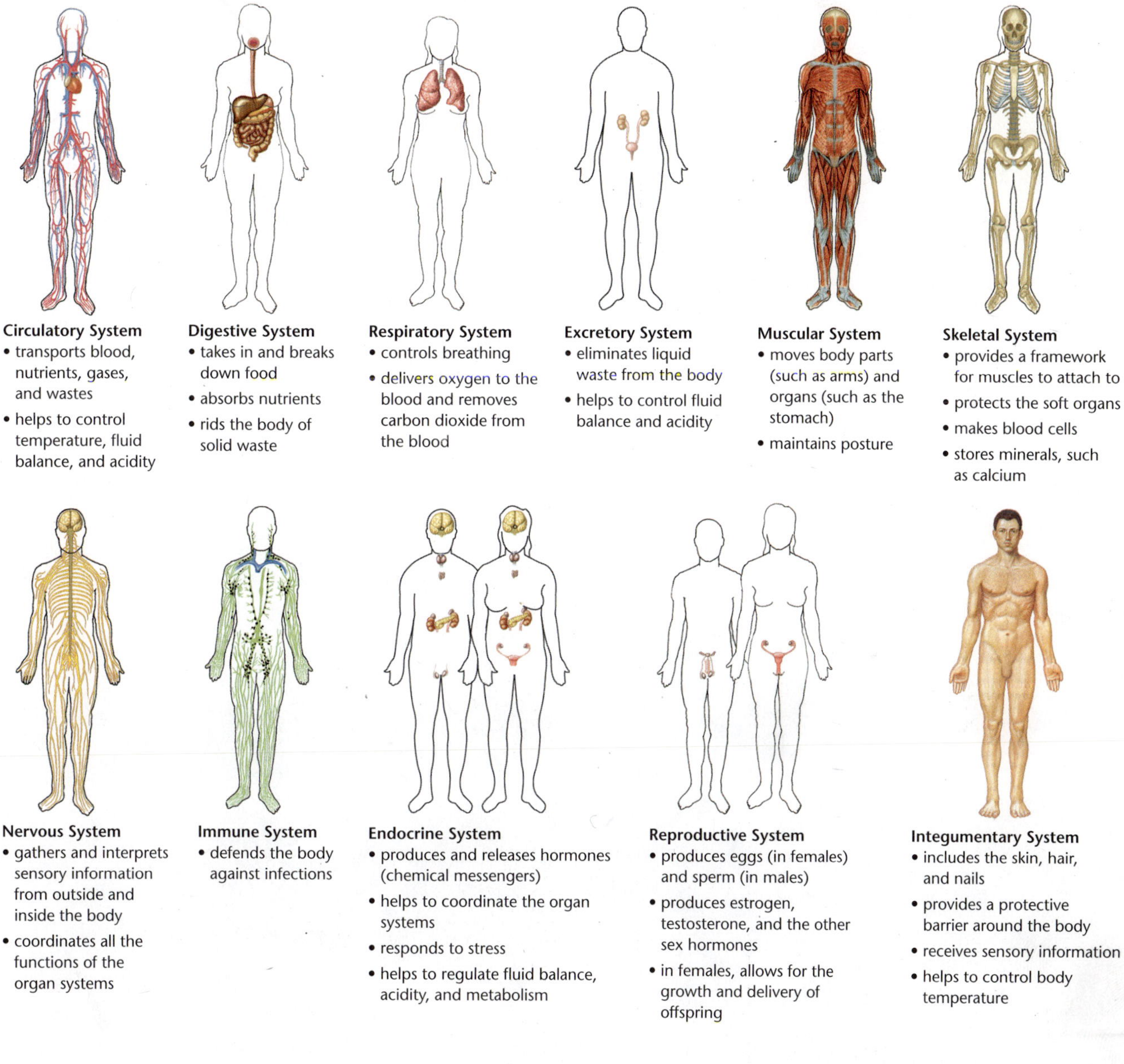

▲ **Figure 1.17** Human organ systems

LEARNING CHECK

1. What is an organ?
2. a) What function do the circulatory and respiratory systems work together to perform?
   b) Identify two other examples of two or more organ systems working together to perform a certain function.

ACTIVITY LINK
Activity 1.17, on page 49

Inquiry Focus

Activity 1.16

THINKING ABOUT CHANGES TO ORGANS

In *A Voyage to Arcturus*, a strange novel that is part science-fiction and part fantasy, the main character awakes on an Earth-like planet where he discovers that his body has new organs. One is a tentacle-like limb sprouting from his heart, whose function is to perceive the inner beauty of all things. Another is a plum-sized lump on his forehead that enables him to read minds and communicate telepathically with other beings on the planet.

What To Do

1. Imagine that you are the character in a story that you are writing. In your story, one day you find that you have awoken on the Moon, on Mars, or on a planet that you have made up.
   a) Describe changes to two of your organs that are appropriate to the conditions of the Moon or planet.
   b) Invent two new organs that you (your character) discovers upon awakening.
2. Now bring your imagination and your ideas back down to Earth. What kinds of changes can happen to real organs and organ systems here, on Earth? Name at least two changes and what could cause them.
3. It is possible for people to live and carry on a healthy, productive life if they lose an organ.
   a) Identify at least four organs that you know or think a person can live without.
   b) Describe how the body adjusts to the absence of each of these organs. (In some cases, the adjustment requires the help of technology. Be sure to indicate what, if any, technology is needed.)

Numeracy Focus

Activity 1.17

THE BEAT THAT GOES ON AND ON

Do you take your heart for granted Do you ever pause to think how amazing it is? Your heart pumps approximately 4 L of blood through your body each minute. You know this pumping action as the beating of your heart. Every minute of every day, for your whole life, your heart continues to beat. Determine how many times your heart has beaten from the moment you were born until your last birthday.

What To Do

1. Determine how many times your heart beats in one minute.
   - Gently place your middle finger and ring finger against either wrist until you find a pulse.
   - Use a stopwatch to keep time while you count the beats you feel in one minute.
2. Use the following equation to calculate how many times your heart has beaten from the moment you were born until your last birthday.

$$\text{Beats from birth until last birthday} = \text{number of beats counted in 1 minute} \times 60 \times 24 \times 365 \times \text{your age}$$

60: number of minutes in one hour
24: number of hours in one day
365: number of days in one year

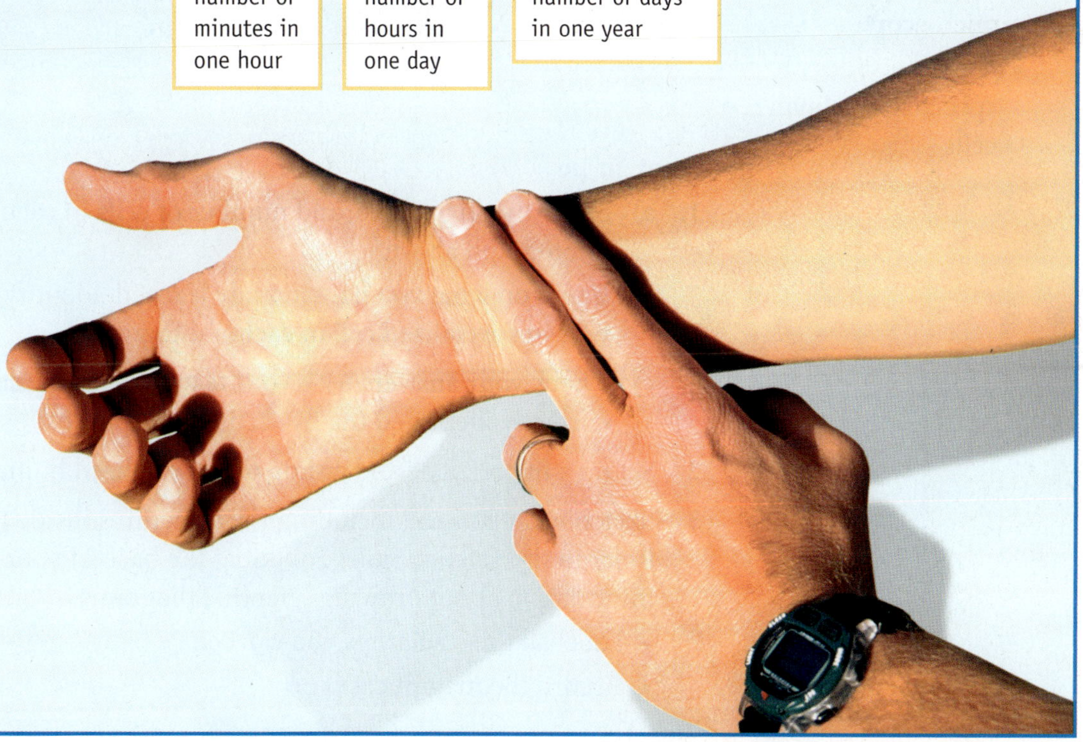

What Did You Find Out?

1. How many times has your heart beaten since you were born?
2. How do you think your answer would compare with the number of beats calculated by a marathon runner who is the same age? Explain.
3. How accurate do you think your answer is? (Hint: Think of how your heartbeat changes when you play sports.) Explain your reasoning.
4. Why do you think it is recommended that you exercise to make your heart beat faster for at least 20 minutes three times a week?

Investigation 1B

Skill Check

- initiating and planning
- ✓ **performing and recording**
- ✓ **analyzing and interpreting**
- ✓ **communicating**

Viewing Specialized Human Cells

In this investigation, you will observe specialized human cells under a microscope and sketch what you observe. Then you will compare what you observed under the microscope with the photographs shown below.

A

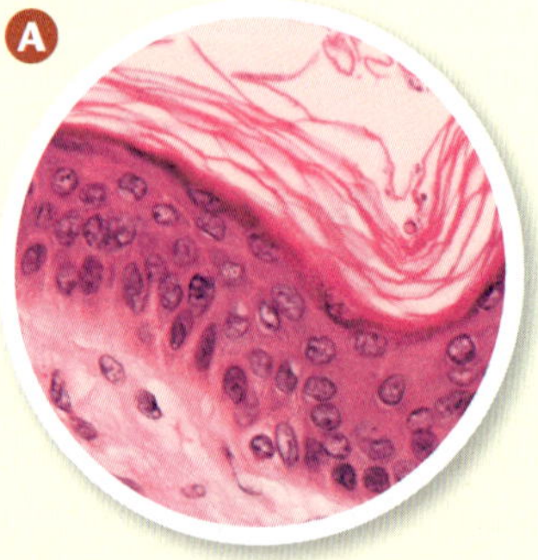

B

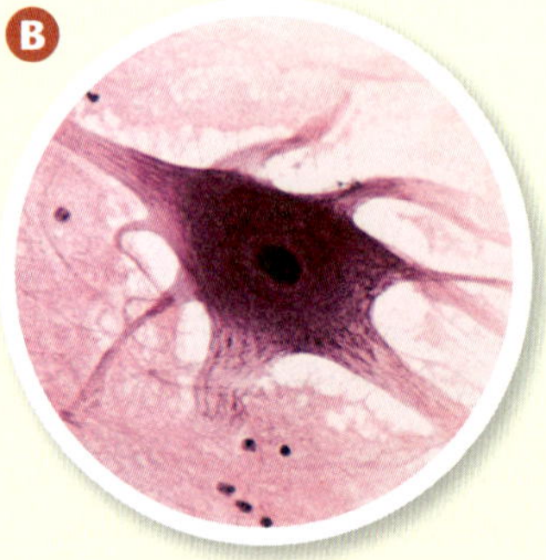

C

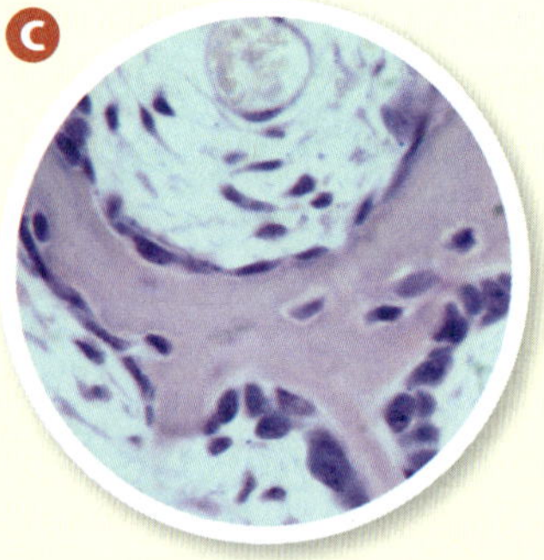

D

E

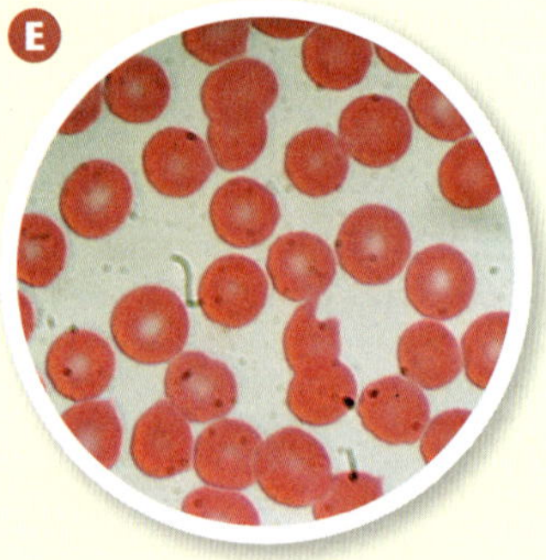

Safety

- Microscope slides are made of glass. If they break, put them in the container for broken glass.
- To unplug a microscope, pull on the plug not the cord.

What You Need

- microscope
- prepared slides of specialized human cells

What To Do

1. **a)** Study the shape, size, and number of cells in each photograph above.
   b) Based on what you have already learned, identify the type of specialized cell in each photograph.
   c) Check your answers with your teacher to make sure you have correctly identified the five cells in the photos.
2. Set up a microscope and a slide of a specialized human cell.
3. Sketch what you see, including the structures inside the cell. Refer to the Science Skills Toolkit at the back of your textbook for information about drawing scientific diagrams.
   - Label all the structures you can see.
   - Record the magnification.

4. a) Identify the type of specialized cell you sketched by matching your sketch with one of the photographs. Compare the similarities and differences.
   b) Label the type of specialized cell you sketched.
5. Repeat steps 2 to 4 for each slide.

What Did You Find Out?

1. Which cell was the easiest to identify? Explain why.
2. Which cell was the most difficult to identify? Explain why.
3. How similar were the specialized cells you observed under the microscope to the specialized cells in the photographs? Provide a possible reason for any differences you observed.
4. In your notebook, make a table similar to the one below. Give your table an appropriate title. Include a row for each type of specialized cell you viewed.
   - In the first column, write the name of each type of specialized cell you viewed.
   - In the second column, describe the main features of each type of specialized cell.
   - In the third column, explain how these features help the cell perform its function.

Title ______________________________

Specialized Cell	Features	Function

5. Do all of your sketches of specialized cells include the same organelles? Explain why or why not.

Inquire Further

There are many other types of specialized cells. Use print or electronic resources to identify at least two more types of specialized human cells. Ask your teacher for microscope slides of these cells and compare the photographs with the slides. Make a labelled sketch of each type of specialized cell and describe its function.

Strange Tales of Science

Stomach for Science

In the early 1800s, the stomach was an unknown frontier for scientists. Little was known about the digestive system or what happened to food once it was swallowed. Until one fateful day in 1822, that is, when an unfortunate accident provided a unique "window" into the world of digestion. The following story is pieced together from actual notes and letters from the 1800s. Read it and see if you have the stomach for the price one man paid in the name of science.

June 6, 1822. This trading post on Mackinac Island in Lake Huron was about to witness the creation of the most famous stomach in scientific history.

An accidental discharge of a musket blew open the stomach and chest wall of unsuspecting French-Canadian canoe guide, Alexis St. Martin.

Luckily, Dr. William Beaumont was stationed at the nearby US military camp. He reached St. Martin within minutes of the blast.

Dr. Beaumont has cleaned the wound as best he can. Still, it does not look good for St. Martin. But wait...

Amazing. Your wound has healed in weeks. But it has joined to the chest wall, leaving a hole the size of a chestnut. The bandage will keep food from escaping.
Upon my word, what an opportunity. If I can just get him to agree to...
...to the surprise of all, St. Martin recovers. But is that good news or bad? It seems Dr. Beaumont has plans for that hole in Alexis's stomach.
It could not have been easier. Get the illiterate woodsman to sign a document that he will work as my servant for scant wages. And his stomach will be mine to experiment with day in and day out.
What have I done?
One year later, St. Martin has agreed to travel to Dr. Beaumont's new post in the U.S.
The stomach experiments begin. Food is lowered into St. Martin's stomach and observed. Digestive chemicals are removed and analyzed. Slowly, over several years, the secrets of the stomach are revealed.
"I consider myself but a humble inquirer after truths...a simple experimenter."
"The gastric juice is such a powerful solvent. Even the hardest bone cannot withstand its action."

So... What do you think?

1. Did Beaumont convince St. Martin to return? Create a graphic novel that tells how this story might end.
2. Beaumont achieved fame when he published a book about St. Martin's stomach. The book contained 240 of the experiments he completed. Find out three things Beaumont learned about digestion from his experiments.
3. Years later, Dr. Beaumont was quoted as saying that St. Martin left in part because of "unwillingness to submit himself for public experiments." Would you have been willing to take part in these experiments as St. Martin did? Explain why or why not.
4. Beaumont could have closed the hole in St. Martin's stomach with simple surgery, yet he chose not to. In your opinion, was this acceptable? Explain your reasoning.

Topic 1.3 Review

Key Concept Summary

- All cells begin alike and differentiate into specialized cells.
- Specialized cells have different structures that allow them to perform unique functions.
- Groups of cells working together form tissues.
- Groups of tissues working together form organs, which work together in systems.

Review the Key Concepts

1. **K/U** Answer the question that is the title of this topic. Copy and complete the graphic organizer below in your notebook. Fill in four examples from the topic using key terms as well as your own words.

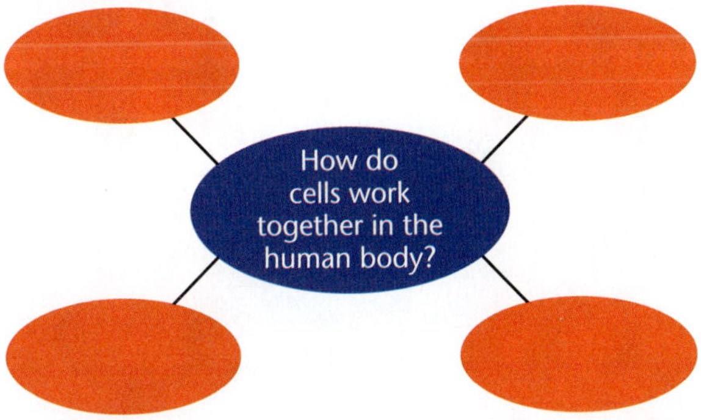

2. **K/U** **a)** What are stem cells?
   b) Why are stem cells important for a multi-celled organism?
3. **K/U** Identify two organs and describe the function of each.
4. **T/I** **a)** Identify each tissue shown below.
   b) For each tissue, describe its function.

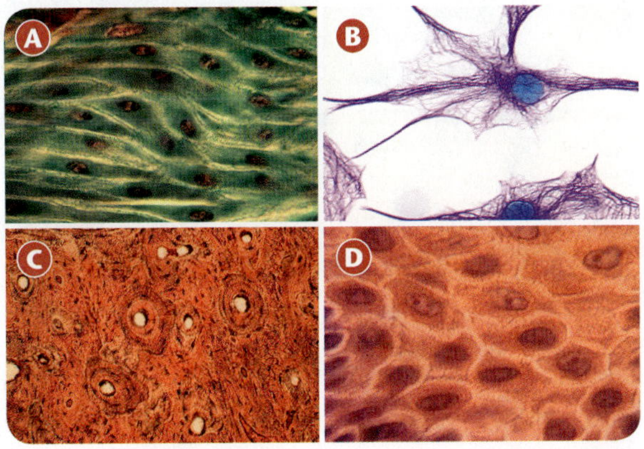

5. **K/U** Draw a flowchart that shows the following terms in order of their complexity, from least complex to most complex: organs, tissues, systems, cells.
6. **T/I** Choose two specialized cells you have studied. Use a Venn diagram to compare the similarities and differences between the two cells.
7. **C** You are the science writer for a community newspaper. Write an article describing one organ system and the role it plays in the body.
8. **A** Think of a human-made system not discussed in this textbook—for example, a computer network, a sewage system, a post office, or a train station. Compare your system to one of the human organ systems shown in **Figure 1.17**.
9. **A** Multiple sclerosis (MS) is a disease that affects the brain and spinal cord, impairing their ability to communicate with each other. Which type of tissue is affected by MS?
10. **C** Use a creative medium of your choice, such as a skit or drawing, to describe how one of the following human cells is adapted for its function: neuron, muscle cell, red blood cell, bone cell, skin cell.

Topic 1.4 How do systems work together in the human body?

Key Concepts

- The respiratory system carries oxygen to and removes carbon dioxide from the blood.
- The circulatory system transports dissolved gases and nutrients through the body.
- The digestive system breaks down food, absorbs nutrients, and eliminates solid waste.
- Organ systems working together carry out important tasks in the body.

Key Skills

- Inquiry
- Literacy

Key Terms

gas exchange
alveoli
capillaries
red blood cells
absorption

In 2009, Canadian astronaut Robert Thirsk began a six-month stay on the International Space Station (ISS) orbiting around Earth. The astronauts on the ISS place their lives in the hands of the space station's advanced life support system. For the astronauts to survive in space, the temperature and pressure within the ISS must be maintained. An adequate supply of oxygen must be provided, and waste gases, such as carbon dioxide, must be removed. Solid waste must also be removed, but urine is recycled to provide the crew with clean water. All of these functions are achieved with the help of advanced technology systems.

All the systems on the ISS must work together to support life on board. The same is true inside your body. Like the life support system on the ISS, your organ systems must work together to keep you alive. For instance, your body needs systems that enable it to take in oxygen and remove carbon dioxide.

Starting Point Activity

Imagine that you are on the ISS for a month-long stay.

1. Name at least three jobs that the ISS needs to perform to keep you and the other astronauts alive.
2. Brainstorm to create a list of the organ systems you already know about. How are the life support systems on the ISS similar to the organ systems in your body?

Canadian astronauts Julie Payette and Robert Thirsk working together and with other astronauts on the International Space Station during a 2009 mission.

The respiratory system carries oxygen to and removes carbon dioxide from the blood.

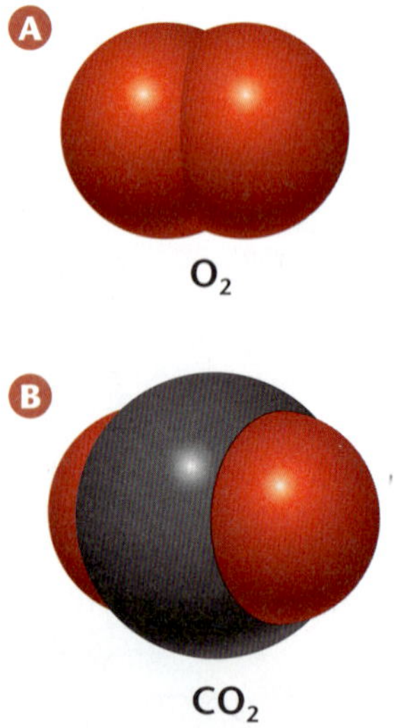

▲ **Figure 1.18** The respiratory system is responsible for the exchange of oxygen (A) and carbon dioxide (B).

Even when you are at rest, a lot of activities are occurring inside your body. For example, your body is sending messages, transporting nutrients, and creating new cells. The cells in your body need a lot of energy to perform these activities. Where does this energy come from? If you answered food, you are only partly right. Cells also need oxygen to release the energy that is stored in food molecules such as glucose. They do this through cellular respiration. Each time you breathe in, the respiratory system takes in the oxygen that your cells require to carry out cellular respiration.

Carbon dioxide and water are also produced when cells carry out cellular respiration. Your body gets rid of carbon dioxide every time you breathe out. The process of taking in oxygen and releasing carbon dioxide is called **gas exchange** (see **Figure 1.18**). Gas exchange occurs in your lungs.

Components of the Respiratory System

The respiratory system includes many different organs that work together for gas exchange to take place. **Figure 1.19** shows the path that air follows when you inhale.

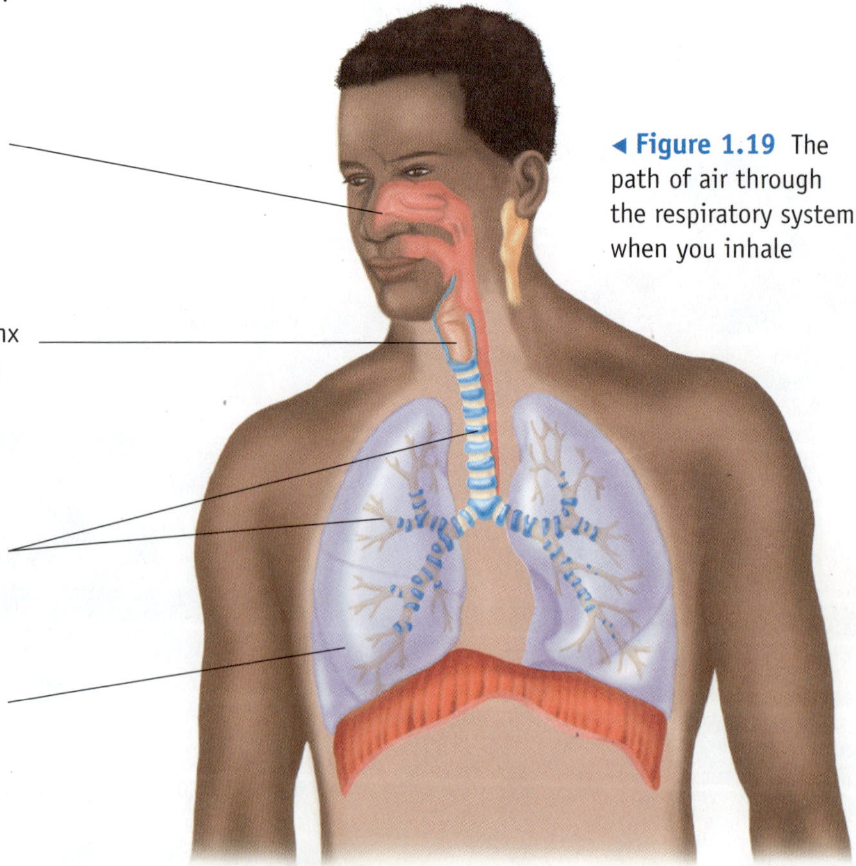

◀ **Figure 1.19** The path of air through the respiratory system when you inhale

Gas Exchange Takes Place in the Alveoli

Once air reaches the lungs, the actual exchange of gases occurs between the blood and the **alveoli**. Alveoli are clusters of tiny air sacs in the lungs. The wall of each alveolus is a single layer of cells.

Alveoli are surrounded by a network of tiny blood vessels called **capillaries**. The wall of each capillary also is a single layer of cells. The ultra-thin walls of both the alveoli and the capillaries allow the exchange of gases between the air and the blood, as shown in Figure 1.20.

Once the air enters the capillaries, oxygen from the air is taken up by the **red blood cells**. The red blood cells are responsible for transporting gases in the bloodstream. Oxygen diffuses through the walls of the alveoli, through the capillary walls, and into the red blood cells.

The blood also releases carbon dioxide into the lungs. The path that carbon dioxide follows is the reverse of the path that oxygen follows. Carbon dioxide diffuses from the blood through the capillary walls, through the walls of the alveoli, and into the alveoli. Once in the lungs, the carbon dioxide is exhaled with the next breath.

gas exchange: the process of taking in oxygen and releasing carbon dioxide

alveoli: air sacs in the lungs where gas exchange occurs (singular is alveolus)

capillary: the smallest blood vessel

red blood cells: blood cells that carry oxygen and carbon dioxide in the blood

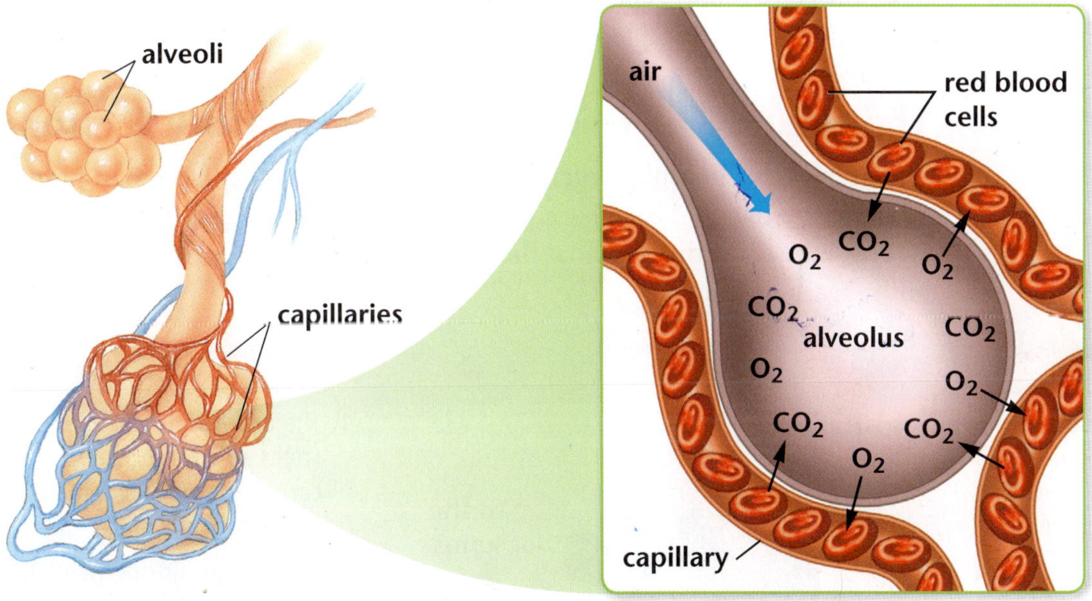

▲ Figure 1.20 Gas exchange occurs between the air in the alveoli and the blood in the capillaries.

LEARNING CHECK

1. Why do you breathe?
2. Where does gas exchange occur?
3. Draw a flowchart showing how air travels through the respiratory system when you breathe in.
4. Figure 1.20 shows that capillary walls are very thin. What would happen to a person with a disease that thickened the capillary walls?

ACTIVITY LINK

Activity 1.20, on page 66.

The circulatory system transports dissolved gases and nutrients through the body.

The respiratory system carries oxygen to and removes carbon dioxide from the blood. The system that transports these gases between the lungs and the cells is the circulatory system.

How the Circulatory System Works

The cells in the body require a constant supply of oxygen and nutrients. They also require the removal of carbon dioxide and other wastes. The circulatory system ensures that both delivery and clean-up occur by transporting blood through the body. The blood carries oxygen and nutrients to the cells. It also carries carbon dioxide and other wastes away from the cells. Blood is pumped through the circulatory system by the heart and travels to and from the cells in the blood vessels.

Go to **scienceontario** to find out more

The Heart: The Pump of the Circulatory System

The heart is the muscular organ that drives the circulatory system. It pumps blood to the cells and then back to the heart. The arrows and numbers in **Figures 1.21** show the path that the blood takes as it moves through the body, heart, and lungs.

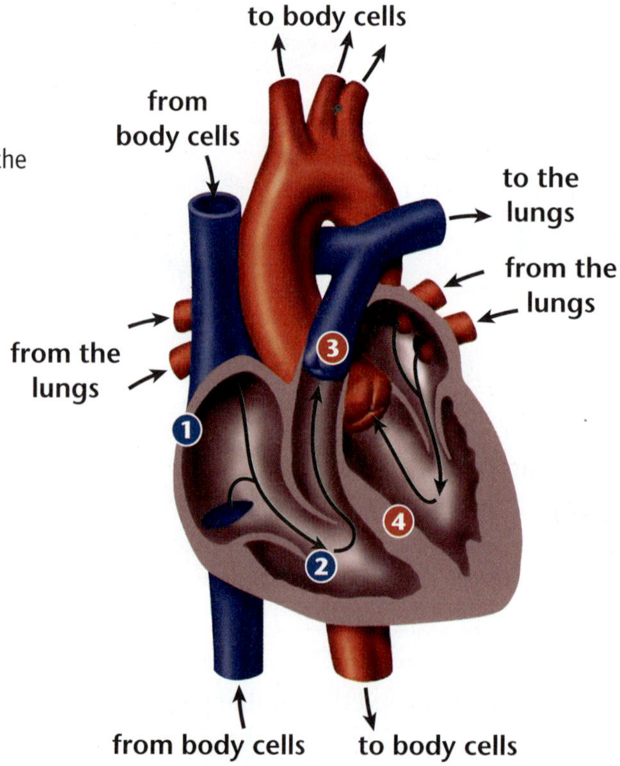

▶ **Figure 1.21** Blood flow through the human heart. The arrows show the direction of blood flow.

1. The upper-right chamber (right atrium) receives carbon dioxide-rich blood from the body.
2. The carbon-dioxide-rich blood moves into the lower-right chamber (right ventricle), which pumps it to the lungs. Inside the lungs, the blood gets rid of the carbon dioxide and picks up oxygen again.
3. The upper-left chamber (left atrium) receives the oxygen-rich blood from the lungs.
4. The oxygen-rich blood moves into the lower-left chamber (left ventricle), which pumps it to the body cells.

Blood Vessels: The Branches of the Circulatory System

There are many different blood vessels in the human body. The main blood vessels are arteries and veins. These blood vessels branch out from the heart as shown in **Figure 1.22**. As they move toward the cells, they branch out and grow smaller and smaller. This allows them to bring blood to all the cells in the body. As they move away from the cells, they combine and grow larger again. The changes in the size of the blood vessels are shown in **Figure 1.23**.

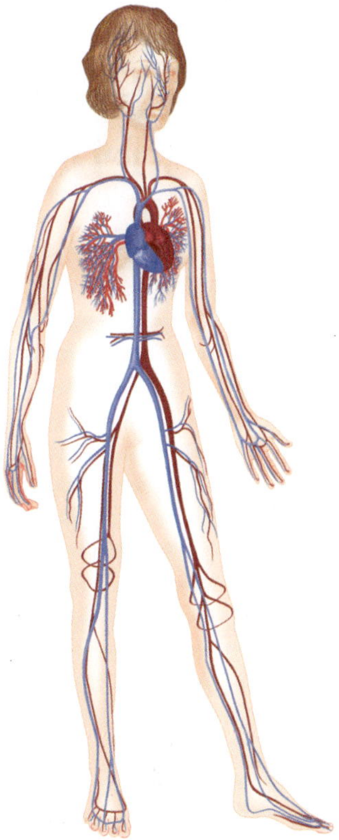

▲ **Figure 1.22** The arteries and veins in the circulatory system branch out from the heart. Oxygen-rich blood is shown in red. Carbon dioxide-rich blood is shown in blue.

Capillaries: The capillaries are the smallest blood vessels. All the work of the circulatory system related to gas exchange takes place in the capillaries. They are one-cell thick. Oxygen and nutrients, plus carbon dioxide and other wastes, diffuse easily through the thin capillary walls.

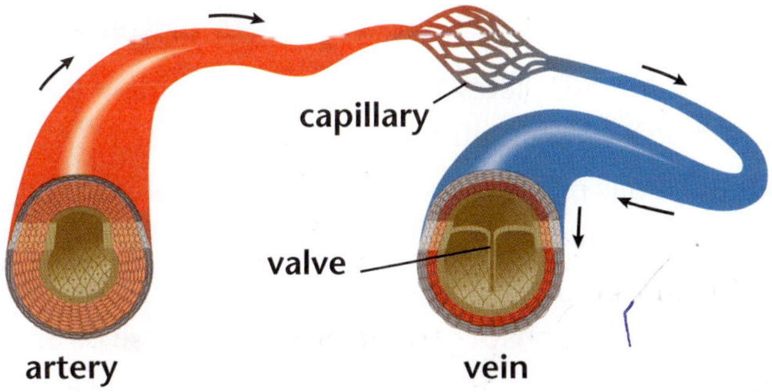

Arteries: Arteries are thick-walled, elastic blood vessels that carry blood away from the heart. The arteries get narrower the farther they are from the heart.

Veins: Veins are thin-walled, inelastic blood vessels. They have valves that keep blood from backing up as it is carried toward the heart.

▲ **Figure 1.23** Arteries carry oxygen-rich blood from the heart to the capillaries, where gas exchange takes place. From the capillaries, carbon dioxide-rich blood moves through the veins back to the heart.

LEARNING CHECK

1. List two functions of the circulatory system.
2. Refer to **Figure 1.23**. Agree or disagree with this statement and give your reasons: "The heart, arteries, and veins exist to get the blood to the capillaries and from the capillaries."
3. Why do you think that the muscle around the left ventricle is larger than the one around the right ventricle? (Hint: How far does each ventricle have to pump blood?)

INVESTIGATION LINK
Investigation 1C, on page 68.

The digestive system breaks down food, absorbs nutrients, and eliminates solid waste.

The digestive system is a 10 m long coil of churning muscle. Here are a few facts about the digestive system that you may find surprising:

- The stomach contains chemicals that are as powerful as battery acid.
- Saliva glands near the mouth create an entire litre of saliva (spit) each day.
- As shown in **Figure 1.24**, the digestive system is home to bacteria that produce over 100 L of gas each year. This gas passes from the digestive system about 14 times a day!

Processes Carried Out by the Digestive System

The digestive system completes the following four tasks in the body:

- **Ingestion**: Food is taken into the body.
- **Digestion**: Food is broken down into nutrients physically (through dissolving and breaking it into smaller bits) and chemically (through chemical reactions).
- **Absorption**: During **absorption**, nutrients diffuse or are moved into the blood. Energy from these nutrients is made available to cells through cellular respiration.
- **Elimination**: Solid waste passes from the digestive system out of the body.

absorption: the process by which nutrients pass from the digestive system to the blood

Food takes about 20 to 30 h to move from ingestion to elimination. **Figure 1.25** describes what happens each step of the way.

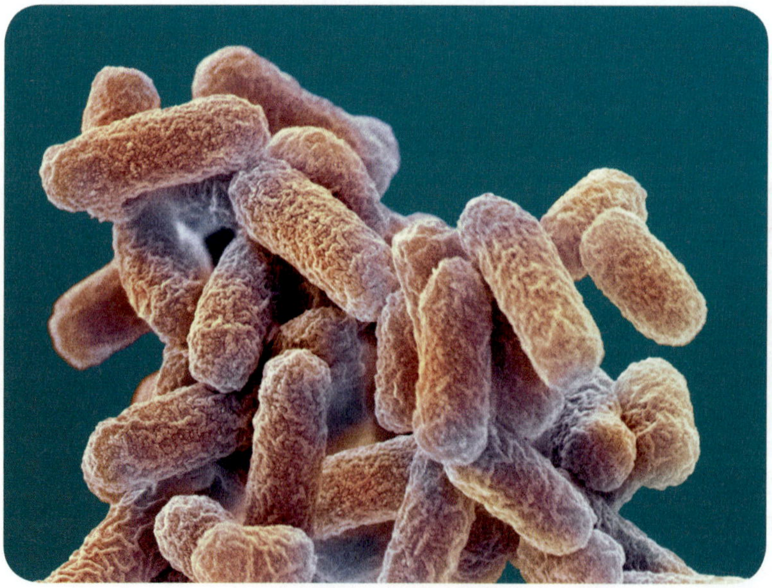

▶ **Figure 1.24** Bacteria like these are a vital part of your digestive system. As they break down food, they release gases such as methane as a byproduct. The gas you pass comes from them!

ACTIVITY LINK

Activity 1.21, on page 67.

1. Ingestion takes place as food enters the mouth. Digestion begins with chewing, as the tongue, teeth, and saliva break down the food.
2. The esophagus pushes the food into the stomach using wave-like muscular contractions. These contractions continue to move the food through the digestive system.
3. Stomach muscles contract to mix the food. At the same time, the stomach releases powerful acids and other chemicals that further break down the food.
4. Digestion continues in the small intestine. Nutrients from the food are absorbed into the bloodstream here.
5. Undigested food passes into the large intestine where water and some nutrients are reabsorbed.
6. Any undigested materials that remain are called feces. Feces are stored in the rectum and eliminated through the anus.

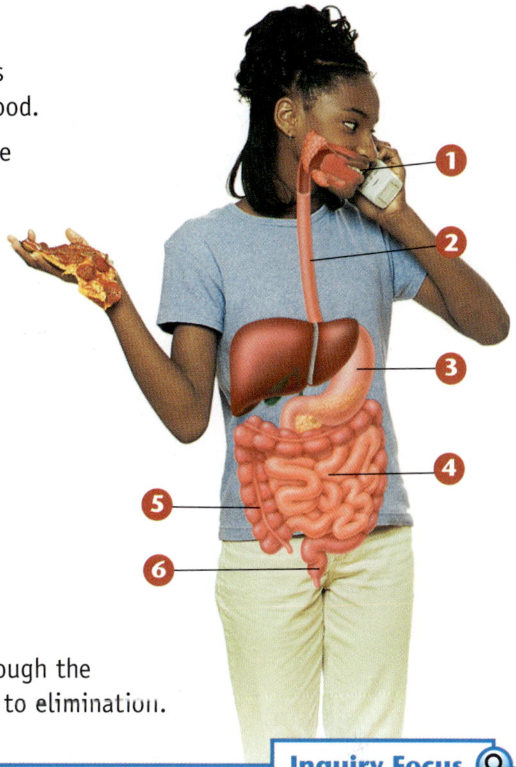

▶ **Figure 1.25** Food moves through the digestive system from ingestion to elimination.

Inquiry Focus

Activity 1.18

CATCHING THE WAVE

Wave-like muscle contractions called peristalsis move food through your digestive system. You can model this process using a tennis ball, liquid soap, and a knee-high nylon stocking with a hole at the toe-end.

1. Stretch the nylon stocking in different directions, observing changes in the length and width of the stocking.
2. Soak the stocking and ball in water for a few seconds. Then apply one or two squeezes of liquid soap to each. Using your hands, spread the soap throughout the stocking and around the ball.
3. Put the ball in the stocking at the knee end, where the stocking is reinforced. Push the ball until it is below the band of reinforced material. With your free hand, squeeze the stocking above the ball between your thumb and first finger. Observe what happens.
4. Continue to squeeze the ball until it exits the toe end.

LEARNING CHECK

1. Identify four tasks carried out by the digestive system.
2. Using Figure 1.25, create a flowchart to show the path that food travels through the digestive system. On your flowchart, identify each stage and organ involved.
3. If a person needs to have part of his or her small intestine removed, how might this affect digestion?

INVESTIGATION LINK

Investigation 1D, on page 70.

Organ systems working together carry out important tasks in the body.

Most tasks in the body need the support of two or more organ systems working together. Take cellular respiration, for instance—summarized in **Figure 1.26**. This task requires oxygen and food. The respiratory system brings oxygen into the lungs when you breathe. The digestive system breaks food down into nutrients such as glucose.

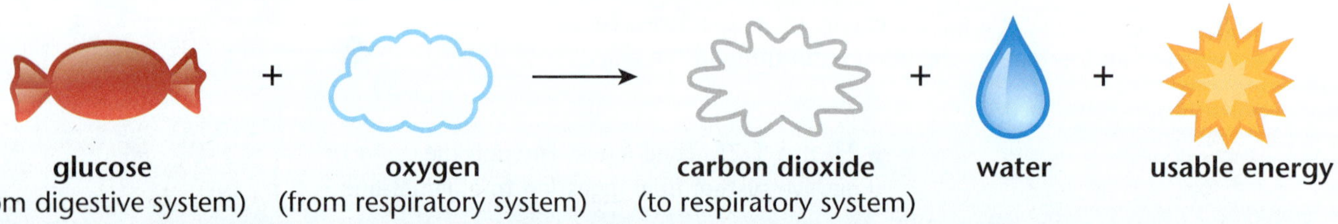

▼ **Figure 1.26** The reaction that occurs during cellular respiration

Now the circulatory system enters the picture. It transports glucose and other nutrients from the digestive system to the cells. The circulatory system also transports oxygen from the lungs to the cells. Now the cells have what they need for cellular respiration: oxygen and glucose.

The teamwork doesn't end there, however. The circulatory system also transports carbon dioxide waste from the cells to the lungs of the respiratory system. Through gas exchange in the lungs, the carbon dioxide waste is removed from your body when you breathe out.

How the Organ Systems Work Together

In the example in **Figure 1.26**, all the systems have to perform their role for the overall task to be completed successfully. In this way, the organ systems are like the runners in a relay race. Each runner needs to pick up the baton from another runner, run with it, and then pass it to the next runner to complete the race. In your body, organ systems work together in a similar way to complete tasks such as cellular respiration.

Literacy Focus

Activity 1.19

WHICH ORGAN SYSTEMS WORK TOGETHER?

1. Determine which organ systems are working together in each of the following scenarios.

When you run, you begin to breathe heavier and faster. Your heart beats more quickly, bringing more oxygen to your cells. Which organ systems are working together here?

When you lift weights, your arms bulge and your brain signals them to lift despite the resistance. Which two organ systems are working together to raise the weights?

When you finish exercising, you are hot, tired, and sweating. After a bottle of juice, you feel a lot better. Which organ systems are working together in this scenario?

2. Think of two other scenarios in which organ systems are working together. Test a partner to see if he or she can identify these organ systems.

LEARNING CHECK

1. How are organ systems like runners in a relay race?
2. Using **Figure 1.26**, identify three organ systems that play a role in cellular respiration. Then name two other organ systems that you think also play a role in cellular respiration, and give reasons for your choices. (Hint: Refer to **Figure 1.17** back on page 47.)
3. Describe a task other than cellular respiration that is completed by several organ systems working together.

INVESTIGATION LINK
Investigation 1C, on page 68.

Inquiry Focus

Activity 1-20

HOW DO YOU BREATHE?

Lung tissue does not have any muscle cells. What makes your lungs expand and contract? A large muscle called the diaphragm plays a key role in this process. It is located directly beneath the lungs. Build a model to find out how your diaphragm helps you breathe.

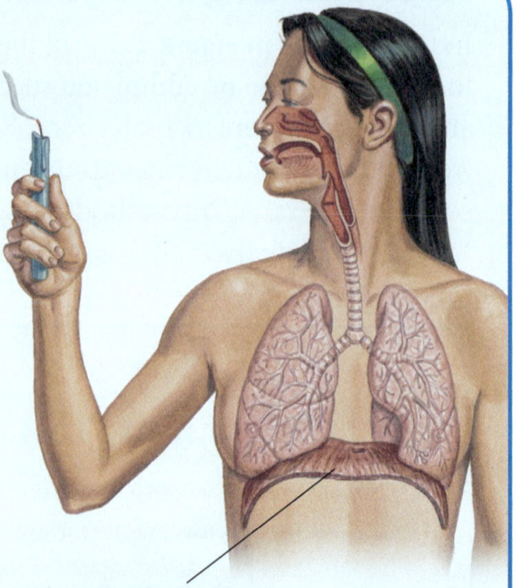

The diaphragm is a large muscle located below the lungs.

Safety

What You Need

- 2 small balloons
- 2 plastic straws
- 2 small elastic bands
- modelling clay
- 500 mL plastic cup with hole in bottom
- large balloon with neck cut off
- large elastic band

What To Do

1. Inflate the balloons to stretch them. Then let out the air.
2. Follow these steps to build your model:
   - Insert a straw into the neck of each small balloon. Use an elastic band to hold the balloon and straw together tightly.
   - Fit the straws through the hole in the cup. Use modelling clay to completely seal the hole around each straw.
   - Stretch the large balloon over the mouth of the cup. Use a large elastic band to hold the balloon in place.

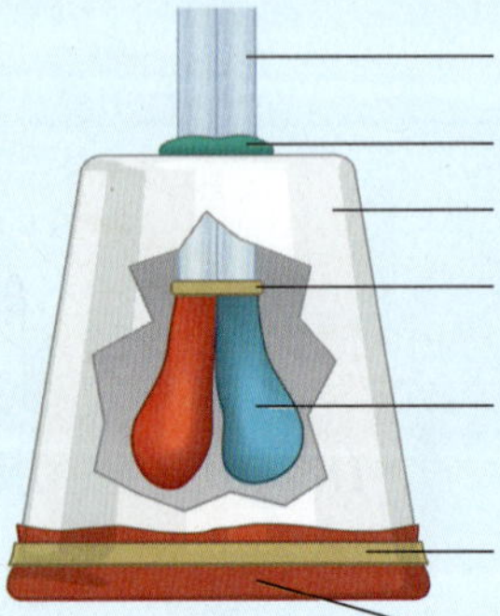

3. Use one hand to hold the cup. Use your other hand to pull down the centre of the large balloon slowly. Then gently let the balloon go.

What Did You Find Out?

1. a) What happened when you pulled down the centre of the large balloon?
   b) What happened when you let the balloon go?
2. Put your hand just below your chest cavity. Take a breath.
   a) When you inhale, does your diaphragm move up or down?
   b) When you exhale, does your diaphragm move up or down?
3. How does your model simulate inhaling and exhaling?

Activity 1.21

A TUBE WITH TWISTS

The digestive system is a tube with many twists. The shape of this tube varies along its length. Most adult digestive systems are 9 to 10 m long. They are divided as follows:

- esophagus: 25 cm
- stomach: 15 cm
- small intestine: 6 to 8 m
- large intestine: 1.5 to 2 m
- rectum: 12 cm

In this activity, you will make a 3-D model of the digestive system.

What You Need

- various art materials
- round-tipped scissors
- tape
- glue

What To Do

1. Make a 3-D model of the digestive system. Your model must
   - be to scale
   - include labels for each structure and its length
   - show where the circulatory system connects to the digestive system

Hint: Where are nutrients from food absorbed into the bloodstream?

What Did You Find Out?

1. a) What is the longest structure in the digestive system?
   b) Why do you think this is the longest structure?
2. Do you think your stomach is always the same size? Explain.

Investigation 1C

Skill Check

✓ initiating and planning

✓ performing and recording

✓ analyzing and interpreting

✓ communicating

Safety

- Always take a pulse at the wrist, never at the neck.
- Make sure you do not over-exert yourself.
- Let your teacher know if you have any health conditions that prevent you from participating in physical exercise.

What You Need

- electronic heart monitor (if available)
- various pieces of sports equipment
- graph paper

The Effect of Exercise on Breathing Rate and Heart Rate

The circulatory system and the respiratory system work together to supply your body with the oxygen your cells need. In this investigation, you will look for evidence of the connection between these two systems. In Part 1, you will learn how to take a pulse safely. Taking a person's pulse lets you determine heart rate—the number of times the heart beats in one minute. You will compare heart rate to breathing rate—the number of times a person inhales and exhales in one minute. Then, in Part 2, you will design your own investigation to determine the effect of exercise on heart rate and breathing rate.

What To Do

Part 1 Measuring Resting Heart Rate and Breathing Rate

1. Create a data table to record your measurements and calculations.
2. The resting heart rate is the number of times a person's heart beats per minute while that person is completely at rest. You will find your partner's resting heart rate by taking your partner's pulse. To take a pulse, locate the artery in your partner's wrist. Gently press your index finger and one or two other fingers against the artery. (Don't use your thumb. It has its own pulse.) Count the number of pulses in 15 s. Then multiply that number by 4. This will give you the number of times the heart beats in 1 min, which is the heart rate (number of beats per minute). Record your partner's resting heart rate in the data table.
3. Repeat step 2 two more times. Add the three values for heart rate together, and divide by three. This will give you your partner's average resting heart rate.
4. The resting breathing rate is the number of times a person breathes per minute while that person is completely at rest. To determine your partner's resting breathing rate, count the number of times your partner breathes (one inhale and one exhale) in 15 s. Then multiply that number by 4. This will give you the number of times your partner breathed in 1 min, which is the breathing rate (breaths per minute). Record your partner's resting breathing rate in the data table.
5. Repeat step 4 two more times. Add the three values for breathing rate together, and divide by three. This will give you your partner's average resting breathing rate.
6. Switch roles with your partner and repeat steps 2 to 5.

Part 2 Recovery Time

7. With a partner, state a hypothesis about the time it takes for heart rate and breathing rate to return to their resting rate after light exercise, medium exercise, and intense exercise.
8. Design a procedure to test your hypothesis. As part of your procedure, make decisions about the following:
   - activities to represent light, moderate, and intense exercise (for example: walking, jogging, and running)
   - how long to carry out each activity
   - the time interval between measuring heart rate and breathing rate (for example, taking measurements every 30 s or every 60 s)
9. Write down the procedure you plan to follow. Include the data table you intend to use to record your measurements. Show the procedure to your teacher for approval.
10. Carry out your procedure.
11. Use your completed table to plot recovery rate data on a graph. Title and label the axes of your graph.

What Did You Find Out?

1. Interpret your graph. Are the patterns that you observe what you would have expected? Explain why or why not.
2. a) Identify all the variables that you controlled in your investigation.
   b) Is it possible that there were variables that were not controlled in your investigation? Identify at least one other variable that you might not have controlled, and explain how you think this might have affected your results.
3. In step 5, you determined an average breathing rate. In step 3, you determined an average heart rate.
   a) How did the average breathing rate and average heart rate compare with the individual values for breathing rate and heart rate that you counted?
   b) Explain why using an average breathing rate and an average heart rate improves the accuracy of your overall results.
4. Did your results support your hypothesis? If not, explain why that might be the case.

Investigation 1D

Skill Check

initiating and planning

✓ performing and recording

✓ analyzing and interpreting

✓ communicating

Safety

- Take extreme care when using dissecting instruments, particularly scalpels. Make cuts away from your body.
- Keep sharp dissection tools pointing down when held in your hand.
- Your frog is preserved in a chemical solution. Wear plastic gloves, goggles, and an apron at all times. If some of the chemical comes into contact with your skin, wash it off immediately.
- Clean up the work area and wash your hands thoroughly when finished.

Frog Dissection

Follow your teacher's instructions to perform a frog dissection. Alternately, your teacher may have you complete a virtual dissection.

What To Do

Part 1: Respect for Life

1. Before you begin your dissection, discuss the following quote as a class. How is it important in terms of the dissection you will complete?

   "Respect for living things and the environment is... considered essential for meaningful work in science and technology."

   From *Marineland: Life systems*

Part 2: Making Incisions

2. Rinse the frog in water.
3. Place the frog in the dissection tray on its back. Pin its limbs to the tray.
4. Use forceps to lift the frog's skin between the rear legs. Use the scalpel to cut through the lifted skin, making the incisions shown in the diagram. Be careful to cut only the skin.
5. Use the forceps to peel back each flap of skin. Use a scalpel to help separate the skin from the muscle layers below. Pin the skin flaps to the dissection tray.

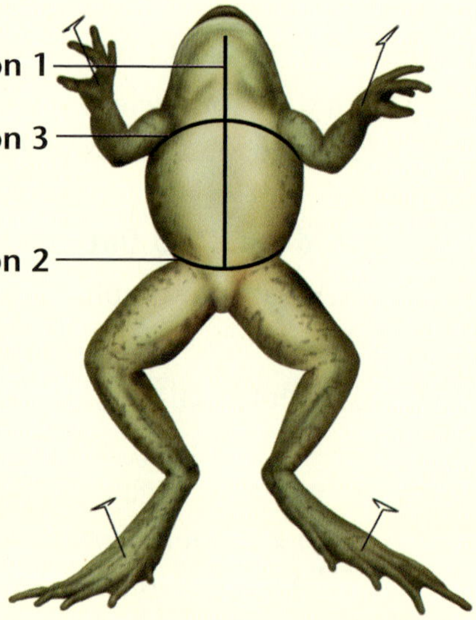

6. Repeat the three incisions you made in step 4, but this time cut through the muscle and bone layers.
   - Use dissection scissors to cut through the muscles. Be careful to cut only the muscle layer or you may damage the organs underneath.
   - Use dissection scissors to cut through the chest bones. When you reach the front legs, turn the scissor blades sideways, so you cut only through the bones.
   - Separate the muscle flaps from the organs below. To do so, use the forceps to pull back and hold the muscle flaps. Then use the scalpel to separate the muscle from the organ tissue.
   - Pin the muscle flaps to the dissection tray. They should be pulled back far enough to allow easy access to the internal organs.

Part 3: Internal Examination

7. In your science notebook, draw an outline of your frog. The first organs you will see in your internal examination are the liver and heart. Draw and label these organs in your frog diagram.
8. The heart and liver cover the digestive organs below them.

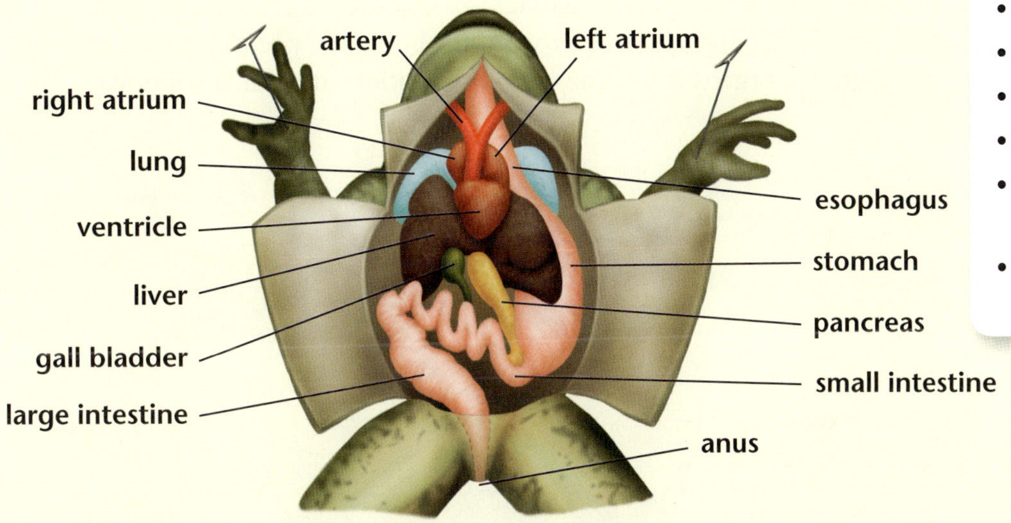

Use the forceps and probe to pick up these organs and hold them to the side. Use the labelled diagram below to find the organs of the digestive system, from the mouth to the anus. Draw and label all the organs you know in your frog diagram.

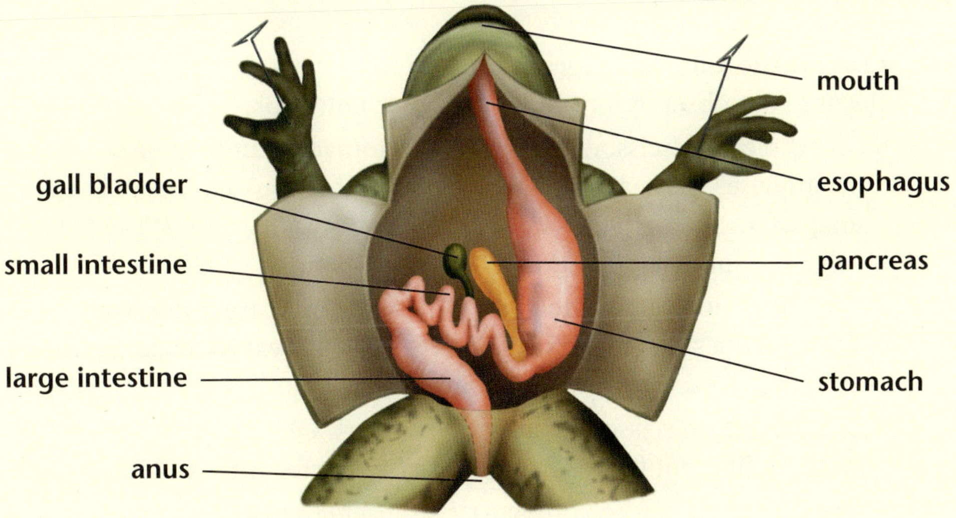

The digestive system

What You Need

- preserved frog
- dissection tray
- dissection pins
- dissection scissors
- forceps
- scalpel
- probe
- magnifying glass
- gloves, goggles, and lab apron
- paper towels for clean up

9. Two organs secrete substances into the digestive system to aid digestion. These are the gall bladder and the pancreas. Use the diagram of the digestive system to help you find them. Hint: The pancreas is a thin, yellowish ribbon.

10. Use the labelled diagram below to find the components of the circulatory system. Draw and label the heart, as well as any visible blood vessels, in your frog diagram. Use the magnifying glass to observe the connections between the circulatory blood vessels and the digestive organs. Describe your observations in your notebook.

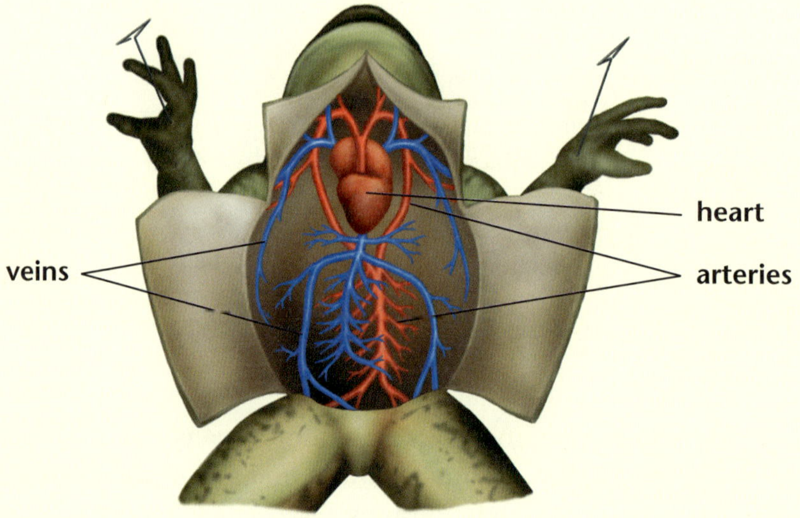

The circulatory system

11. Observe the following digestive and circulatory organs in greater detail. Record your observations in your science notebook.
    - Use dissection scissors to cut out the stomach. Cut it open lengthwise. You may find the remains of the frog's last meal. Use a magnifying glass to look at the stomach's muscular walls. Describe what the surface looks like.
    - Use dissection scissors to cut out the small and larger intestine. Unwind the small intestine and stretch it out next to the large intestine. Describe how they compare in size and shape.
    - Use dissection scissors to cut out the heart. Observe how the frog's heart is different from a human heart. Describe these differences.
12. Dispose of your frog according to your teacher's instructions.
13. Rinse and dry all equipment, including the dissection tray.

What Did You Find Out?

1. Identify two of each of the following that you observed during the dissection:
   a) tissues
   b) organs
   c) organ systems
2. a) Frogs eat insects. Create a flowchart that shows the path of an insect as it moves through a frog's digestive system.
   b) Write a brief paragraph explaining how the organs of the digestive system work together to digest the insect.
3. a) Based on your observations, how do the frog's circulatory and digestive systems connect?
   b) Explain why the interaction of the digestive and circulatory systems is necessary for the frog's survival.
4. Some people refuse to dissect a real animal. They believe that students can use software to study animal organ systems without cutting up the animals. Other people think that dissecting real animals is useful for students to better understand how organ systems work in animals. What do you think?

Inquire Further

Design a procedure to investigate the frog's respiratory system. Include two What Did You Find Out? questions. With your teacher's approval, exchange procedures and questions with a partner and investigate your frog's respiratory system.

Go to **scienceontario** to find out more

Making a DIFFERENCE

April Dutheil is from Haida Gwaii, a collection of about 150 islands off the northwestern coast of British Columbia. These islands, also known as the Queen Charlotte Islands, are home to the Haida. Approximately 5000 people live in communities scattered about the islands. April's community is 25 minutes from an ambulance and 40 minutes from a hospital. When April was in high school, she realized there was a need to improve health care on the islands. She met with her local fire chief and medical first responder to discuss ways to make improvements. They decided that providing free CPR training would be the most effective way to help, since some communities could not afford CPR training for their firefighters. April applied for funding and organized free classes that taught CPR to firefighters, teachers, and students.

April has since completed her Emergency Medical Responder training. As a result she is able to work on an ambulance in Northern British Columbia during the summers. This training is provided by the Canadian Red Cross. The program provides the skills and knowledge needed to reduce the harm caused by an injury or sickness. The training helps maintain life and minimize pain during an emergency until the next level of health care can take over.

April believes young people can make a difference in their communities. "If you have a vision and believe in it, you can make it happen, despite what others may believe."

What changes could be made to improve health care in your community?

Topic 1.4 Review

Key Concept Summary

- The respiratory system carries oxygen to and removes carbon dioxide from the blood.
- The circulatory system transports dissolved gases and nutrients through the body.
- The digestive system breaks down food, absorbs nutrients, and eliminates solid waste.
- Organ systems working together carry out important tasks in the body.

Review the Key Concepts

1. K/U Answer the question that is the title of this topic. Copy and complete the graphic organizer below in your notebook. Fill in four examples from the topic using key terms as well as your own words.

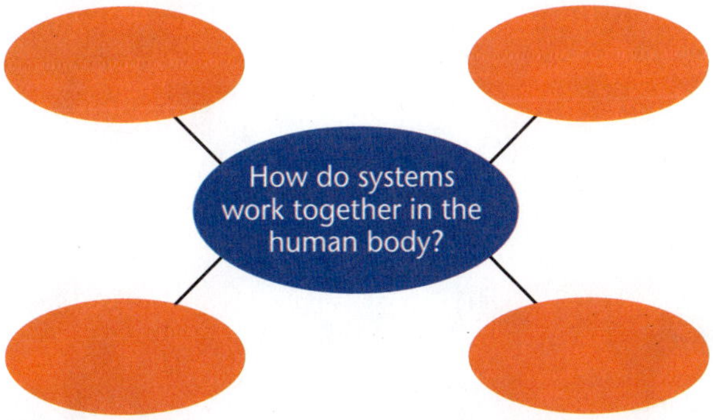

2. K/U What organ systems are involved in

a) supplying body cells with nutrients?

b) supplying body cells with oxygen and removing carbon dioxide from cells?

3. K/U Using **Figure 1.21**, create a flowchart that traces the path that blood takes through the circulatory system.

4. K/U Identify two characteristics of alveoli that make gas exchange easier.

5. K/U How do nutrients pass from the digestive system to the circulatory system?

6. T/I Explain how your digestive system would be affected if your circulatory system failed.

7. T/I A A condition called anemia often results from too few red blood cells. People who are anemic are often tired. Explain why this is so using what you know about the respiratory and circulatory system.

8. C The diagram below shows four disorders that can impair the proper function of the respiratory system. Predict how each disorder would impair respiratory system function.

a) pneumonia: alveoli fill with thick fluid

b) bronchitis: airways (the branches leading to alveoli) are inflamed due to infection or irritation

c) asthma: airways are inflamed and constricted

d) emphysema: alveoli burst and fuse into enlarged air spaces

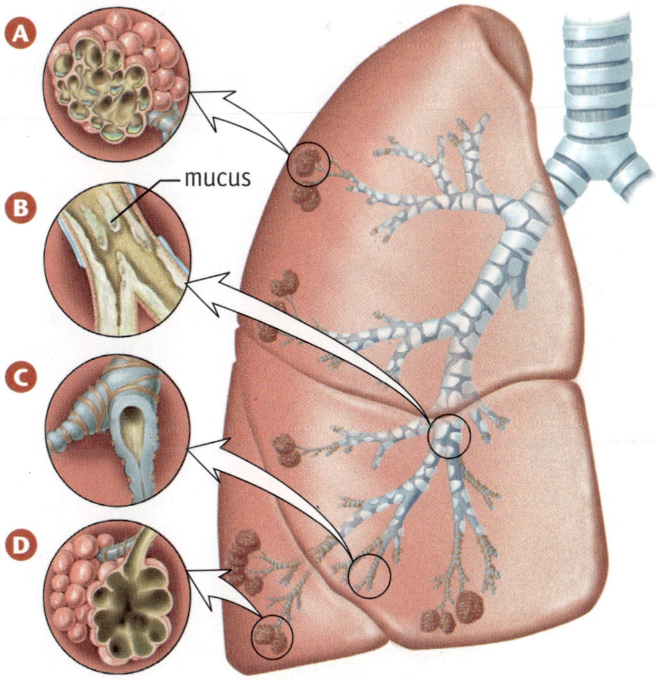

Topic 1.5 How do technology, substances, and environmental factors affect human health?

Key Concepts

- Medical imaging technologies are used to explore, diagnose, and treat the human body.
- Exposure to various technologies, substances, and environmental factors can impair health.
- Technology will affect human health in new ways in the future.

Key Skills

Inquiry
Literacy
Research

Key Terms

medical imaging technologies

The ability to see inside the body using technology such as an X ray machine is little more than 100 years old. Before then, doctors had to trust their senses and their wits to infer what might be happening inside a patient's body. If direct observation of an organ or other internal body part was necessary, doctors had only one option. They had to cut the body open. In the early 1800s, the prospect of dealing with serious wounds from accidents or the battlefield carried an additional challenge—anesthetic was not used in surgery until the 1840s!

Today, with X ray machines and other medical imaging technologies such as CT scans and ultrasound, doctors can observe, diagnose, and treat patients without ever opening the body. In some cases, with the addition of optical fibre technology, doctors can perform delicate surgery with only the tiniest of incisions.

A medical kit from the 1800s. Notice the bone saw, which was used in amputation procedures.

In the past, as in this depiction of a field hospital during the 1800s, severe injuries often had only one life-saving procedure: amputation.

Starting Point Activity

Before modern imaging technologies were developed, doctors relied on one main set of diagnostic tools—their senses. Use your sense of touch to try to feel the organs in the model digestive system that your teacher has set up.

1. Visit the "digestive-system-in-a-box" model that has been set up. The box represents the part of the digestive system that is found in the abdomen.
2. Try to feel the organs in the model digestive system through the layer of foam. What does the foam represent in the body?
3. Draw a diagram to show the shape and placement of the organs based on what you discovered by touch.
4. Find the figure in Topic 1.4 that you can use to check your diagram for the correct placement of the organs. How correct was your diagram?
5. Technology for "seeing" inside the body, such as X ray machines, was invented only in the twentieth century. In what ways do you think such technology has helped improve the life and lifespan of people who are sick or injured?

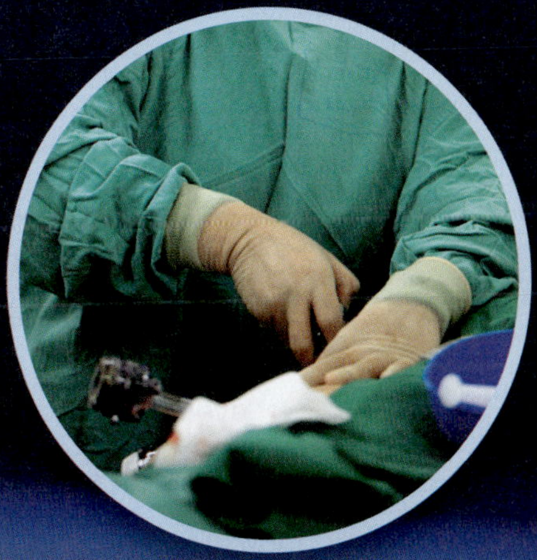

A modern surgeon repairs a leg injury using a specially designed scope that lets her see inside and operate on a leg through a tiny incision.

Medical imaging technologies are used to explore, diagnose, and treat the human body.

medical imaging technologies: technologies that are used to make images of cells, tissues, and organs

Medical diagnosis has come along way since the 1800s. We now have a variety of **medical imaging technologies** that allow doctors to observe what is going on inside a patient. **Table 1.4** shows common medical imaging technologies that are currently used to explore, diagnose, and treat injuries and disease.

Table 1.4 Medical Imaging Technologies

Technology	Description	Purposes	Image
X ray	• Involves sending electromagnetic radiation through the body to make an image	• To view hard tissue, such as bone • To diagnose bone injuries and malformations	A broken wrist 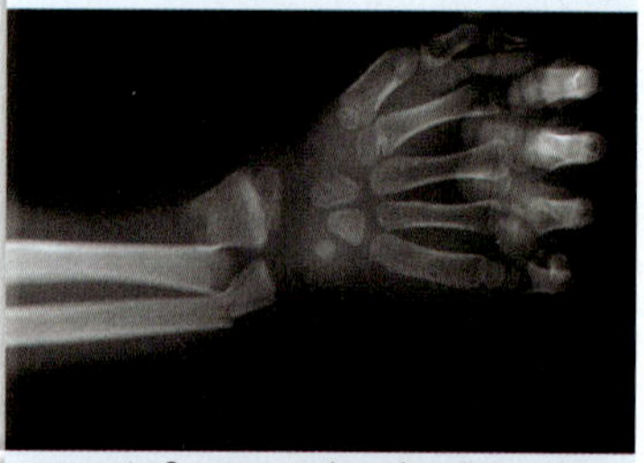
CT scan (computerized axial tomography)	• An X ray source and sensor rotate around the body while slowly moving along the length of the body. A computer converts the data from the sensor into a 3-D image that looks like slices of the body.	• To view hard tissue, such as bone • To diagnose bone injuries and malformations	A fracture in the hip 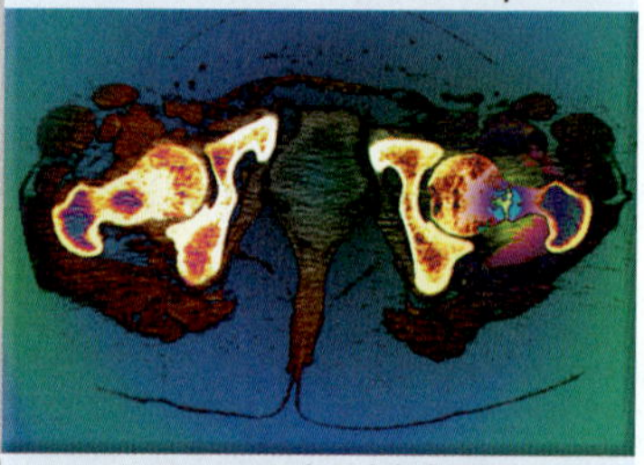
Ultrasound	• Involves directing sound waves at a body part and measuring reflected sound waves to make an image	• To view soft tissue • To monitor fetal development, observe organ function, and detect cancer	A 23-week-old fetus 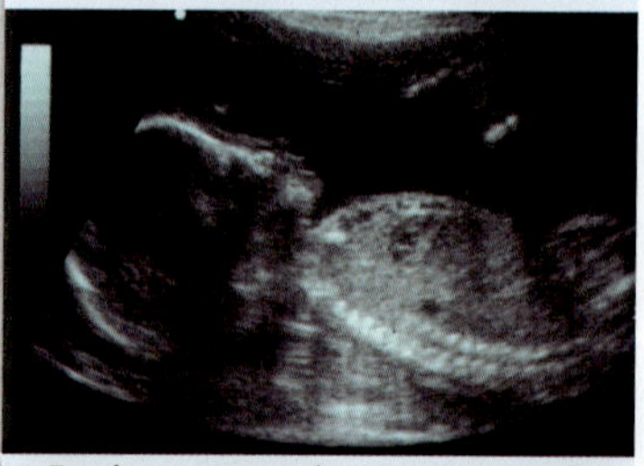
MRI scan (magnetic resonance imaging)	• Involves passing radio waves through a magnetic field around the body, creating multiple images on a computer • Produces images that are similar to those produced by a CT scan, but shows soft tissue in much greater detail	• To contrast soft tissue (such as organs) and hard tissue (such as bones) • To diagnose disease in organs and soft tissues	Brain cancer (orange areas) 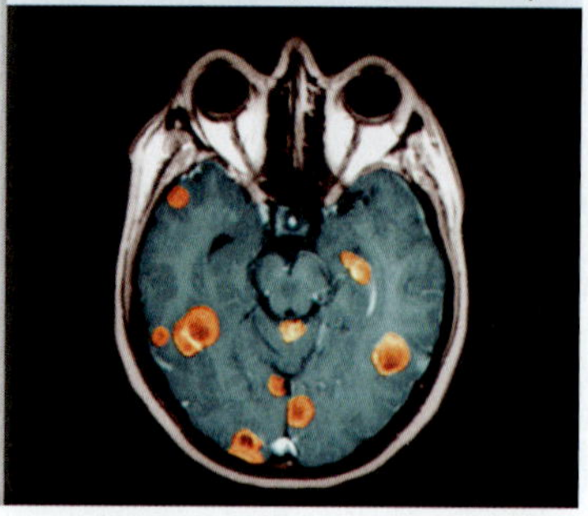

Technology	Description	Purposes	Image
PET scan (positron emission tomography)	• Involves scanning small amounts of radioactive materials, which have been taken into the body • Reveals details of tissues and organs • Produces more detailed images if combined with another imaging technology, such as a PET-CT scan or PET-MRI	• To view soft tissues • To diagnose cancer or track cancer treatments	No tumours after treatment 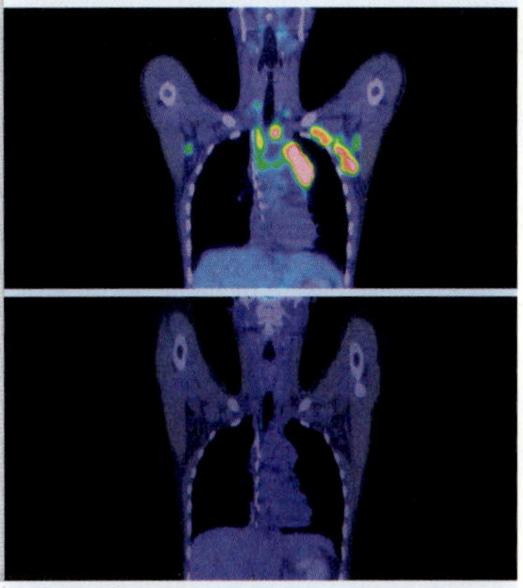
Endoscopy	• Is conducted with a scope made up of a tiny camera and a light, which are attached to a flexible tube that is inserted into the body	• To view internal body parts without cutting open the body • To diagnose diseases, take tissue samples, and perform surgeries	Endoscopic surgery 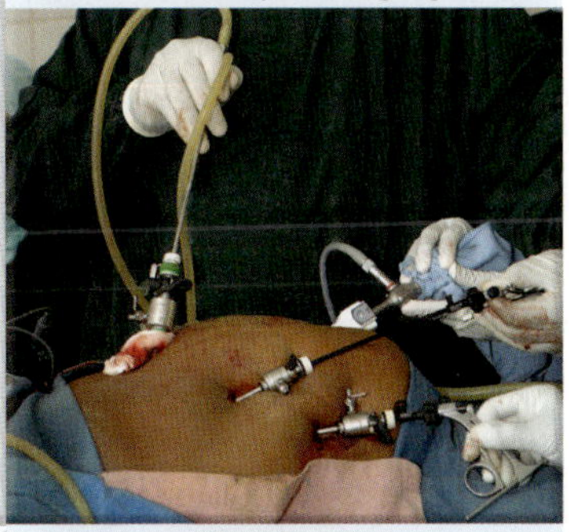
Microscopy	• Is conducted using a variety of microscopes including light microscopes and electron microscopes, which provide much greater enlargement and resolution	• To view small objects, such as cells • To diagnose various diseases	Blood cells 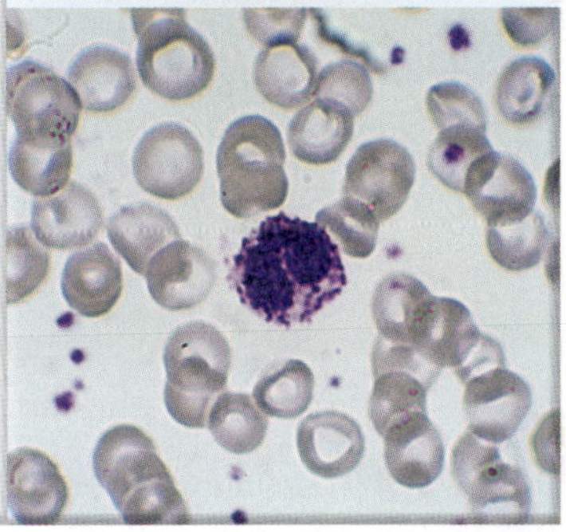

LEARNING CHECK

1. Why was the development of medical imaging technologies important?
2. Identify three general purposes of using medical imaging technologies.
3. A 16-year-old female patient comes to your walk-in clinic with a suspected bladder infection. Which medical imaging technology from **Table 1.4** would you use to check her urine for white blood cells, which indicate an infection?
4. A 44-year-old male is brought to the emergency room after a fall. He cannot put weight on his ankle. Which medical imaging technology from **Table 1.4** would you use to determine the extent of his injury?

INVESTIGATION LINK

Investigation 1E, on page 86

ACTIVITY LINK

Activity 1.24, on page 84

Exposure to various technologies, substances, and environmental factors can impair health.

Air pollution, pesticides, loud noise—it seems that just waking up in the morning can be harmful. Exposure to various technologies, substances, and environmental factors can indeed affect your health. However, the health risk posed often depends on the degree or length of exposure. The images and text below explore some of the possible effects of exposure to several harmful technologies, substances, and environmental factors. As you read, keep in mind that some of these agents also have positive effects. It's up to you to weigh the risks.

Inquiry Focus

Activity 1-22

WHAT ARE THE HEALTH RISKS?

Analyze the health risks that you are exposed to. Then create a plan to reduce your exposure.

1. Examine the activities in the following list. In your notebook, record the activities that can be applied to your life over the past year.
   - [?] You smoke.
   - [?] You use a cellphone.
   - [?] You had an X ray or CT scan.
   - [?] One of your friends or family members smokes.
   - [?] You listen to music at a high volume.
   - [?] You go out in the sunlight without sunscreen.
2. As a class, discuss and assess the health risks of each activity listed in step 1.
3. Based on the results of your discussion, rank the activities in order, from highest to lowest health risk, as a class.
4. Assess your personal risk level by applying this ranking to the activities you recorded in step 1. Develop an action plan to reduce your health risks due to these activities.

Harmful Technologies

- Studies suggest that extensive cellphone use may be linked to brain damage and cancer, especially in children. However, more research is needed to determine how much exposure results in a significant threat to health.
- Despite their benefits, X rays and CT scans emit radiation. The radiation levels are generally considered to be safe. Pregnant women, however, should avoid these technologies.

Harmful Substances

- Smoking and second-hand smoke increase the risk of lung, heart, throat, and mouth disease. This is especially true for heavy and long-time smokers. Smoking is also a contributing factor to atherosclerosis. As atherosclerosis develops, the arteries are increasingly blocked by a build-up of fatty deposits, slowing blood flow. If blood flow becomes very limited or blocked, a heart attack can result.
- Pesticides are chemicals that are used to control and kill weeds and insects. Unless you eat foods that are certified organic, they are likely to contain at least some pesticide residue. Pesticides have been linked to skin, eye, and lung irritations. They may also affect the nervous and reproductive systems.

Harmful Environmental Factors

- While some exposure to sunlight is essential for good health, prolonged exposure brings the risk of too much radiation. This can damage the skin and eyes, as well as increase the chance of developing skin cancer.
- Even if you do not live in an urban area, it is difficult to escape the effects of air pollution. Particles and other contaminants in the air irritate the eyes, throat, and lungs. They can also trigger life-threatening attacks in people with asthma.

LEARNING CHECK

1. How might smoking affect the circulatory system's ability to function?
2. Why might some people engage in risky behaviour, such as smoking or sunbathing, even if they know the risks?

INVESTIGATION LINK

Investigation 1F, on page 88

Technology will affect human health in new ways in the future.

Many of the health-care technologies that you may encounter in the next few decades are still literally in the lab today. Extensive development and testing are required before a new technology is ready for use. This means that the technologies described below may not be available for some time. However, they will most likely be worth the wait. These technologies hold great potential for treating diseases. Some may even cure diseases that we're struggling with today.

▲ **Figure 1.30** The i-pill helps to target the delivery of medication.

The i-Pill

The i-Pill or "intelligent pill" will soon let doctors control the delivery of medication electronically. This could be especially helpful for treating diseases such as Crohn's disease. Crohn's disease causes inflammation of the digestive system. Large doses of the medication used to treat Crohn's disease can make patients very ill. The i-Pill is shown in **Figure 1.30**. It can deliver the medication directly to where it is needed. It then releases a pre-measured amount at that location. To do all this, the i-pill contains a microprocessor, battery, pH sensor, temperature sensor, wireless transceiver, fluid pump, and reservoir for the medication.

Regenerative Medicine

Imagine re-growing a severed fingertip or growing a kidney in the lab to replace a kidney that has been damaged! This may well be the future of regenerative medicine. Regenerative medicine involves producing new cells, tissues, and organs to replace damaged body parts. These cells are grown in the human body or in a lab. For example, scientists can already apply a powder that is a mix of protein and connective tissue (often used to repair tendons) to a fingertip to re-grow tissue. The powder activates cells that are capable of regenerating. Scientists believe that in the future it will be possible to actually re-grow entire arms and legs.

Scientists can also grow tissues (such as heart valves) and organs (such as bladders) from human cells in a lab. Once the techniques are mastered, you may be able to have a new heart valve grown from your own tissue if a replacement becomes necessary. This means that your body will not reject the new valve.

Artificial Blood

The human blood supply is limited by how much is donated. To solve this problem, scientists are researching artificial substitutes for real blood. The "fake blood" currently being developed does not carry out all the functions performed by real blood. Instead, it only transports oxygen. As a result, artificial blood products are classified according to the way that they transport this gas. One type of artificial blood actively being researched is fluorocarbon-based. Fluorocarbons are chemicals that are closely related to the non-stick coating on frying pans. They carry and release large amounts of oxygen. Another type of artificial blood imitates how real blood carries oxygen, by using specific proteins. Recently, scientists have also started exploring stem cells as a way to produce blood.

Inquiry Focus

Activity 1.23

MEDICAL TECHNOLOGY BREAKTHROUGH!

The device shown below is used to treat blood clots. It was an important medical technology breakthrough. Make your own medical technology breakthrough. Choose a disease or disorder and design a technology to diagnose or treat it.

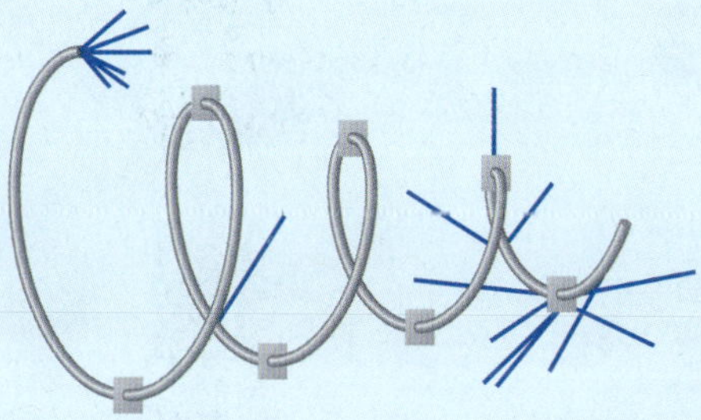

This device is inserted into a blood vessel as a straight wire and placed in a blood clot. Once it heats inside the body, it reshapes into a coil and attaches to the clot. Then the coil and the clot are removed and blood flow is restored.

1. Choose a disease, disorder, or injury that you are familiar with. You may also choose one of the conditions listed below:
   - amputated limb
   - collapsed vein
   - broken toe
   - cut that will not heal
   - paralysis
   - severe burn

   Identify the problem that you want to solve. For example: A blood clot in an artery can block blood flow and cause a heart attack. A clot buster is needed to remove the clot.
2. Design a technology that solves the problem you identified.
3. Describe your medical technology in detail using words, pictures, or a graphic organizer.

LEARNING CHECK

1. How do you think the i-pill will change medical treatment?
2. What is artificial blood?
3. Many scientists research how to grow tissue. Why might other scientists research how to destroy tissue?

Literacy Focus

Activity 1-24

INTERPRETING X RAYS

On an X ray, bone appears white, air appears black, and other structures appear in various shades of grey. Test your diagnostic skills by interpreting the X rays below.

1. Compare images A and B. Which image shows a fracture?

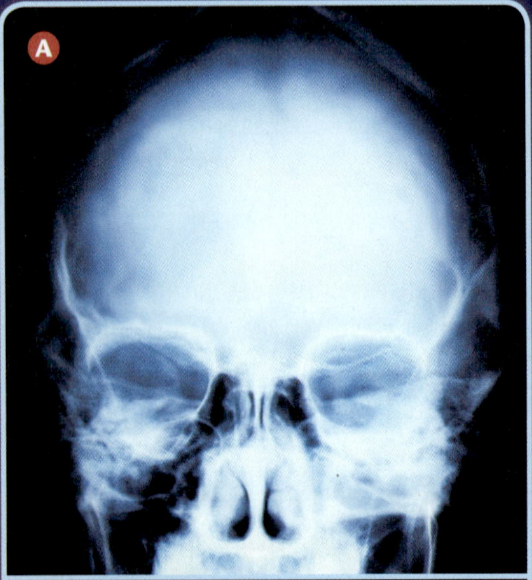

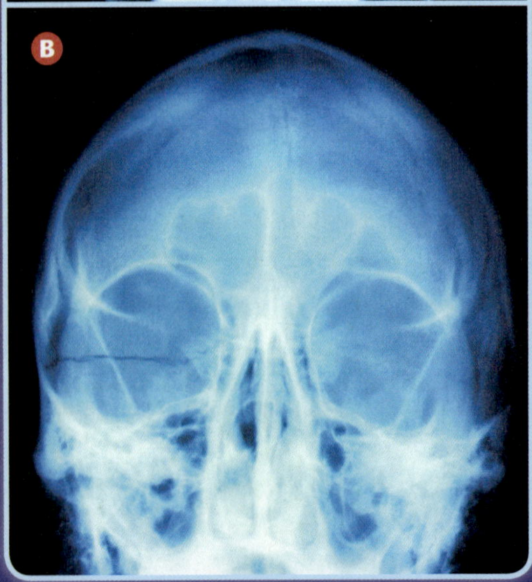

2. a) Compare images C and D. Which image shows damage?
   b) What do you notice about the bones and joints?
   c) What do you notice about the tissues around the bones?

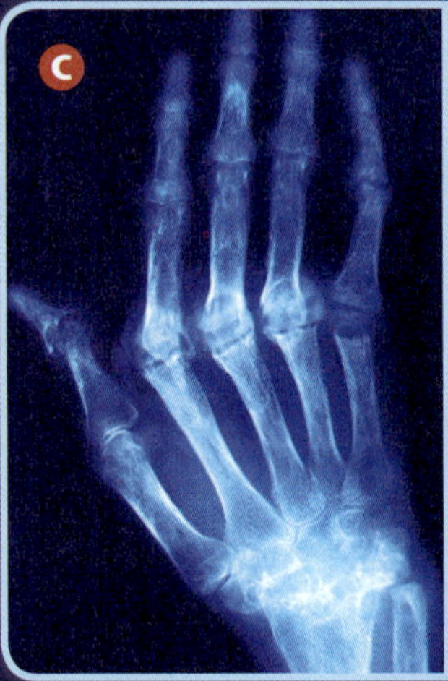

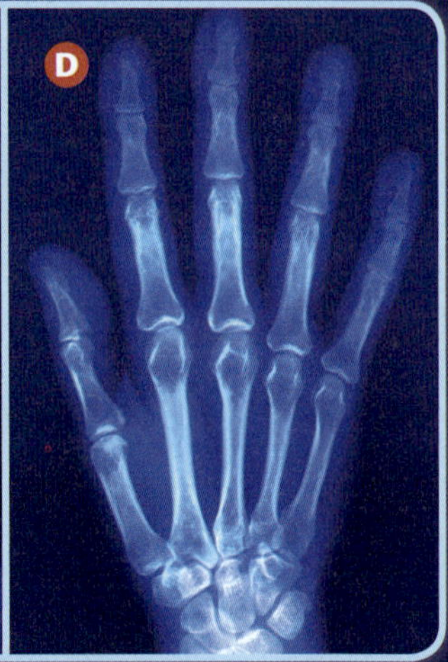

3. What does this X ray show?

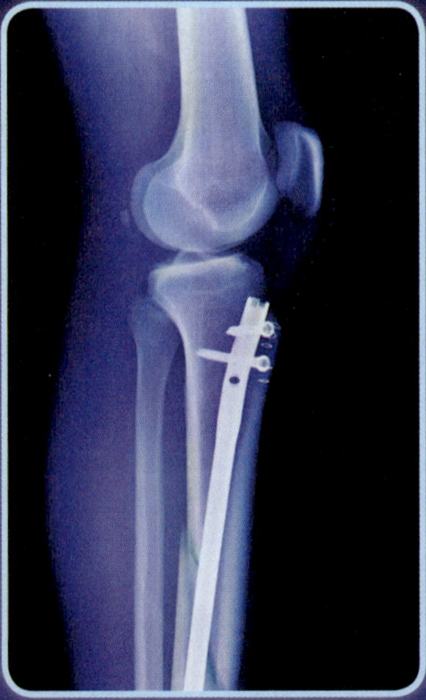

4. Identify the image(s) that you would use to
   a) decide on a treatment for a problem
   b) assess the success of the treatment

Research Focus

Activity 1.25

DETERMINING THE DIAGNOSIS

You are the chief pathologist in a large urban hospital. You are provided with the following information about a 57-year-old female patient who died under suspicious circumstances. You are asked to determine the cause of death and provide your reasoning.

1. Read the following notes from the treating emergency physician:

   June 5: A 57-year-old female admitted at 2:17 P.M. died immediately upon arrival before treatment was possible. The patient's brother, who brought her to the hospital, reported that the patient had felt fine in the morning. However, she had been extremely stressed by outbursts at a family lunch when she announced that she had changed her will. At about 1:30 P.M., the patient began complaining of chest pain. She had discomfort described as pressure on the chest, pain in both arms, shortness of breath, and nausea. The patient's brother stated that he believed she had been poisoned. He also stated that the patient was a smoker but had no other health problems.

2. Examine the microscope image (A) of a cross-section taken from one of the patient's arteries. For comparison, also examine the microscope image (B) of a cross-section taken from a healthy artery.

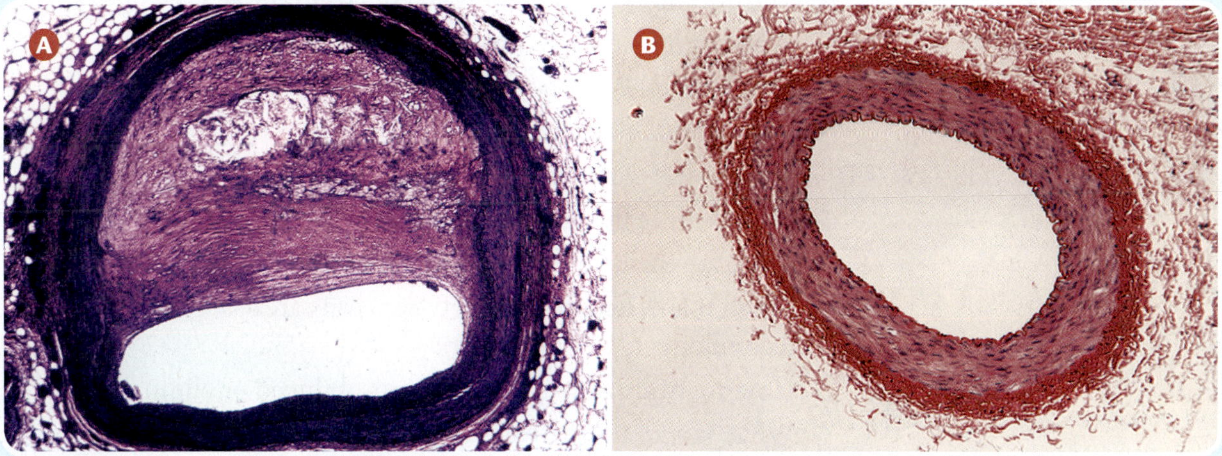

3. Try to determine the condition that probably led to the patient's death.
4. Research this condition using the resources suggested by your teacher. Describe the causes, symptoms, and risk factors for this condition.
5. Complete a brief pathologist's report to identify the cause of death. You must describe the cause of death using information from step 4. You must also explain how you came to your conclusion.

Investigation 1E

Skill Check

- ✓ initiating and planning
- ✓ performing and recording
- ✓ analyzing and interpreting
- ✓ communicating

Advances in Medical Technology

Advanced medical imaging technologies are changing how doctors practise medicine. These technologies allow doctors to diagnose and treat diseases earlier, more easily, and more safely than in the past. However, there are some health and safety concerns associated with these technologies. In this investigation, you will research a medical imaging technology and present your findings.

What To Do

1. Choose one of the following medical imaging technologies. Refer to the descriptions of these technologies on pages 78 and 79.
   - CT scan
   - PET scan
   - microscope
   - X ray
   - endoscope
   - ultrasound
   - MRI scan
2. Write down what you have already learned about the medical imaging technology you chose.
3. Use library and/or Internet resources to research this technology. Focus on the questions you want answered. For example:
   - When and where was the technology developed?
   - What does the technology do?
   - How does the technology work?
   - What is the technology best used for?
   - What are the benefits of the technology?
   - What are the limitations of the technology?
   - What, if any, health and safety concerns are associated with the technology?
   - How are health and safety concerns reduced or eliminated?
   - What, if any, alternative is available to perform the same function or make the same diagnosis as this imaging technology? What are the benefits and limitations of this alternative?

What Did You Find Out?

1. What are the main features of the medical imaging technology you chose?
2. Based on what you learned about the health risks, what is your opinion about using this technology? Support your opinion with information from your research.

3. Use your findings to create a pamphlet, poster, or Web page that will educate patients about the pros and cons of treatment with this medical imaging technology.
   - ☑ Summarize your findings.
   - ☑ Decide on your audience.
   - ☑ Use words and graphics that appeal to your audience.
4. If a friend was advised to use the medical imaging technology you chose, what advice would you give about its features and safety?

Inquire Further

Canada is a world leader in the export of medical isotopes. Use library and Internet resources to answer the following questions about this technology:

- What are medical isotopes?
- How are medical isotopes used?
- What process is used to make medical isotopes?
- In which other countries are medical isotopes made?
- What are the costs and benefits of using medical isotopes to treat diseases?
- How would a shortage of medical isotopes affect Canadians and other people around the world?

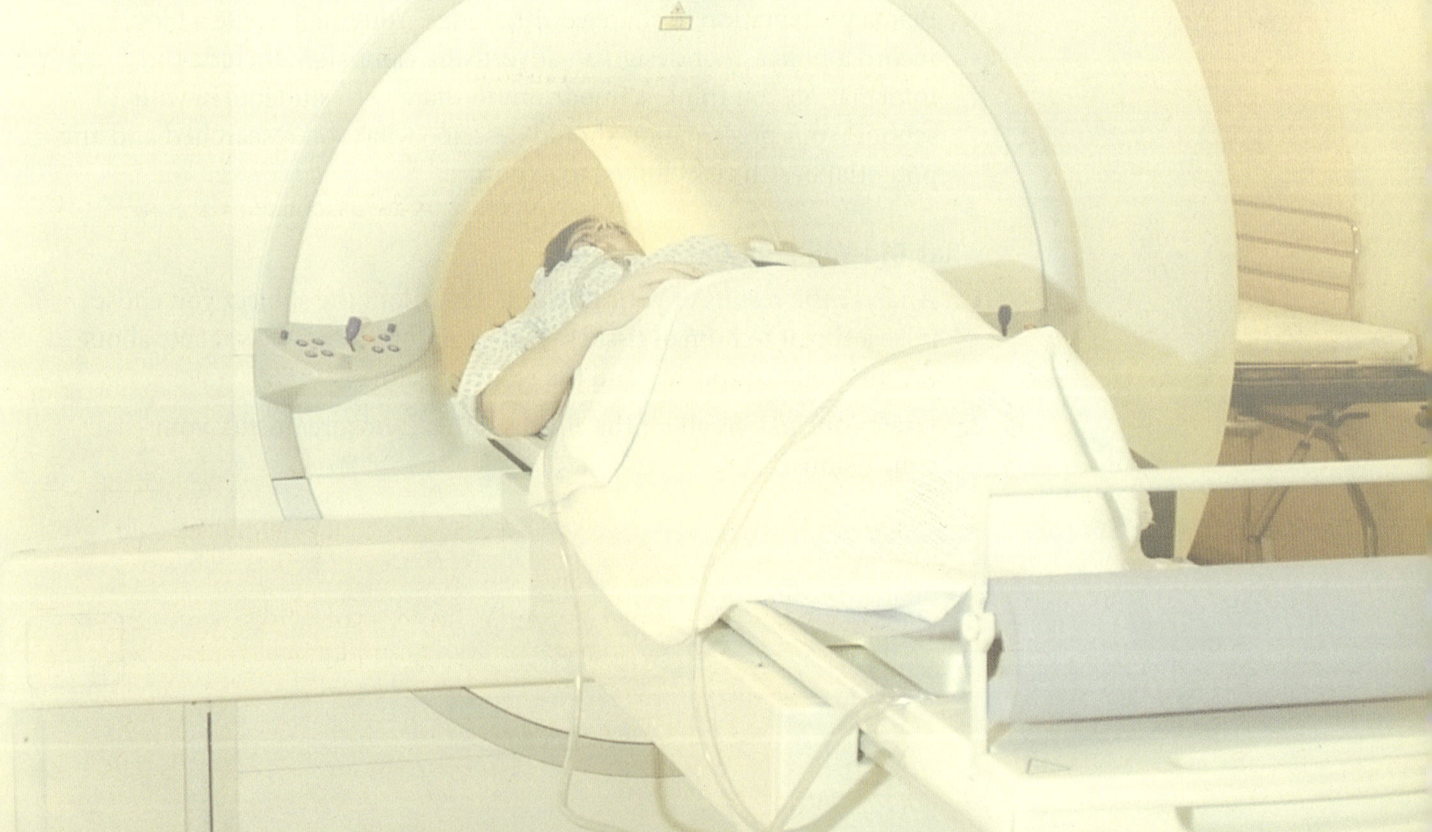

Investigation 1F

Skill Check

✓ initiating and planning
✓ performing and recording
✓ analyzing and interpreting
✓ communicating

How Much Exposure Is Too Much?

Create a presentation about the health effects of exposure to a technology, substance, or environmental factor.

What To Do

1. The chart below lists a variety of technologies, substances, and environmental factors that can affect health. Choose one of these potentially harmful agents.

cellphone	food additives	preservatives	electricity lines
personal audio player	pesticides	cigarette smoke	air pollution
exposure to sunlight	tanning beds	X ray or CT scan	heavy metals

2. Write down what you already know about this technology, substance, or environmental factor, including any health risks.
3. Research the substance, technology, or environmental factor you chose. Look for information about its impact on the tissues, organs, and organ systems in the human body. Create a bibliography of the resources you use as you carry out your research.
4. Plan a presentation to share your findings. You might write a blog, record a podcast, or design an advertising campaign. Include the information you think is important to share with students in your school. Your presentation should describe what you researched and any potential health risks linked to exposure.

What Did You Find Out?

1. Analyze the results of your research. How does the subject you chose pose a threat to human tissues, organs, and systems? Be specific about the amount of exposure and the related health risks.
2. Draw conclusions about the effects of this exposure. Justify your conclusions.

3. a) In your opinion, what do most students know about the effects of this exposure? Explain.
   b) What do most students *not* know about the effects of this exposure?
   c) How aware do you think most students are about their exposure to potentially harmful agents? Explain.
   d) What do you think is important for students to know about the technology, substance, or environmental factor you researched?
4. Explain how the following factors could affect students' choices and decisions about exposing themselves to potentially harmful agents.
   a) peer pressure
   b) popular media
   c) lack of knowledge about health risks

Inquire Further

Your health depends on the food you eat. How safe is your food? Food can be exposed to heavy metals, pesticides, preservatives, colouring agents, and other additives. To what substances is your food exposed? What are the potential effects of this exposure on human tissues, organs, and systems? Do additional research to find answers to these questions.

Note: There is a lot of incomplete, misleading, and false information about food and food safety on the Internet. With your classmates and teacher, discuss how to tell a reputable source of information from one that is not. Be sure to find and use at least three sources of reputable information to help you answer these questions.

Case Study Investigation: What's the Price of Peak Performance?

What's the Issue?

In today's society, the pressure to be the best can be intense. When Canadians between 12 and 17 were asked if they would take performance-enhancing substances that would make them faster, stronger, or simply more buff, one out of five said they would, despite the risks involved. These substances have the potential to seriously harm the human body. Would you take a chance with your health to be the best?

Some people involved in athletic activities take performance-enhancing substances to be the best.

The Science behind the Issue

What are the risks of using performance-enhancing substances? How can these substances affect your cells, tissues, organs, and systems? The answers to these questions vary depending on the substance. Three of the most popular performance-enhancing substances are creatine, steroids, and human growth hormone.

Creatine

Creatine occurs naturally in the body. It helps muscles release energy. If creatine is something your body uses anyway, what's the problem with taking it? To get the performance-enhancing effect, athletes need to take a lot more creatine than is usually present in the body. What happens to the body when large amounts of creatine are taken on a regular basis? Dr. Peter Yu of the University of Saskatchewan wondered the same thing. The Canadian scientist found that the body changes creatine into another substance called formaldehyde. Formaldehyde is poisonous and can cause serious side-effects when present in large amounts. These side-effects include damage to the circulatory system and kidneys.

Steroids

Steroids are hormones that enhance the production of muscle tissue in the body. If athletes want to bulk up, steroids can help them do it faster. Steroids also help athletes recover from training more quickly. However, the side-effects are dangerous—even deadly. They include changes in behaviour, such as episodes of rage or depression, as well as severe acne, liver damage, and increased risk of infection. Steroids also affect the sex hormones. Males may develop larger breasts and infertility, while females often gain a deeper voice and increased body hair.

Human Growth Hormone

Farmers in some countries (not Canada) give dairy cows growth hormones to help them produce more milk. Growth hormones can also enhance the performance of human athletes. Human growth hormone promotes the production of new muscle cells. It also gives athletes more energy. Despite the fact that human growth hormone is naturally found in the body, it can cause problems when taken in large amounts. Side effects include joint pain, swollen limbs, high blood pressure, and diabetes.

Would you consider risking your health to win a medal?

Over To You

1. Using your knowledge of how organs and systems work together in the body, suggest how using creatine could lead to the build-up of poisonous substances in an athlete's body.
2. Build on your knowledge of performance-enhancing substances by researching and writing a brief paragraph about a substance not covered in this Case Study Investigation. Possible choices include diuretics, androstenedione (andro), and stimulants such as caffeine and amphetamines.
3. The Olympics and other top competitions test athletes for banned performance-enhancing substances. If athletes test positive, they are stripped of their medals. What criteria would you use to determine which substances should be banned or allowed?
4. Some of your peers may be thinking of using performance-enhancing substances despite the risks. Design a campaign to demonstrate the risks of using these substances. Hint: Risks can involve harm to families and friendships as well as harm to the body.

Making a DIFFERENCE

As a 14-year-old, Kristopher Knowles campaigned across Canada on a walking tour to educate people about organ donations. Increasing the rate of organ donation is a personal issue for Kristopher. He has been waiting for a new liver most of his life. The Ontario teen has biliary atresia, a liver disease that can be fatal. Because Kristopher's liver is severely damaged, he continues to wait for a transplant.

Kristopher's hope is for Canada to create a system of presumed consent. Such a system requires people to indicate only if they do not wish to have their organs donated after they die. This type of system has increased organ donations in other countries. Currently in Canada, people must sign their organ donor cards to indicate that they wish to donate.

What could you do to raise awareness about a health care issue that is important to you?

Prashanthi Baskaran was a high school student when she began researching atherosclerosis. Prashanthi was motivated to learn about atherosclerosis after her uncle was diagnosed with the disease. Her research focuses on connections between gingivitis and atherosclerosis. Gingivitis is a swelling of the gums that surround the teeth. The chronic inflammation that comes with gingivitis may link the two diseases.

How is Prashanthi making a difference? Her work could one day help uncover methods for early detection of atherosclerosis. Prashanthi's advice for students who want to use science to help make a difference is to "develop a passion for something you love." Prashanthi has also volunteered her time with a local pharmacy and other community organizations. In 2008, Prashanthi was named one of Youth in Motion's Top 20 Under 20™.

How could you help promote health in your community?

Topic 1.5 Review

Key Concept Summary

- Medical imaging technologies are used to explore, diagnose, and treat the human body.
- Exposure to various technologies, substances, and environmental factors can impair health.
- Technology will affect human health in new ways in the future.

Review the Key Concepts

1. K/U Answer the question that is the title of this topic. Copy and complete the graphic organizer below in your notebook. Fill in four examples from the topic using key terms as well as your own words.

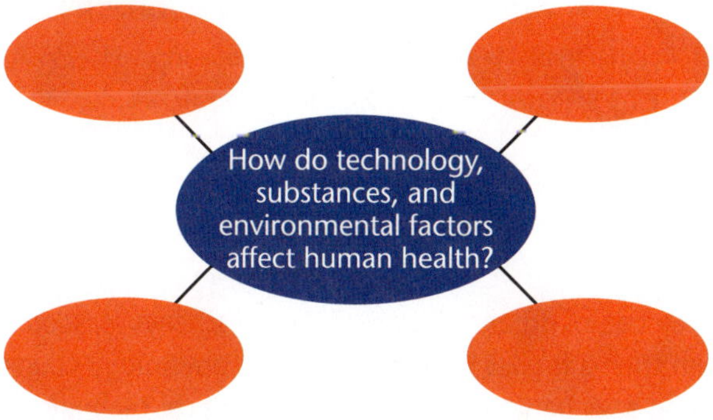

2. K/U Explain how ultrasound has improved health care.

3. a) K/U Identify the medical technology shown here.

b) What is it best used for?

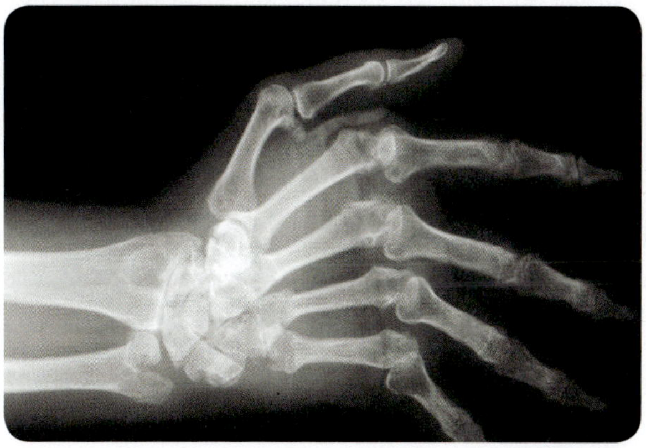

4. a) K/U How might exposure to cellphone radiation affect children?

b) A Why do you think children are at higher risk from exposure to radiation?

5. a) K/U What is the i-Pill?

b) What is the importance of i-Pill technology?

6. T/I What factors would you consider when deciding on a medical technology to diagnose a problem?

7. T/I A What would you tell a friend who asks you about the health risks of smoking?

8. A Consider the following patient cases.

a) A 25-year-old female patient is experiencing severe pain in her hips. You cannot diagnose the problem using an external exam. What imaging test would you order?

b) You are a medical technician who is taking a tissue sample of a 19-year-old male patient's small intestine. Which technology would you use?

9. C You have learned that pesticides can be harmful to human health. Write a letter to the editor of your local paper explaining why pesticides pose a health risk and what people can do to reduce the risk.

SCIENCE AT WORK

CANADIANS IN SCIENCE

▲ Masood Hassan is a radiological technologist at Sunnybrook Health Sciences Centre.

Radiological technologists—or "rad techs," as they are commonly known—make it possible for doctors to locate problems hidden inside the body. This knowledge is often essential in diagnosing and treating a patient. Rad techs perform several types of radiography procedures. They carry out "plain" radiography, which use X rays to detect fractures, foreign objects, and malformations. They also take images that screen for breast cancer and show disease in the human heart. Maintaining radiation safety is another important aspect of the job.

Masood Hassan is a recent graduate from The Michener Institute for Applied Health Sciences in Toronto. The program is offered jointly with the University of Toronto. He now works at Toronto's Sunnybrook Health Sciences Centre. This centre is home to a regional trauma centre. As a result, it has a special need for radiological technologists.

How much do you have to know about organs and organ systems to be a radiological technologist?

"You must have a basic knowledge of organs and organ systems," says Masood. To gain this knowledge, Masood took a higher level anatomy and physiology course as part of his training. Masood says he was attracted to radiological technology because it involved so many of the sciences. Physics helped him understand how X rays are generated. Computer skills are important because most images are now captured digitally. However, Masood also had to study chemistry in case he was required to work in a facility that used older, film-based technology.

What is the most important skill required for the job?

"The most important skill, in my opinion, would be communication with the patient. To get good X rays, you need to be able to communicate with the patient in a way that they understand what you want, so that they position themselves in a way that you can get a good picture. This can be a very big challenge in a cosmopolitan city where many people are not fluent in English. You have to be prepared to use non-verbal ways of communicating, to point and show them what you need."

What do you enjoy most about your work?

"I personally like problem-solving. Sometimes patients come to you in a cast which is not removable and the surgeons want to see a specific part of the bone and you have to find a way to manipulate your equipment to get the view that you're looking for."

Put Science To Work

The study of human biology contributes to these careers, as well as many more!

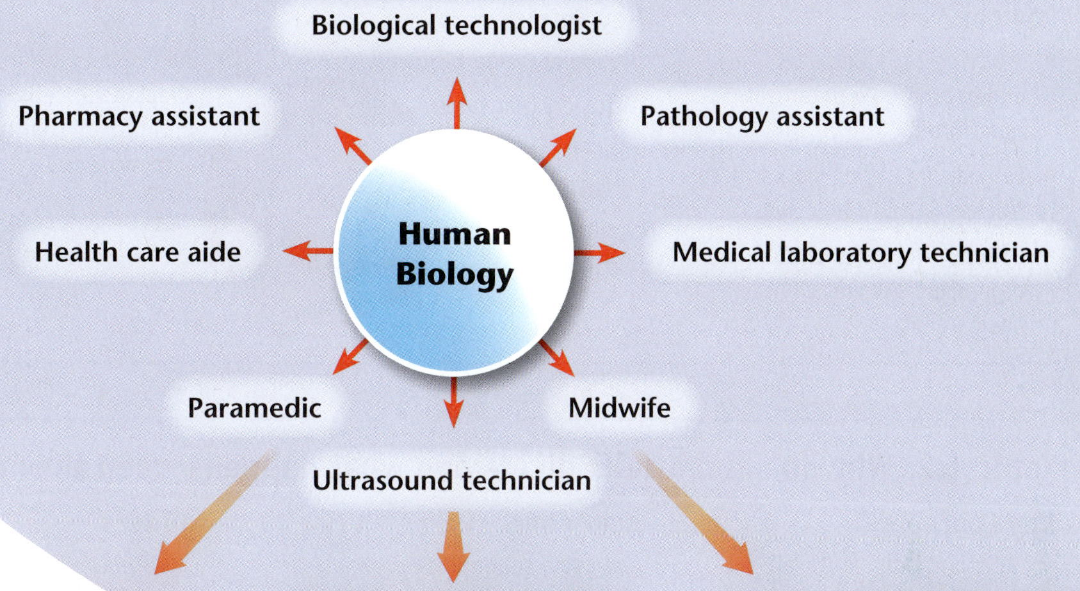

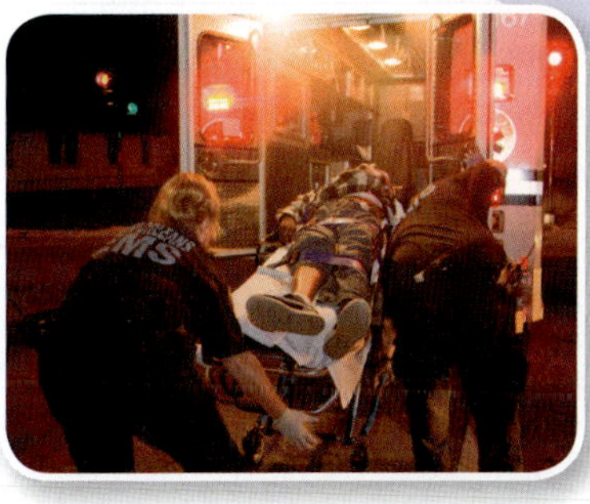

▲ Paramedics work for ambulance services. They respond to emergency calls, complete initial patient diagnosis, provide emergency treatment, and safely convey patients to the hospital if necessary.

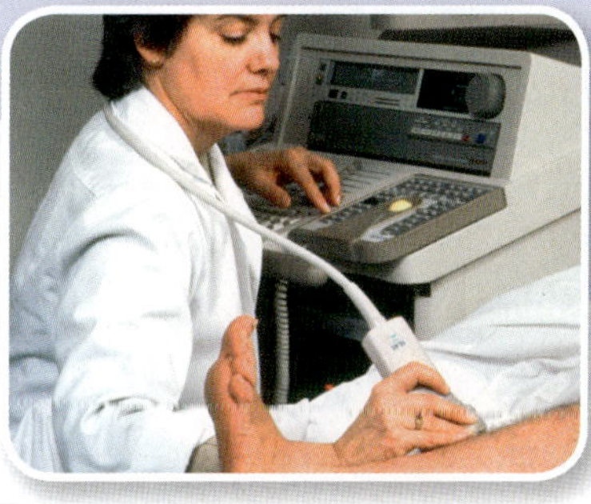

▲ Ultrasound technicians use ultrasound medical imaging technology to generate images used to diagnose and assess medical conditions.

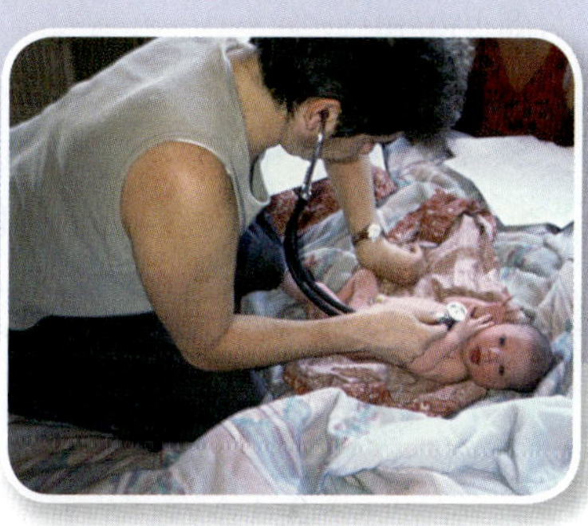

▲ Midwives deliver babies in hospitals, birthing centres, and private homes. They care for women during pregnancy and act as labour coaches. They also offer care to new mothers and infants.

Over To You

Work Life Learning

1. If you could interview Masood Hassan, what questions would you ask him about his work?
2. Why is it important for a radiological technologist to understand human biology?
3. Research a career involving human biology that interests you. If you wish, you may choose from the list above. What are the essential skills needed for this career?

Go to **scienceontario** to find out more

Unit 1 Summary

Topic 1.1: Why are cells important?

Key Concepts

- Studying cells helps us understand how organisms function.
- Cellular organelles work together to carry out life functions.
- Cellular processes enable organisms to meet their basic needs.

Key Terms

organelle (page 12)

diffusion (page 16)

concentration (page 16)

osmosis (page 17)

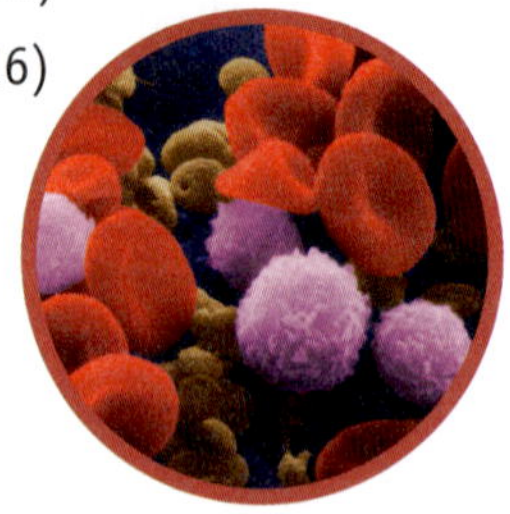

Big Ideas

- All animals are made of specialized cells, tissues, and organs that are organized into systems.

Topic 1.2: Why do animal cells divide and what happens when they do?

Key Concepts

- Cells must divide for an organism to survive.
- Hereditary material is passed on during cell division.
- Animal cells have a life cycle that includes both growth and division.
- New animal cells are created during the cell cycle.
- Uncontrolled, rapid division of animal cells can be cancer.

Key Terms

cell cycle (page 26)

interphase (page 26)

mitosis (page 26)

cytokinesis (page 26)

regeneration (page 27)

prophase (page 28)

metaphase (page 28)

anaphase (page 28)

telophase (page 28)

Big Ideas

- All animals are made of specialized cells, tissues, and organs that are organized into systems.

Topic 1.3: How do cells work together in the human body?

Key Concepts

- All cells begin alike and differentiate into specialized cells.
- Specialized cells have different structures that allow them to perform unique functions.
- Groups of cells working together form tissues.
- Groups of tissues working together form organs, which work together in systems.

Key Terms

cell specialization (page 41)

cell differentiation (page 41)

tissue (page 44)

organ (page 46)

organ system (page 47)

Big Ideas

- All animals are made of specialized cells, tissues, and organs that are organized into systems.

Topic 1.4: How do systems work together in the human body?

Key Concepts

- The respiratory system carries oxygen to and removes carbon dioxide from the blood.
- The circulatory system transports dissolved gases and nutrients through the body.
- The digestive system breaks down food, absorbs nutrients, and eliminates solid waste.
- Organ systems working together carry out important tasks in the body.

Key Terms

gas exchange (page 58, 59)
alveoli (page 59)
capillaries (page 59)
red blood cells (page 59)
absorption (page 62)

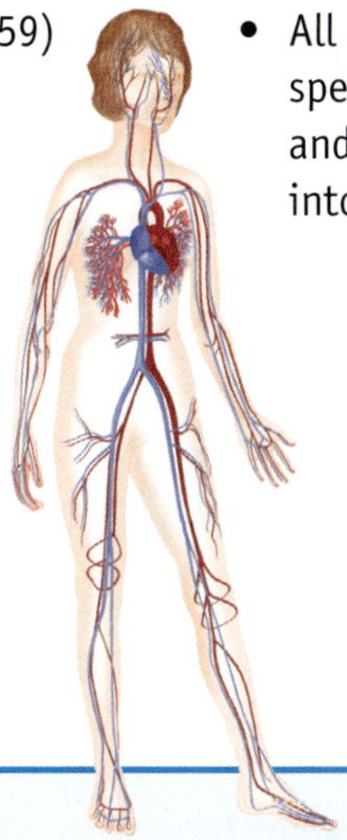

Big Ideas

- All animals are made of specialized cells, tissues, and organs that are organized into systems.

Topic 1.5: How do technology, substances, and environmental factors affect human health?

Key Concepts

- Medical imaging technologies are used to explore, diagnose, and treat the human body.
- Exposure to various technologies, substances, and environmental factors can impair health.
- Technology will affect human health in new ways in the future.

Key Terms

medical imaging technology (page 78)

Big Ideas

- All animals are made of specialized cells, tissues, and organs that are organized into systems.
- Although technology and chemicals can be used to improve human health, they can also constitute a health hazard.

Unit 1 Project

Inquiry Investigation: How Disease Affects Organs

Some diseases affect the function of tissues and organs and cause health problems that affect organ systems. Examples include asthma, diabetes, arthritis, allergies, atherosclerosis, sickle-cell anemia, Crohn's disease, hepatitis B, and cirrhosis.

Investigate Question
What health problems result when disease affects a person's tissues, organs, and organ systems?

Initiate and Plan

1. Choose one disease to research.
2. Plan by writing at least 10 questions to answer the inquiry question. For example:
   - Which organ or system does the disease affect?
   - How does the organ become diseased?
   - What health problems does a person affected by this disease have?
   - What are signs and symptoms of this disease?
   - What are possible treatments?

Perform and Record

3. Use electronic, print, and human sources to find answers to your questions. Include a picture or diagram of a healthy organ and of a diseased organ.
4. Use the diagrams of the healthy organ and the diseased organ to create a model of each.

Analyze and Interpret

1. Use a graphic organizer to compare the healthy organ and the diseased organ.
2. If the disease can be prevented, use the information you have gathered to describe how.
3. How might the diseased organ affect other organs or systems in the body?

Communicate your Findings

4. Create a pamphlet to outline the information you have discovered. Use appropriate scientific language to communicate your findings.

Assessment Criteria

Review your project. Did you …

- ✔ show knowledge of the disease and organ chosen? K/U
- ✔ create models of a healthy organ and a diseased organ? T/I
- ✔ create an information pamphlet that includes ways to prevent the disease? C
- ✔ use an appropriate format and terminology to communicate the information to your classmates? C
- ✔ explain which medical technology is used to diagnose and/or treat the disease? A
- ✔ discuss how other organs or organ systems in the body are affected by this disease? A

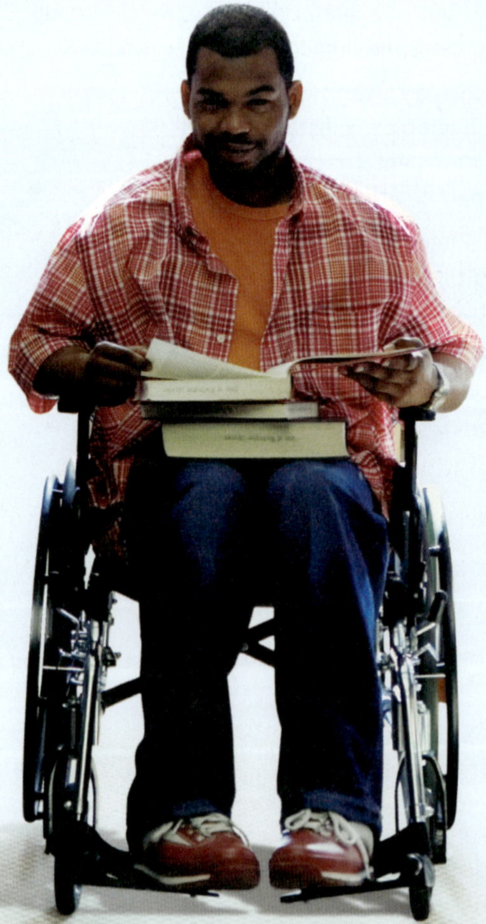

An Issue to Analyze: Encouraging Healthy Lifestyles

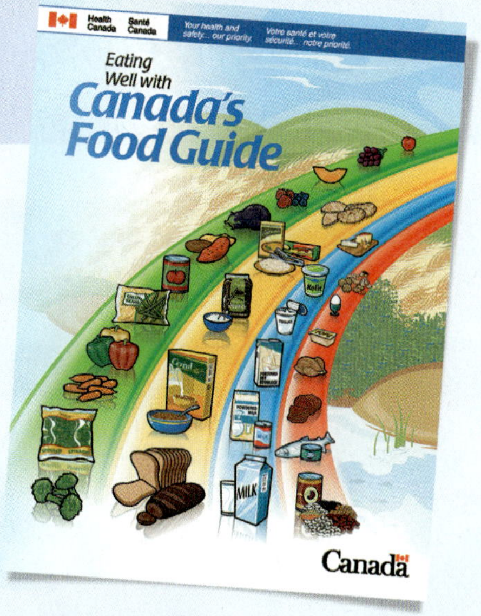

Diseases may be caused by genetics, viruses, or bacteria. Many diseases, however, are the result of lifestyle choices. Unhealthy diet, lack of exercise, and the use of tobacco, alcohol, and other drugs can lead to chronic (long-term) diseases such as diabetes, heart disease, and lung disease.

Issue

Chronic diseases linked to lifestyle choices are on the increase. This puts a strain on health-care systems and makes it hard for people to enjoy life. What kinds of resources and information can help Canadians learn about and make healthier choices?

Initiate and Plan

1. Plan your research by writing at least 10 questions that will help you assess the issue. Here are some examples.
   - How can healthy and unhealthy diets affect our chances of developing chronic disease?
   - What factors affect the chances of developing a chronic disease?
   - How do factors in our environment affect our chances of developing chronic disease?
   - What percentage of health-care spending goes to treating chronic disease?
   - What government agencies and programs currently encourage Canadians to live healthier lives? What messages are they sending out?
2. Determine possible sources of information.
3. Choose a graphic organizer or other method to organize your findings.
4. Show your research plan to your teacher.

Perform and Record

5. Gather and record the information to answer your questions.

Analyze and Interpret

1. Use a PMI chart or a cost-benefit analysis to evaluate the effects that changing to a healthier lifestyle can have on the chances of developing chronic disease.
2. Find three public health messages about healthy lifestyles. Describe them. How effective are they?
3. Create a media plan to encourage Canadians (including your peers) to live a healthier lifestyle.

Communicate your Findings

4. Your classmates are media buyers. Present your media plan to improve the health of Canadians. Use a slide show presentation, poster, or a written or oral report to present your plan.

Assessment Checklist

Review your project. Did you …

- ✔ research how diet, exercise, and environmental factors can affect the health of a person? **K/U**
- ✔ consult credible resources to determine what current government programs exist to educate the public? **T/I**
- ✔ use graphic organizers to record your research? **C**
- ✔ present your findings in a persuasive manner? **C**
- ✔ create a media plan that includes both a message and a delivery method? **A**

Unit 1 Review

Connect to the Big Ideas

1. All animals are made of specialized cells, tissues, and organs that are organized into systems. Organ systems have many parts that work together to perform a function. Choose one of the following organ systems: circulatory, digestive, respiratory.

   Use a series of drawings and words to do the following.

   a) Describe the function of the organ system.

   b) Name the organs that form the system. Identify and describe as many types of tissues that form one organ as you can.

   c) Identify and describe the specialized cells that form each tissue.

   d) Use a t-chart to compare the human system you chose and the same system in the frog.

2. Technology and chemicals can be used to improve human health. However, they also can be hazardous to health. Conduct research on a technology of your choice, such as microwave ovens or cell phones. Discover the health risks associated with the technology and how to reduce the risks. Develop an action plan for the safe use of the technology. Present your findings in a letter of concern to your school newspaper.

Knowledge and Understanding K/U

3. Draw an oval to represent an animal cell. Add the following organelles and cell parts and label them: cell membrane, cytoplasm, nucleus, nuclear membrane.

4. What is the benefit of animal cells differentiating into specialized cells?

5. Examine the diagram at the top of the next column, which shows molecules of carbon dioxide outside a cell and inside a cell.

   a) Identify the cellular process shown in the diagram.

   b) Describe the evidence that supports your answer to part a).

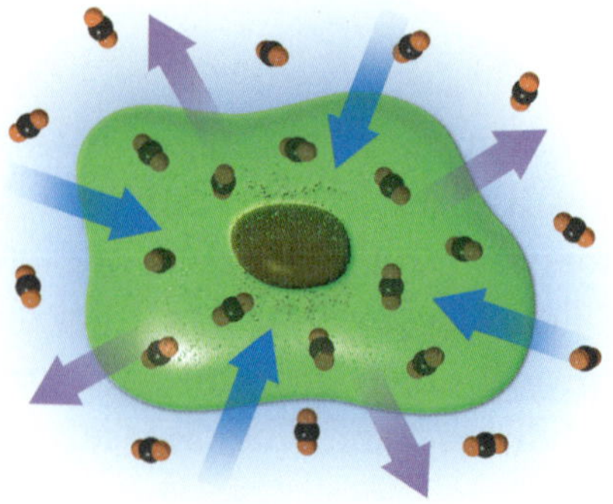

6. a) Identify the stages of the cell cycle shown in the three photos below. They are in the correct order.

   b) Sketch the cell as it would appear before photo A.

   c) Sketch the cell as it would appear after photo C.

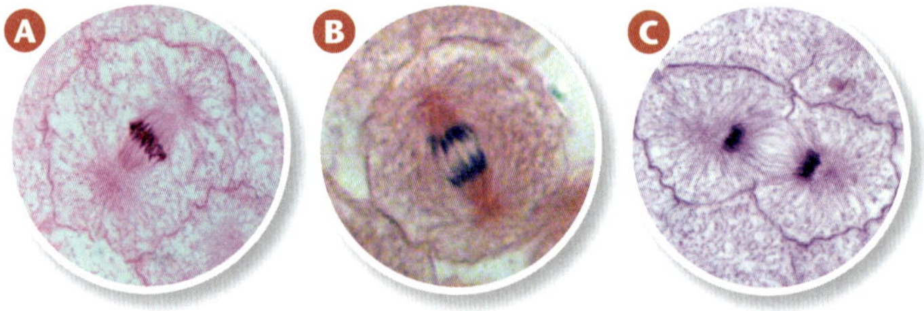

7. Describe what is happening in each of the three photos in question 6.

8. Explain how cells, tissues, organs, and organ systems are related.

9. Draw a spider map to identify and describe the organ and vessels of the circulatory system.

10. a) Which organ system is responsible for the exchange of carbon dioxide and oxygen?

    b) Use a diagram and words to explain what happens during this process.

11. Write a short paragraph (two or three sentences) to explain how the respiratory system and the circulatory system work together.

12. Use a diagram and words to explain how the digestive and circulatory systems work together.

13. Describe two examples of medical imaging technology that you learned about. Explain their purposes.

14. a) Identify two technologies that can impair health, and explain how they can do so.
  b) Identify two substances that can impair health, and explain how they can do so.
  c) Identify two environmental factors that can impair health, and explain how they can do so.

15. Cellular respiration takes place in the mitochondria of cells. Muscle cells have many more mitochondria than the cells of most other organs. Explain why this does or does not surprise you.

16. Your teacher announces a surprise quiz. For some students in the class, their heart starts to beat faster and their rate of breathing increases. Which two body systems are interacting in this example?

17. As you view slides of cells under a microscope, you observe a cell with long finger-like extensions and another cell that is round and disk-like. Use what you have learned to identify these cells and explain how each structure helps the cells perform their function. Which body system is responsible for controlling and coordinating this interaction?

Thinking and Investigation T/I

18. You are judging at an elementary school science fair. One student has made models of the four types of tissues. Develop a set of criteria to help assess how well the design of each tissue model suits the function of each type of tissue.

19. You are asked to create a model of alveoli and capillaries. List at least two design features you need to consider and explain your thinking.

20. One goal of medical research is to grow specialized cells, tissues, and organs in the laboratory.
  a) Identify a benefit of achieving this goal.
  b) Explain why this is a challenging goal.

21. State a hypothesis that could explain why single-celled organisms are found both in aquatic ecosystems and within the bodies of many-celled organisms.

22. Sketch a line graph that shows how certain cells in a person's body are dividing if those cells are cancerous. Be sure to label the *x*-axis and the *y*-axis appropriately.

23. A student observed a number of cells at different stages of the cell cycle. The student calculated the percentage of time that the cells spent during each of the stages. The table below shows the student's results.
  a) The stages of the cell cycle are listed in alphabetical order. List them, instead, based on their correct sequence, starting with the phase during which the nuclear membrane disappears.
  b) According to the table, the observed cells spent 79 percent of their time in interphase. Explain why this is a result you would expect.

Stage of Cell Cycle	Percentage of Time Spent in Each Stage
Anaphase	2 percent
Interphase	79 percent
Metaphase	2 percent
Prophase	13 percent
Teleophase	5 percent

Communication C

24. You are editing a wiki about cells. Use words and diagrams to clearly define the process of diffusion.

25. Use a graphic organizer to help explain to a Grade 4 class the path of a glucose molecule from dinner plate to body cell.

26. A recent movie portrays a monster bacterium that is unicellular and the size of King Kong. Explain to your friends why this is not realistic.

27. West Nile Virus is carried by mosquitoes and can cause a disease that is fatal to those who contract it. One response to the risk of West Nile Virus is to spray pesticides (some of which can cause cancers) in and around water sources that contain mosquitoes. Discuss the pros and cons of this response. Research and summarize other methods of prevention.

28. Make either a crossword puzzle or a word jumble puzzle using as many key terms from Unit 1 as you can. Trade your puzzle with a classmate who made a different kind of puzzle. Solve each other's puzzles.

29. Sometimes a living cell is compared with a factory. Write a paragraph or use a t-chart to compare the parts and functions of a cell with what happens in a factory. Use the diagram below to guide your answer.

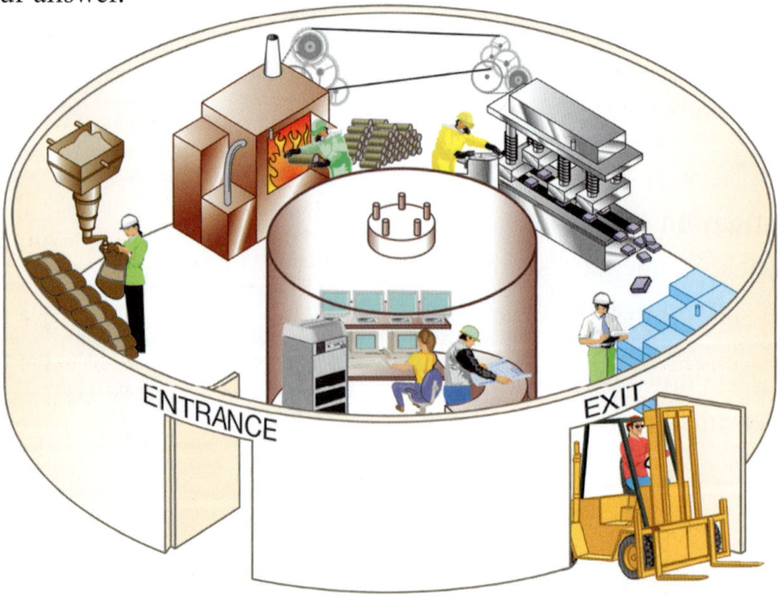

Application A

30. Explain why your heart is pounding after you run up a flight of stairs.

31. Describe how a variety of medical imaging technologies could be helpful in diagnosing and treating lung cancer.

32. Many forest firefighters wear kerchiefs around their mouth and nose when they are walking through ashes. Explain why this is important for their respiratory systems.

33. If you were in a mineshaft and the elevator broke, leaving you far below ground until it could be repaired, what would you worry about most—a lack of food, water, or air? Explain your answer.

34. Treatments for many types of cancer involve killing cells that divide rapidly using chemicals (chemotherapy) or radiation. These treatments often kill the cancer cells by causing mutations in them. Sometimes, however, the treatment of cancer can cause surrounding normal cells to become cancerous. Why might this occur?

35. An unknown disease is causing the number of red blood cells in a person's body to decrease. Identify at least two possible consequences of this.

Literacy Test Prep

Read the selection below, and answer the questions that follow it.

In 2003, Sabrina Shannon, aged 13, died after eating cafeteria french fries that had come in contact with dairy products. Sabrina was allergic to dairy products. In Ontario, more than 42 000 teens have severe, life-threatening allergies to foods. A severe allergic reaction that affects all or most organ systems is called anaphylaxis. Common symptoms include

- flushed face, hives, swollen or itchy lips, tongue, or eyes
- tightness in the throat, mouth, or chest
- wheezing or coughing, difficulty breathing or swallowing
- choking, vomiting, nausea, diarrhea, stomach pains
- dizziness, unsteadiness, sudden fatigue, rapid heartbeat
- loss of consciousness

If left untreated, anaphylaxis can be fatal, so recognizing its symptoms and getting immediate treatment is crucial. People with severe allergies must learn how to avoid the things they are allergic to and be prepared to manage an unexpected reaction by always carrying an epinephrine auto-injector (EpiPen).

In 2006, Sabrina's Law came into effect in Ontario. It ensures that all schools have policies and procedures in place for students at risk of anaphylaxis. School staff are trained to recognize the signs and give medication if needed. Sabrina's Law helps all students be and feel safe at school and may prevent another student from Sabrina Shannon's fate.

Multiple Choice

In your notebook, choose and record the best or most correct answer.

36. Death from anaphylaxis can be prevented by
- **a)** avoiding cafeteria french fries
- **b)** carrying an epinephrine auto-injector
- **c)** Sabrina's Law
- **d)** recognizing symptoms and immediate treatment

37. The information in the bulleted list is used to
- **a)** compare and contrast ideas
- **b)** describe the steps in a process
- **c)** summarize ideas
- **d)** provide details in order of importance

38. Which of the following symptoms of anaphylaxis are related to the respiratory system?
- **a)** tightness in the throat, mouth or chest, wheezing
- **b)** choking, vomiting, nausea, diarrhea, stomach pains
- **c)** dizziness, unsteadiness, sudden fatigue, rapid heartbeat
- **d)** loss of consciousness

39. Sabrina's Law helps Ontario students be safe by
- **a)** banning potential allergic substances in schools
- **b)** ensuring that people know what to do when a student has a severe allergic reaction
- **c)** requiring students to carry epinephrine auto-injectors
- **d)** not allowing students with severe allergies to eat cafeteria food

Written Answer

40. Many people are allergic to nuts and nut products. Many schools have adopted a nut-free policy. Explain why this might be effective in keeping some students safe at school. Use specific details from the selection and your own ideas to support your answer.

Unit 2 Chemical Reactions and Their Practical Applications

Big Ideas

- Chemicals react with one another in predictable ways.
- Chemical reactions are a necessary component of chemical products and processes used in the home and workplace.

In the movie *Backdraft,* fire is described as if it is alive. In fact, one character in the movie calls fire, "The Animal." Fuelled by oxygen, wood, and other flammable materials, fire does indeed seem to take on a life of its own. It can creep and slither low to the ground like a stealthy python on the hunt. It can erupt with ferocious intensity like a cornered lion. Starve it of oxygen, though, and fire withers, smoulders, and eventually dies.

The people who fight fire—in cities, in forests, on windswept terrain—are like the knights of legend confronting the dragon. Outfitted with special protective garb, firefighters are trained to understand and combat fire and other chemical reactions that pose a risk to the lives and property of others.

HOW is fire linked to chemical reactions? Why do firefighters need special clothing and equipment to battle fires? Who else works with chemicals in their jobs? What special clothing and equipment do they use, and why do they need it?

?

Unit 2 At a Glance

In this unit you will learn that many of the products and processes used in the home and in the workplace are the result of chemical reactions. You will also use the fact that chemical compounds react with one another in certain, predictable ways to learn how to name compounds, write their formulas, and write chemical equations to describe their reactions.

***Think** about answers to each question as you work through the topic.*

Topic 2.1: How do chemical reactions affect your daily life?

Key Concepts

- Chemical reactions support our lives and assist us at home and at work.
- Chemical compounds require safe handling to minimize their hazards.

Chemical Reactions and Their Practical Applications

Topic 2.4: What are acids and bases, and how do they react?

Key Concepts

- Acids and bases are compounds with specific properties.
- An acid and a base react in a neutralization reaction to produce a salt and water.
- Chemical reactions involving acids, bases, and other compounds require safe handling to minimize hazards.

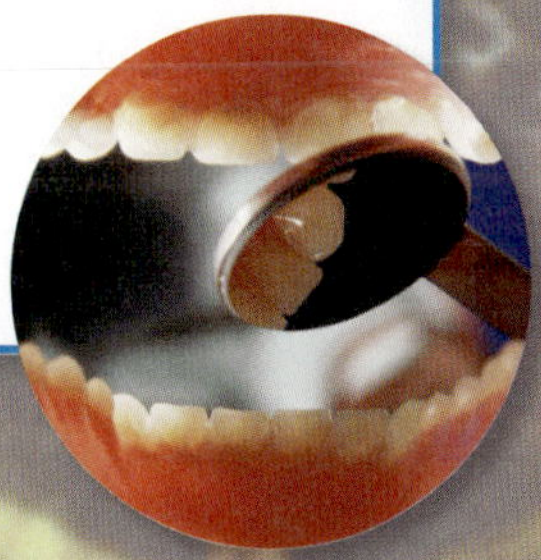

Topic 2.2: How can we understand, describe, and name chemical compounds?

Key Concepts

- Chemical compounds are formed from elements in the periodic table.
- Chemical compounds are represented using chemical names and chemical formulas.
- Reactive elements can become more stable when they form compounds.
- Chemical compounds are described as either ionic or molecular.
- Ionic compounds are named with the metal ion first and then the non-metal ion ending in "ide."
- Molecular compounds are named using numerical prefixes.

Topic 2.3: What happens during a chemical reaction, and how can it be described?

Key Concepts

- During a chemical reaction, chemical compounds are changed into different compounds with different properties.
- The four types of chemical reactions can be described using word equations.
- Chemical reactions can be described using chemical equations.
- Atoms and mass are conserved during a chemical reaction.

Looking Ahead to the Unit 2 Projects

At the end of this unit you will have the opportunity to apply what you have learned. In your unit projects, you will investigate how the pH in soda pop changes over time, and you will consider the safety and environmental implications of a business plan to mine e-waste for gold.

Get Ready for Unit 2

Concept Check

1. Complete each sentence with a word from the box below.

compound	element	group	period

a) A(n) ______ is a pure substance that cannot be broken down further by physical or chemical means.

b) A(n) ______ is a substance that can be broken down into elements by chemical means.

c) A horizontal row of elements in the periodic table is called a ______.

d) A vertical column (also called a family) of elements in the periodic table is called a ______.

2. Copy and complete the following table in your notebook.

Facts about Subatomic Particles

	Electrons	Neutrons	Protons
Location		inside the nucleus	
Charge			positive (+)
Relative size	smallest of these particles		

3. Identify the information listed below for the element beryllium. Refer to the periodic table below.

a) symbol

b) name of family

c) number of protons

d) number of electrons

e) atomic number

f) name of family of elements to its left

4. Determine whether each statement below describes a physical property or a chemical property of an element. If the statement describes a physical property, indicate whether it is a qualitative property or a quantitative property.

a) It is a pale yellow gas at room temperature.

b) It can burn or etch glass permanently.

c) Its density is 1.695 g/L.

d) It explodes when it reacts with water.

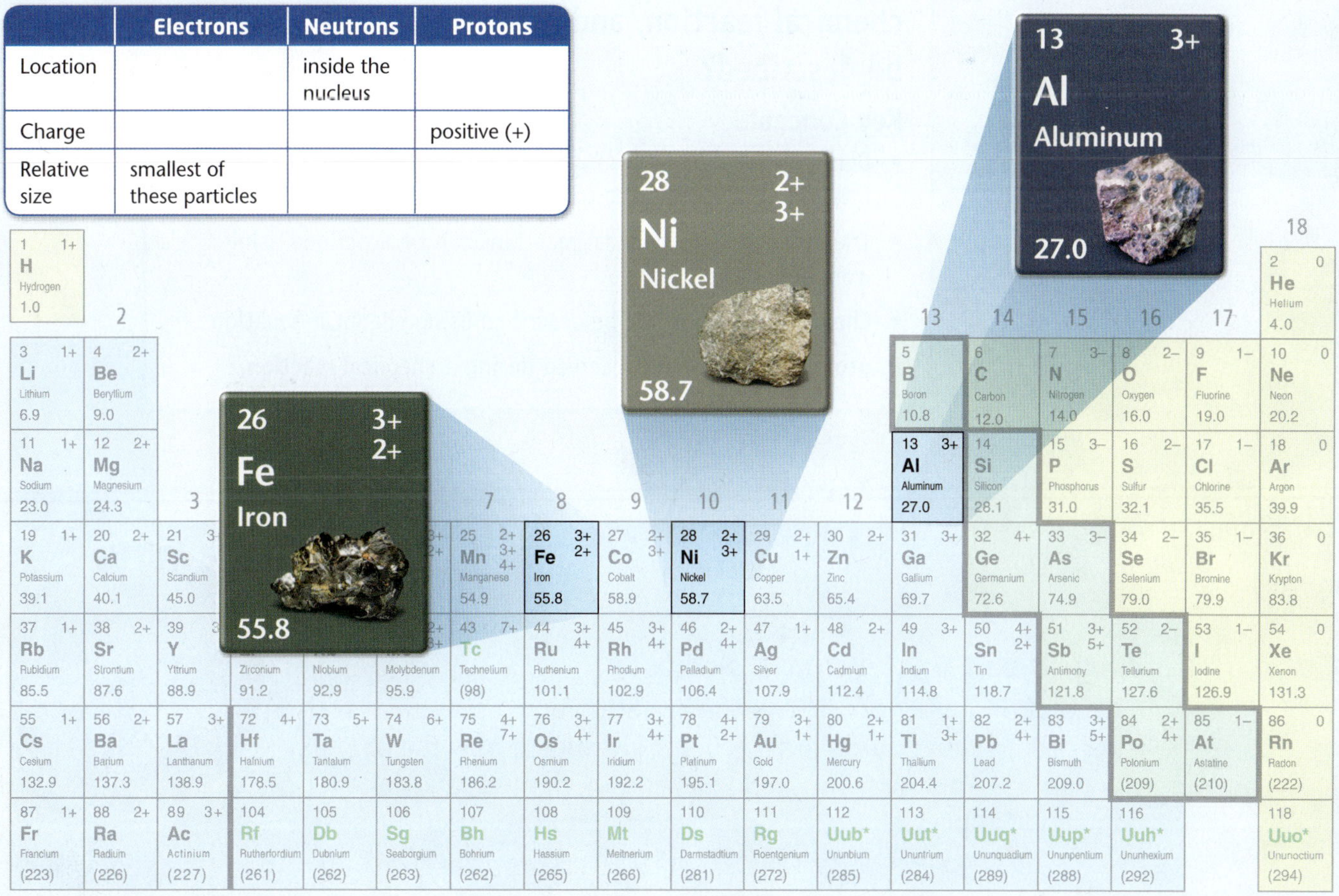

Inquiry Check

5. **Analyze** The chemical formulas of four molecules are shown below:
   - **i)** H_2
   - **ii)** Cl_2
   - **iii)** P_4
   - **iv)** S_8

   a) How many atoms make up each molecule?

   b) What is the name of each molecule?

6. **Analyze** The chemical formulas of six compounds are shown below.
   - **i)** H_2O
   - **ii)** CO_2
   - **iii)** CO
   - **iv)** $NaCl$
   - **v)** H_2O_2
   - **vi)** $NaHCO_3$

   a) Identify the name of the elements that make up each compound.

   b) Identify each compound.

   c) How many atoms of each element are there in each compound?

Numeracy and Literacy Check

7. **Calculate** The densities of three metals are given in the table below. Each of these metals is shown in an "exploded view" on the previous page.

Density of Three Metals

Name and Symbol	Density (g/cm^3)
aluminum (Al)	8.9
iron (Fe)	7.9
nickel (Ni)	2.7

One of these metals has a mass of 10 g and a volume of 1.12 cm^3. Determine the identity and atomic number of the metal. Show all your work.

8. **Draw** Make a sketch of the icon(s) you would expect to see in an activity or an investigation that involves the use of a chemical that can cause burns to the skin.

9. **Write** Skim the pages of Unit 2. Use a main idea web to record the three or four main ideas you will learn in this unit.

Topic 2.1 How do chemical reactions affect your daily life?

Key Concepts

- Chemical reactions support our lives and assist us at home and at work.
- Chemical compounds require safe handling to minimize their hazards.

Key Skills

- Inquiry
- Literacy

Key Terms

chemical reaction
product
reactant
dilute

If something has a "practical application," it has a use that people consider to be important, handy, or helpful. All the products and events in the photos on these two pages involve a chemical reaction. Each of them could be considered a practical application of a chemical reaction.

A car battery

A welder's torch

Fresh-baked bread

Food cooking

Starting Point Activity

Work in small groups to complete these tasks. Make sure that you reach an agreement in each task.

1. As a group, discuss what a chemical reaction is. Come to an agreement on the definition of a chemical reaction.
2. Discuss the photos on these two pages. Explain why each photo involves a chemical reaction.
3. List at least three other chemical reactions that you consider to have practical applications.
4. List at least three chemical reactions that you consider *not* to have practical applications.
5. What makes your answers to question 3 different from your answers to question 4?
6. Compare your lists with those of other groups in the class. Does everyone agree on what should be considered practical and what should not be? Does it matter if "practical application" means different things to different people? Give reasons to justify your answer.

A flare used to signal for help

Food preservatives

Ethanol added to gasoline

Brightening and disinfecting fabrics

Chemical reactions support our lives and assist us at home and at work.

chemical reaction: a change in matter that produces new substances with new properties

products: new substances produced in a chemical reaction

reactants: substances that react together in a chemical reaction

Perhaps the most practical application of chemical reactions is life itself. Your body is fuelled by chemical reactions, and the food that supplies the fuel is formed by chemical reactions. A **chemical reaction** is a change in matter that produces new substances with new properties. Recall that, in a physical change, no new substances are produced. The substance just changes its appearance. A chemical reaction also involves energy. Some chemical reactions store energy, while others release energy. For example, when paper burns, the chemical reaction is releasing energy in the form of heat. The new substances that are produced in a chemical reaction are called **products**. The substances that react together in a chemical reaction are called **reactants**. You can write a chemical reaction as:

reactants → products

The arrow indicates that a chemical change takes place. **Figure 2.1** reviews the reactants and products of the chemical reactions that support and sustain your life and most other life on Earth.

Figure 2.1 Photosynthesis and cellular respiration are examples of chemical reactions. Photosynthesis is an example of a chemical reaction that stores energy. Cellular respiration is an example of a chemical reaction that releases energy.

reactants: carbon dioxide and water
products: sugar and oxygen

Photosynthesis is a series of chemical reactions that stores energy in the form of food (sugar), which you and other organisms depend on.

reactants: sugar and oxygen
products: carbon dioxide and water

Cellular respiration is a series of chemical reactions that releases energy from the food you eat to "power" all the functions and activities inside your body.

Chemical Reactions at Home and at Work

Many different chemical products are found at home, including cleaners, foods, and food ingredients. All of these products are produced using chemical reactions or are used to make chemical reactions happen. One common product found in most homes is vinegar.

Vinegar is produced from chemical reactions that involve yeast and fruit sugars. Vinegar is actually a **dilute** solution of a chemical called acetic acid in water. In its dilute form, household vinegar can be used in recipes or as a cleaner. In its concentrated (non-dilute) form, acetic acid has many applications in industry and the workplace, as shown in **Figure 2.2**. However, concentrated acetic acid is not safe for home use. It is so powerful that it can burn through skin and other body tissues.

dilute: reduced in concentration by being mixed with a liquid, such as water

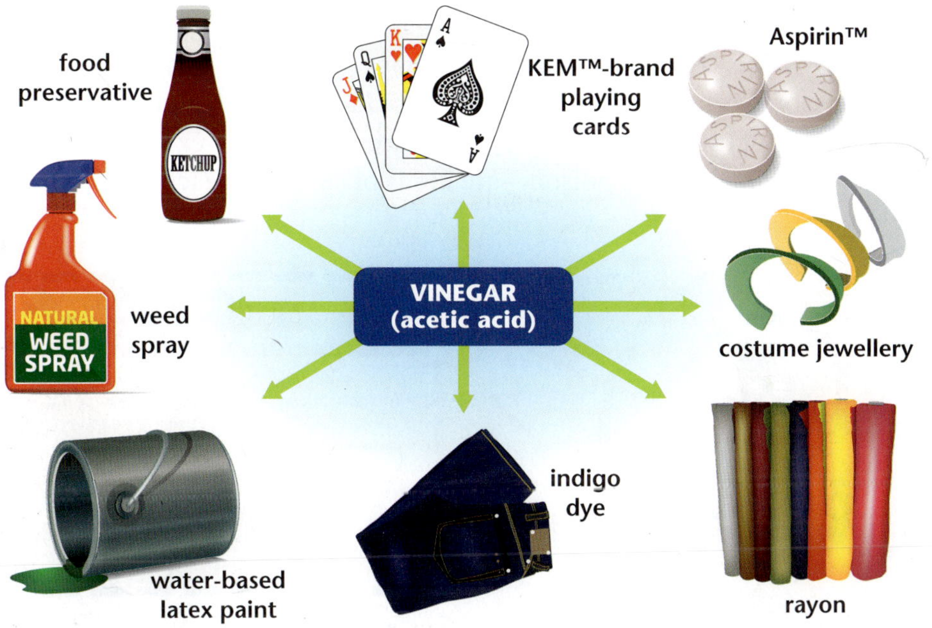

◀ **Figure 2.2** Acetic acid is used to make a variety of products that might surprise you. These include costume jewellery, fabrics, medicines, dyes, paint, weed killers, and a high-quality brand of playing cards.

Inquiry Focus

Activity 2.1

INFLATING A BALLOON

Safety

Use a scoop to put about 15 mL of baking soda inside a balloon. Fit the balloon over the opening of a plastic bottle that is about one-third full of vinegar. Watch the balloon, and feel the bottle. What evidence shows that a chemical reaction is taking place?

LEARNING CHECK

1. Name the reactants in the chemical reaction in Activity 2.1.
2. You put some water in the freezer and later it is solid. Has a chemical reaction occurred? Explain why or why not.

Chemical compounds require safe handling to minimize their hazards.

Hazardous chemicals are not only found in laboratories and industries—they are also found in the home. Wherever you find them, you will find labels that explain possible hazards.

Hazards in the Home

Many of the products in homes, supermarkets, and hardware stores have symbols on them to warn of possible danger. These **H**azardous **H**ousehold **P**roduct **S**ymbols (HHPS) use different shapes and easy-to-recognize icons to display some basic safety information about a product. Figure 2.3 shows the meanings of the HHPS. The four categories of danger—explosive, corrosive, flammable, and poison—are kinds of chemical reactions.

▼ Figure 2.3 These Hazardous Household Product Symbols (HHPS) were established by Health Canada in 2001.

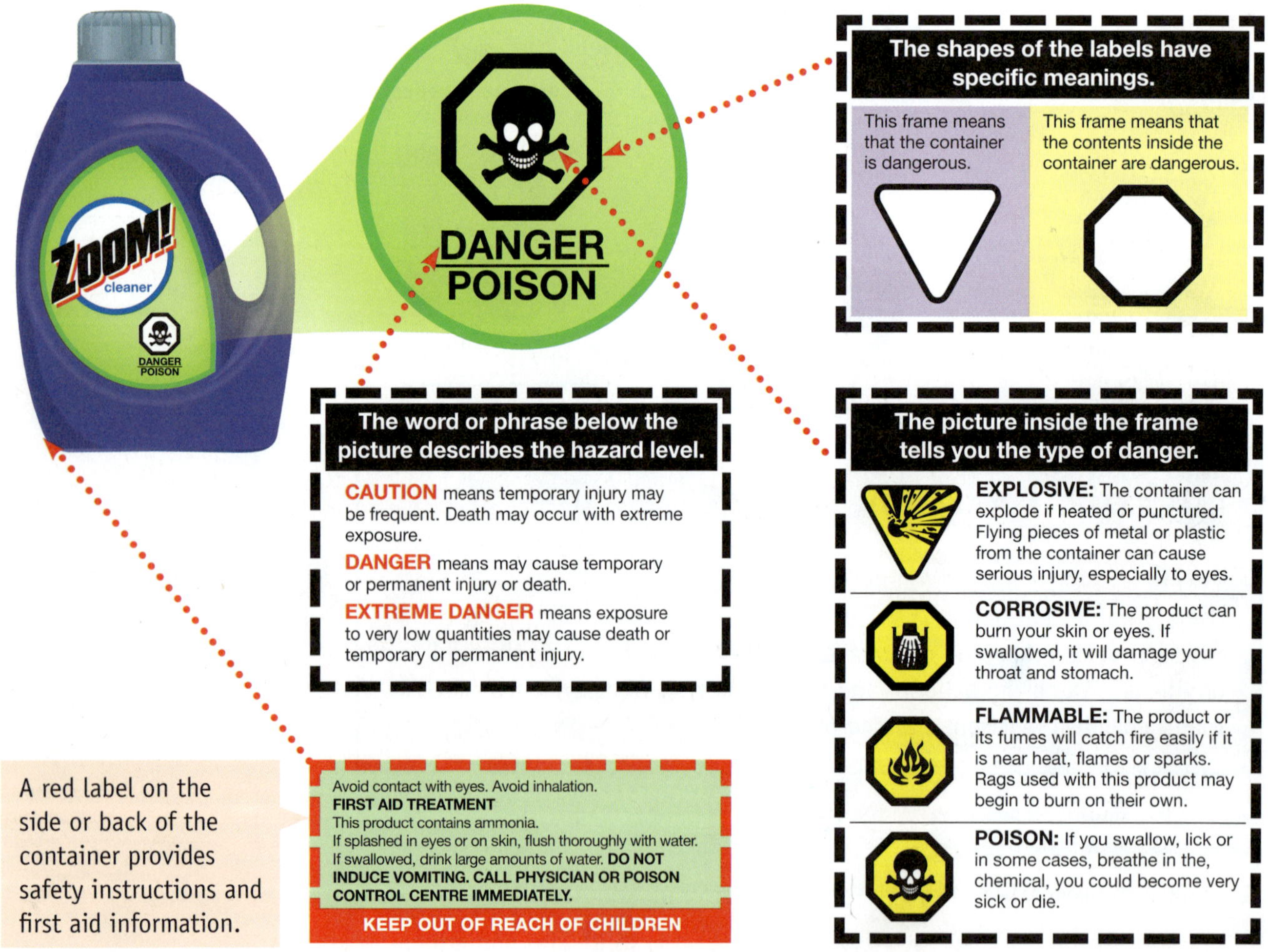

Hazards in the Workplace

Workplaces, such as restaurants, repair shops, industrial plants, and schools, have many hazardous substances. The "Safety in the Science Classroom" section of this book lists the eight WHMIS symbols on page xv. WHMIS stands for **W**orkplace **H**azardous **M**aterials **I**nformation **S**ystem. WHMIS provides detailed information about how to store, handle, and dispose of chemical substances that are used in the workplace. It also provides first aid information.

There are two kinds of WHMIS labels: a supplier label and a workplace label. A supplier label, like the one in **Figure 2.4**, is applied by the people who make the chemical product. A workplace label, like the one in **Figure 2.5**, is applied to a container into which a product has been transferred from its original container. A workplace label is also attached to containers of employer-made products. Both kinds of labels must refer to a **M**aterial **S**afety **D**ata **S**heet (MSDS) for the product. An MSDS contains information about the composition and properties of a chemical substance, as well as steps for handling and storing it safely.

Go to **scienceontario** to find out more

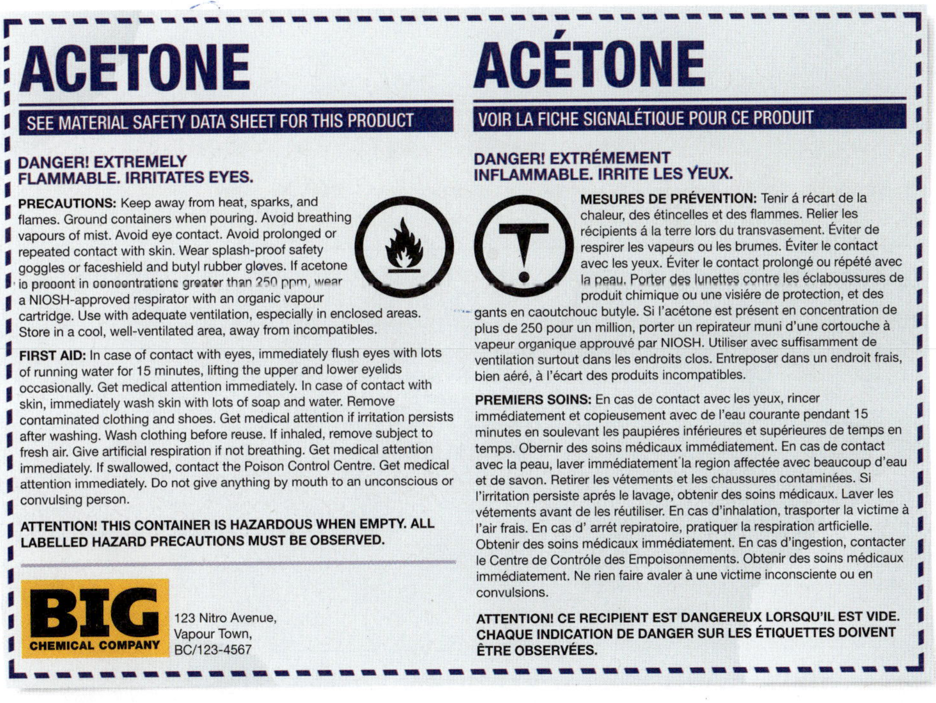

▲ **Figure 2.4** An example of a supplier WHMIS label

▲ **Figure 2.5** An example of a workplace WHMIS label

LEARNING CHECK

1. Study **Figure 2.4**, and then decide what preventative measures you should take when working with acetone.
2. Use a Venn diagram to compare the function of the HHPS system and WHMIS in terms of their intended users.

ACTIVITY LINK

Activity 2.2, on page 116

Literacy Focus

Activity 2-2

BECOMING FAMILIAR WITH AN MSDS

Products that have an MSDS range from potent firefighting substances to hair-care products. By law, certain information must appear on an MSDS, but there is no standard format. In this activity, you will examine the MSDS for a variety of products to determine the types of information that must appear on an MSDS.

What You Need

- MSDS for at least three products (from the Internet or supplied by your teacher)

What To Do

1. Work in groups of three. Each group member is responsible for examining the MSDS for one product.
2. In Canada, there are nine categories of information that must appear on an MSDS. Refer to the MSDS for your product. To the best of your ability, record what you think are the nine categories.
3. When you are done, share your nine categories with your group members. Work together to agree on a final set of nine categories for your group.
4. Compare your group's categories with those of other groups. If possible, work together to agree on a final set of nine categories for the class.
5. Your teacher will tell you the nine categories that are required by law. Compare your group or class categories with the official ones.

ABC GASES
Division of The ABC Group, Inc.

MATERIAL SAFETY DATA SHEET

CHLORINE

1. CHEMICAL PRODUCT AND COMPANY IDENTIFICATION

ABC Gases Division of The ABC Group, Inc.
313 Oxygen Road North Bay, Ontario

TELEPHONE NUMBER: (705) 555-5555
24-HOUR EMERGENCY TELEPHONE NUMBER: (408) 444-4444
Emergency Response Plan NO: 20101

PRODUCT NAME: CHLORINE
CHEMICAL NAME: Chlorine
COMMON NAMES/SYNONYMS: Bertholite, Molecular Chlorine
TDG (Canada) CLASSIFICATION: A, DIA, D2A, D2B, E, C
PREPARED BY: ABC GASES 97050 555-5555
PREPARATION DATE: 3/1/00
REVIEW DATES: 3/7/01

2. COMPOSITION, INFORMATION ON INGREDIENTS

INGREDIENT	% VOLUME	PEL-OSHA[1]	TLV-ACGIH[2]	LD_{50} or LC_{50}Route/Species
Chlorine FORMULA: CL_2 CAS: 7782-50-5 RTECS #: FO2100000	100.0	1 ppm Ceiling	0.5 ppm TWA 1 ppm STEL	LC_{50} 293 ppm/1H (rat)

[1]As stated in 24 CFR 1910, Subpart Z (revised July 1, 1993)
[2]As stated in the ACGIH 1994-95 Threshold Limit Values for Chemical Substances and Physical Agents

3. HAZARDS IDENTIFICATION

EMERGENCY OVERVIEW
Corrosive and irritating to the eyes, skin and mucous membranes. Inhalation may result in chemical pneumonitis and pulmonary edema. Nonflammable oxidizer, may explode or accelerate combustion if contacting reducing agents.

Topic 2.1 Review

Key Concept Summary

- Chemical reactions support our lives and assist us at home and at work.
- Chemical compounds require safe handling to minimize their hazards.

Review the Key Concepts

1. **K/U** Answer the question that is the title of this topic. Copy and complete the graphic organizer below in your notebook. Fill in four examples from the topic using key terms as well as your own words.

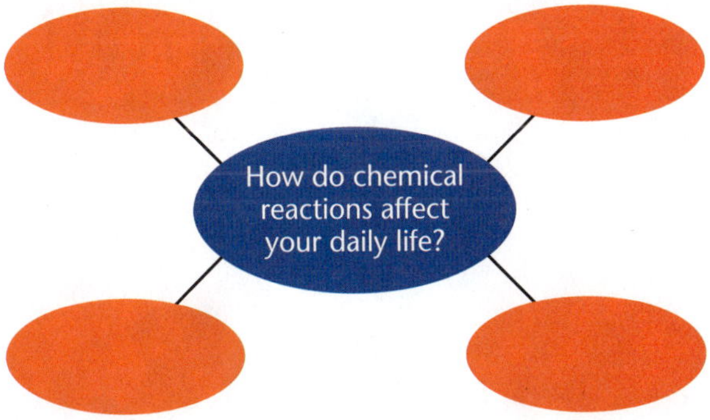

2. **K/U** Acetic acid (vinegar) and sodium hydrogen carbonate (baking soda) react in a chemical reaction to form carbon dioxide gas, water, and a solid substance called sodium acetate.
   a) Explain why this is an example of a chemical reaction and not a physical change.
   b) Identify the reactants in this chemical reaction.
   c) Identify the products in this chemical reaction.

3. **A** Name three substances or products in each of the following workplaces that you think have, or should have, a WHMIS label or hazard warnings on their labels.
   a) a hair salon
   b) an automotive repair shop
   c) a construction site
   d) a school

4. **A** Explain why it would be important for workers in the following workplaces to understand WHMIS.
   a) a restaurant
   b) a hair salon
   c) a construction site
   d) an automotive repair shop

5. **C** **a)** What do the letters MSDS represent?
   b) Name three places where you would expect to find files containing MSDS forms.

6. **C** Examine the product label below.

   a) Name a place in which you would expect to see a product with this label.
   b) Identify the three types of information on this label.
   c) Does this label give you all the information you need to handle the product safely? Explain your answer.

Topic 2.2

How can we understand, describe, and name chemical compounds?

Key Concepts

- Chemical compounds are formed from elements in the periodic table.
- Chemical compounds are represented using chemical names and chemical formulas.
- Reactive elements can become more stable when they form compounds.
- Chemical compounds are described as either ionic or molecular.
- Ionic compounds are named with the metal ion first and then the non-metal ion ending in "ide."
- Molecular compounds are named using numerical prefixes.

Key Skills

- Inquiry
- Literacy
- Research

Key Terms

chemical formula
ion

We use chemical reactions to purify water, to improve our food supply, to treat and prevent diseases, and to produce a wide range of products. Understanding chemical reactions helps you reduce the risks of using them. Part of understanding chemical reactions is knowing how to describe them. Just as you are known by a given name and perhaps a more familiar nickname, chemical compounds have an official name and a common name.

For example, many people add bleach to their laundry. Bleach is used to make clothes look whiter and brighter, as well as to disinfect them. However, there are different types of bleach, and each type uses a different chemical compound.

Starting Point Activity

The official chemical name for a chemical compound is based on the atoms that make up the compound. For instance, the compound sodium chloride is made up of atoms of sodium and atoms of chlorine.

1. Examine items A, B, and C. Pretend that each is a compound.
2. With a partner, create a name for each of them.
3. Use your experience of naming these three compounds to develop a set of rules that you could use to name other compounds.
4. Share and discuss your names and rules with the rest of the class.

A

B

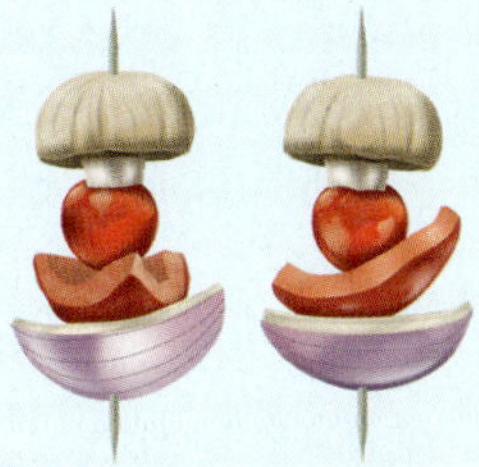

C

For laundry, people use either "chlorine bleach" or "oxygen bleach." But these are common names, too! The official name of the compound used in "chlorine bleach" is sodium hypochlorite. The official name of the compound used in "oxygen bleach" is hydrogen peroxide.

Coming up with and learning how to recognize official names for more than 10^{200} (that's a 1 with 200 zeroes after it) compounds may seem like an impossible task. But there are rules that make this task simpler than you might think.

Chemical compounds are formed from elements in the periodic table.

▼ **Figure 2.6** This is a simple outline of the periodic table. The periodic table records information about the atomic structure and properties of the elements. (Also see the more complete periodic table on page 450.)

The first step to understand how scientists describe compounds is to understand how compounds are formed. All compounds are formed from two or more elements. **Figure 2.6** shows a simple outline of the period table.

The periodic table organizes all the elements in rows and columns. Each element has its own place in the periodic table, based on its properties and its atomic structure. Atomic structure refers to the numbers of electrons, protons, and neutrons that an atom of an element has.

Period 1	H																	He
Period 2	Li	Be											B	C	N	O	F	Ne
Period 3	Na	Mg											Al	Si	P	S	Cl	Ar
Period 4	K	Ca	Sc	Ti	V	Cr	Mn	Fe	Co	Ni	Cu	Zn	Ga	Ge	As	Se	Br	Kr
Period 5	Rb	Sr	Y	Zr	Nb	Mo	Tc	Ru	Rh	Pd	Ag	Cd	In	Sn	Sb	Te	I	Xe
Period 6	Cs	Ba	La	Hf	Ta	W	Re	Os	Ir	Pt	Au	Hg	Tl	Pb	Bi	Po	At	Rn
Group	1	2	3	4	5	6	7	8	9	10	11	12	13	14	15	16	17	18

Periods
Each row in the periodic table is called a *period*. The period number represents the number of electron shells in the atoms of an element.

Families
Each column in the periodic table is called a group or family. All the elements in a group have the same number of electrons in their outer electron shell. They also have similar chemical and physical properties.

Metals
The elements left of the staircase (blue) are metals. All metals except mercury are malleable, shiny, conduct heat and electric current, and are solids at room temperature.

Group 1 Metals
The Group 1 metals are also called alkali metals. They have only one electron in their outer electron shell. This makes them very reactive. In fact, the alkali metals in Group 1 are the most reactive metals. Their reactivity increases as you go down the group. The most reactive Group 1 metal is cesium (Cs).

Non-metals
The elements on the right (yellow) are non-metals. Non-metals are not malleable, do not conduct heat or electric current, and can be solids, liquids, or gases at room temperature.

Group 17 Non-metals
The Group 17 non-metals are also called halogens. Their outermost electron shell is one electron short of being full. This makes the halogens very reactive. In fact, the halogens are the most reactive non-metals. Their reactivity decreases as you go down the group. The most reactive Group 17 non-metal is fluorine (F).

Group 18
The Group 18 elements are all gases. They have a full outer electron shell (eight electrons), which makes them unreactive. They are called the "noble gases" or "inert gases" because they do not react with other elements.

Period 1
There are only two elements in Period 1. Only two electrons will fit in their single electron shell. Helium is a noble gas because its one and only electron shell is full.

Hydrogen
Hydrogen is unique because it has only one electron. It can behave like the Group 1 metals, since it has only one electron in its outer shell. It can also behave like the Group 17 non-metals, since it needs only one electron to complete its outer shell. Some periodic tables put hydrogen in both groups.

Figure 2.7 focuses on the first 18 elements in the periodic table. Look closely at the number of electrons in the outermost electron shell of each element shown. The closer to a full electron shell that an atom has, the more reactive it is. The word *reactive* refers to how likely it is that an atom will take part in a chemical reaction and form a compound. If atoms are more reactive, they are more likely to take part in a chemical reaction. If atoms are less reactive, they are less likely to take part in a chemical reaction. The atoms of the elements in the last column, Group 18, are not reactive at all. That's because the elements in Group 18 have a full outer electron shell.

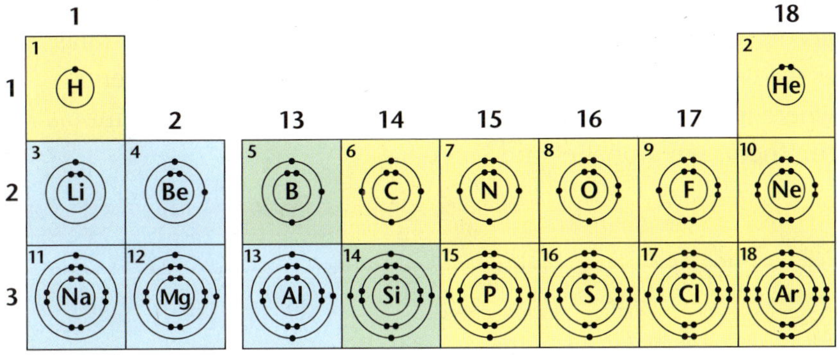

◀ **Figure 2.7** Each cell in the periodic table holds one element. The first 18 elements in the periodic table are shown here, along with their chemical symbol and the electrons in their electron shells.

Inquiry Focus

Activity 2.3

ELECTRONS AND PROTONS OF ELEMENTS

1. Look at this cell from the periodic table, which shows the element fluorine. Four parts are labelled A, B, C, and D. In your notebook, identify what each of the labels is.

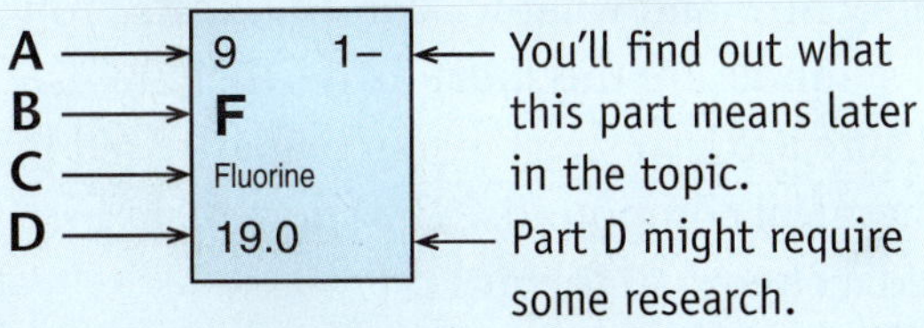

2. Draw the following cells from the periodic table: hydrogen, sodium, magnesium, oxygen, chlorine, and neon. Include labels for the four parts as in question 1.
3. State the number of protons in the nucleus of each of the elements in question 2.

LEARNING CHECK

1. Draw a simple outline of the periodic table. Use shading to identify where the metals and the non-metals are.
2. Name the group of elements that is not reactive. What feature makes the elements in this group not reactive?
3. Name the element in each pair that is more reactive, and explain how you know.
   a) K and Na **b)** F and Cl **c)** Na and Mg **d)** S and Cl
4. Using **Figure 2.7** as a guide, sketch the cells for the elements potassium and calcium. Your sketch must show the chemical symbol and the electron shells with their electrons.

Chemical compounds are represented using chemical names and chemical formulas.

In 1919, a group of chemistry organizations from around the world came together to form the International Union of Pure and Applied Chemistry (IUPAC). The chemists in IUPAC agreed on a set of chemical symbols that are used in the periodic table and in chemical formulas all over the world. As you can see in **Figure 2.8**, chemistry students everywhere in the world learn the same symbols rather than symbols based on their own alphabet and language.

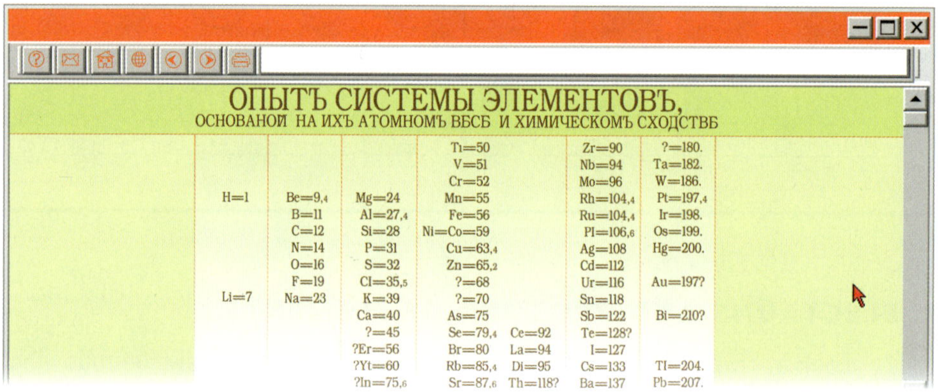

ОПЫТЪ СИСТЕМЫ ЭЛЕМЕНТОВЪ,
ОСНОВАНОЙ НА ИХЪ АТОМНОМЪ ВѢСѢ И ХИМИЧЕСКОМЪ СХОДСТВѢ

			Ti=50		Zr=90	?=180.
			V=51		Nb=94	Ta=182.
			Cr=52		Mo=96	W=186.
H=1	Be=9,4	Mg=24	Mn=55		Rh=104,4	Pt=197,4
	B=11	Al=27,4	Fe=56		Ru=104,4	Ir=198.
	C=12	Si=28	Ni=Co=59		Pl=106,6	Os=199.
	N=14	P=31	Cu=63,4		Ag=108	Hg=200.
	O=16	S=32	Zn=65,2		Cd=112	
	F=19	Cl=35,5	?=68		Ur=116	Au=197?
Li=7	Na=23	K=39	?=70		Sn=118	
		Ca=40	As=75		Sb=122	Bi=210?
		?=45	Se=79,4	Ce=92	Te=128?	
		?Er=56	Br=80	La=94	I=127	
		?Yt=60	Rb=85,4	Di=95	Cs=133	Tl=204.
		?In=75,6	Sr=87,6	Th=118?	Ba=137	Pb=207.

▸ **Figure 2.8** Chemical symbols are an international language used by all chemists and students of chemistry, everywhere in the world.

chemical formula: a group of letters and subscript numbers that represent the make-up of a chemical compound

Chemical Formulas

We use short forms to simplify how and what we communicate. You already know that chemical symbols are the short forms that are used to represent the elements. There are also short forms that are used to represent the make-up of chemical compounds. The short form for a chemical compound is called a **chemical formula.**

Chemical formulas are made up of letters and subscript numbers.

- The *letters* are the chemical symbols. They tell you which elements are in the compound.
- The *subscript numbers* tell you how many atoms of these elements are in the compound.

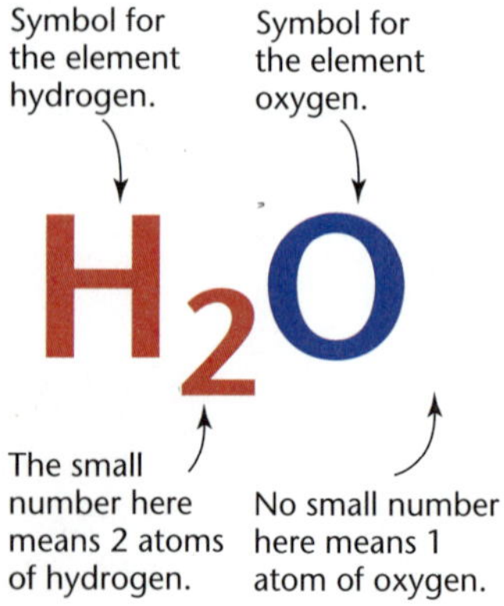

▴ **Figure 2.9** The chemical formula for the compound water, H_2O, tells you that there are two atoms of hydrogen (H) for every one atom of oxygen (O).

Using a periodic table, you can determine which elements and how many atoms of each of these elements make up a compound. For example, the chemical formula for water is H_2O. As you can see in **Figure 2.9**, the chemical formula for water tells you that the compound is made up of the elements hydrogen (symbol H) and oxygen (symbol O). The subscript$_2$ beside the symbol H tells you that there are two hydrogen atoms for every one oxygen atom in the compound. Why doesn't the oxygen (symbol O) have a subscript$_1$ beside it? When there is only one atom of an element in a compound, you don't use a subscript$_1$ beside the symbol. The $_1$ is understood.

Literacy Focus

Activity 2.4

INTERPRETING CHEMICAL FORMULAS

1. Copy this table into your notebook, or use the table that your teacher gives you.
2. Follow the example in the first row to record the number of atoms of each element in the compounds.

The Chemical Formulas of Common Compounds

Name of Compound	Examples of Common Uses	Chemical Formula	Number of Atoms of Each Element
calcium carbonate	chalk for writing on chalkboard	$CaCO_3$	• 1 atom calcium (Ca) • 1 atom carbon (C) • 3 atoms oxygen (O)
sodium phosphate	heavy-duty cleaner	Na_3PO_4	
magnesium chloride	de-icer for roads	$MgCl_2$	
monosodium glutamate (MSG)	flavour-enhancer for foods	$NaC_5H_8NO_4$	
hydrogen peroxide	bleach and disinfectant	H_2O_2	
glucose	sweetener (glucose is a simple sugar)	$C_6H_{12}O_6$	
carbon dioxide	addition of fizz to pop	CO_2	
freon-12	refrigerator coolant (now banned because it harms the ozone layer)	CCl_2F_2	
HFC-32 (difluoromethane)	refrigerator coolant (now used because it does not harm the ozone layer)	CH_2F_2	

LEARNING CHECK

1. a) What does the subscript in a chemical formula indicate?
   b) What does having no subscript mean?
2. For the compound ammonia, NH_3, how many nitrogen atoms are there, and how many hydrogen atoms are there in each molecule?
3. Write the chemical formula for a compound that is made of one atom of carbon (C) and four atoms of hydrogen (H).
4. Write the chemical formula for a compound that has two atoms of nitrogen and four atoms of oxygen.

Reactive elements can become more stable when they form compounds.

You may have noticed patterns in chemical formulas. For example, some elements tend to form compounds with each other. Some elements appear in compounds more often than other elements. Some elements—the noble gases in Group 18—never appear in compounds. These patterns exist because of the atomic structure of the elements.

When elements form compounds, they become more stable. As you have learned, the noble gases rarely form compounds because they already have a stable electron-shell structure—their outer electron shell is full. All the other elements achieve this full, stable electron-shell structure in one of three ways:

1. Metals lose electrons to form positive ions.
2. Non-metals gain electrons to form negative ions.
3. Non-metals share electrons.

ion: an atom or a group of atoms that has an electrical charge, either positive or negative

The term **ion** refers to an atom that has a positive electrical charge or a negative electrical charge. **Table 2.1** summarizes the three ways that elements can achieve a stable electron-shell structure.

Inquiry Focus

Activity 2.5

BUILDING IONS

In this activity, you will use common materials to make models of atoms and ions.

What You Need

- variety of materials to represent nuclei and electrons

What To Do

1. Choose one element from Group 1, 2, 16, or 17.
2. Build a model of an atom of the element you chose. Use **Figure 2.17** on page 121 and the periodic table on page 450 for reference.
3. Sketch and name the atom.
4. Add or remove electrons as necessary to your atom to form an ion with a stable electron-shell structure.
5. Sketch and name the ion.

What Did You Find Out?

1. Compare your model of an ion with your classmates' models.
   (a) What do all the models have in common?
   (b) How are the models different? Explain.
2. How does your model of an ion compare with the model of an atom you built in step 2?

Table 2.1 The Three Ways That Elements Become Stable

1. Metals lose electrons to form positive ions.

> The charge on the Group 1 metal ions is +1 because they have lost one electron. The Group 2 metal ions have a charge of +2, and the Group 3 metal ions have a charge of +3.

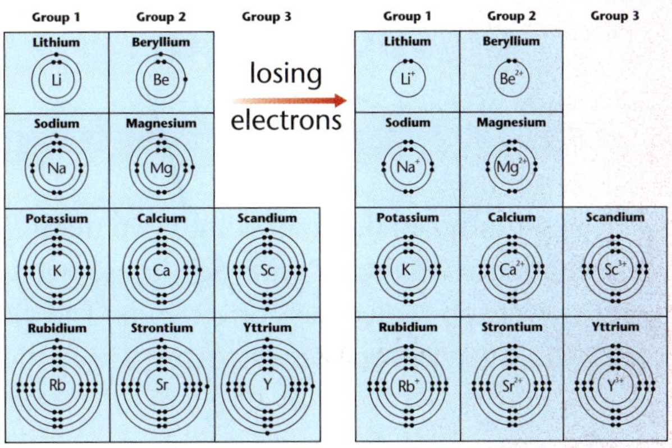

Metal atoms can lose electrons to become stable. Because they have lost electrons, which have a negative charge, the charge on metal ions is positive. All metal ions have a stable electron-shell structure.

2. Non-metals gain electrons to form negative ions.

> The charge on the Group 17 non-metal ions is −1 because they have gained one electron. The Group 16 non-metal ions have a charge of −2, and the Group 15 non-metal ions have a charge of −3.

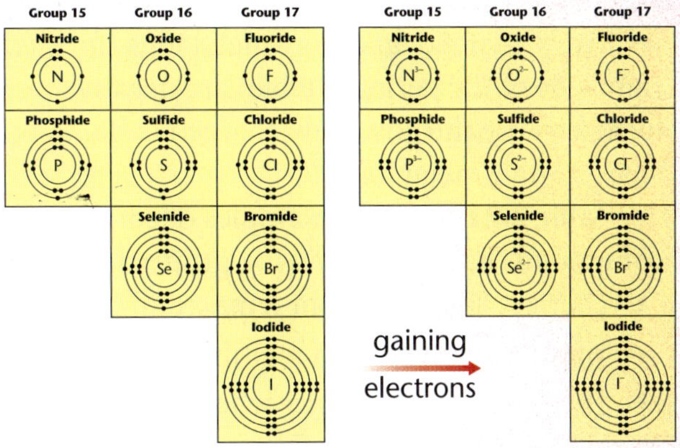

Non-metal atoms can gain electrons to become stable. Because they have gained electrons, which have a negative charge, the charge on metal ions is negative. Notice that the name of a negative ion ends in "ide." All non-metal ions have a stable electron-shell structure.

3. Non-metals share electrons.

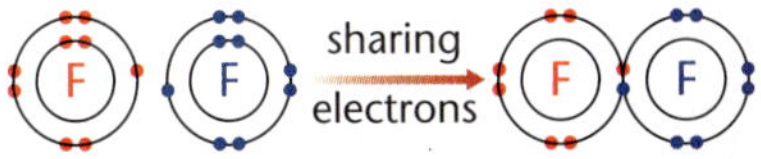

Non-metal atoms can also share electrons with other non-metal atoms to become stable. Their electron shells overlap. Since electrons have not been lost or gained, there is no charge on the atoms when electrons are shared.

LEARNING CHECK

1. Helium, like other noble gases, has a full, and therefore stable, outermost electron shell structure. How many electrons are in helium's outermost shell? What about the other noble gas elements? Why is there a difference?
2. How can metal elements achieve a stable electron-shell structure like those of the noble gases?
3. How can non-metal elements achieve a stable electron-shell structure like that of the noble gases?

Chemical compounds are described as either ionic or molecular.

Compounds can be divided into two main types, based on the differences in their properties. These two types are called ionic compounds and molecular compounds. The differences in their properties are due to the types of elements from which they are made.

Ionic Compounds

Metal ions (formed from metals on the left side of the periodic table) are positively charged, and non-metal ions (formed from non-metals on the right side of the periodic table) are negatively charged. Ionic compounds form because the positively charged metal ions attract the negatively charged non-metal ions.

Table 2.2 lists some examples of common ionic compounds. Ionic compounds have the following properties:

- They are solids at room temperature.
- They have a very high melting point.
- They conduct electricity when they are melted or dissolved in water.

Table 2.2 Examples of Ionic Compounds and Their Uses

Chemical Formula	Chemical Name (common name, if there is one)	Common Use
$NaCl$	sodium chloride (table salt)	seasoning for food
$CaCl_2$	calcium chloride (road salt)	de-icer for roads in the winter
CaO	calcium oxide (lime)	plaster
MgO	magnesium oxide (magnesia)	laxative
$CuBr_2$	copper(II) bromide	lasers and photographic processing

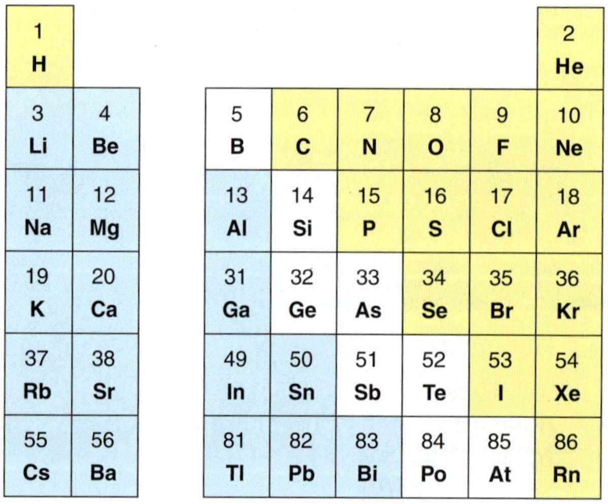

Molecular Compounds

Non-metal atoms can share electrons with other non-metal atoms including hydrogen. This is how molecular compounds are formed.

Table 2.3 lists some examples of common molecular compounds. Molecular compounds have the following properties:

- They may be solids, liquids, or gases at room temperature.
- They have lower melting points than ionic compounds.
- They do not conduct electric current when they are melted or dissolved in water, except in the case of certain acids.

Go to **scienceontario** to find out more

Table 2.3 Examples of Molecular Compounds and Their Uses

Chemical Formula	Chemical Name (common name, if there is one)	Common Use
CH_4	methane	heating
CO	carbon monoxide	production of acetic acid
$C_{12}H_{22}O_{11}$	sucrose (table sugar)	sugar
CCl_4	carbon tetrachloride	dry cleaning fluid
CH_3OH	methanol	windshield washer fluid

Literacy Focus

Activity 2.6

IONIC OR MOLECULAR?

1. Make a table like the one below to record your answers.
2. Identify the types of atoms in each compound. Then state whether each compound is ionic or molecular. Use the periodic table to help you. (You do not have to know the names of these compounds or their properties to do this.)

Chemical Formula	Types (metal or non-metal)	Ionic or molecular	Chemical Formula	Types (metal or non-metal)	Ionic or molecular
$MgBr_2$			SiF_4		
PH_3			Ag_3P		
P_4O_{10}			O_2F_2		
NaI			C_8H_{18}		

LEARNING CHECK

1. What type of elements combine to form ionic compounds?
2. What type of elements combine to form molecular compounds?

Ionic compounds are named with the metal ion first, followed by the non-metal ion ending in "ide."

Sometimes you are given the chemical formula of an ionic compound, and you are asked to name it. Sometimes you are given the name of an ionic compound, and you are asked to write its chemical formula. You will learn both of these skills here.

Naming a Simple Ionic Compound from Its Chemical Formula

An ionic compound has a two-part name. The first part of the name is the name of the metal ion. The metal ion has a positive charge. The second part of the name is the name of the non-metal ion, but it's changed so that it ends with "ide." The non-metal ion has a negative charge. Use **Figure 2.10** to learn how to name an ionic compound if you are given its chemical formula.

STEP 1	Look at the chemical formula: $CaCl_2$. Use the periodic table to name the metal ion.	Ca = calcium
STEP 2	Use the periodic table to name the non-metal ion.	Cl = chlorine
STEP 3	Change the ending of the non-metal ion to "ide."	chlor<u>ine</u> → chlor<u>ide</u>
STEP 4	Write the first part of the name from step 1 with the second part of the name from step 3.	calcium chloride

▲ **Figure 2.10** Follow these four steps to name an ionic compound from its chemical formula. Calcium chloride, $CaCl_2$, is used as an example.

Writing the Chemical Formula of a Simple Ionic Compound from Its Name

Figure 2.11 shows how to write the chemical formula of an ionic compound if you are given its name. You will need a periodic table with the ion charges for the elements in the upper right-hand corner of each cell. Turn to page 450, and make sure that you can find the ion charges for the elements before you continue. **Table 2.4** shows the names of some of the common non-metal ions.

Table 2.4 Common Non-metal Ions

Element Name	Element Symbol	Ion Symbol	Ion Name
nitrogen	N	N^{3-}	nitride
oxygen	O	O^{2-}	oxide
fluorine	F	F^{-}	fluoride
phosphorus	P	P^{3-}	phosphide
sulfur	S	S^{2-}	sulfide
chlorine	Cl	Cl^{-}	chloride
selenium	Se	Se^{2-}	selenide
bromine	Br	Br^{-}	bromide
iodine	I	I^{-}	iodide

STEP 1	Look at the name of the compound: aluminum oxide. Use the periodic table to find the symbols for the ions.	aluminum = Al oxide = oxygen = O
STEP 2	Write the ion charges above the symbols for the ions.	Al^{3+} O^{2-}
STEP 3	Drop the + and – signs, and criss-cross the ion charges to get the subscripts: Al_2 and O_3. If the charges are the same, they cancel. Use no subscripts.	Al^{3+}_{2} O^{2-}_{3}
STEP 4	Write the chemical formula.	Al_2O_3

◂ **Figure 2.11** Follow these four steps to write the chemical formula of a compound from its name. Aluminum oxide, Al_2O_3, is used as an example.

LEARNING CHECK

1. Explain how ionic compounds are named.
2. Name these ionic compounds.
   a) NaBr **b)** LiF **c)** $MgBr_2$ **d)** AlI_3 **e)** K_2S
3. How do you know how many of each type of element there are in an ionic compound?
4. Write the chemical formula for these ionic compounds.
   a) cesium fluoride
   b) strontium chloride
   c) barium oxide
   (Hint: The charges are the same)
   d) potassium phosphide
   e) aluminum nitride

ACTIVITY LINK

Activity 2.8, on page 136

Molecular compounds are named using numerical prefixes.

The rules for naming molecular compounds are different from the rules for naming ionic compounds. Why? There is only one way that two specific ions can react to form an ionic compound. But there are many ways that atoms of two non-metal elements can react to form a molecular compound. For example, **Table 2.5** shows six different molecular compounds that contain only nitrogen and oxygen.

Table 2.5 Six Molecular Compounds That Contain Nitrogen and Oxygen

Chemical Formula	IUPAC Name	What It Is
NO	nitrogen monoxide	pollutant from car exhaust
N_2O	dinitrogen monoxide	used by dentists (laughing gas)
NO_2	nitrogen dioxide	used to make nitric acid
N_2O_3	dinitrogen trioxide	deep blue liquid
N_2O_4	dinitrogen tetroxide	used in rocket fuel
N_2O_5	dinitrogen pentoxide	dissolves in water to form nitric acid

Naming a Molecular Compound from Its Chemical Formula

Molecular compounds have a two-part name. Both parts of the name are taken from the names of non-metals. To decide which non-metal atom to name first, find the one with the lower group number on the periodic table. For example, if the compound contained carbon and oxygen, carbon would be first because it is in Group 14, which has a lower group number than oxygen's group, Group 16. Even if the non-metals are in different periods, the rule is the same. If the compound contained phosphorus and fluorine, for example, phosphorus would be named first because it is in Group 15, which has a lower group number than fluorine's group, Group 17. The fact that phosphorus and fluorine are in different periods on the periodic table does not affect the naming. When you have found the non-metal to name first, use that element's name as the first part of the compound name. The second part of the name is taken from the name of the second non-metal. However, you have to change the ending of the name to "ide."

Because elements can combine in more than one way, a numerical (number-indicating) prefix is used to tell how many of each type of element are in the compound. Look at the examples of numerical prefixes in **Table 2.6**. Then use **Figure 2.12** to see how to name a molecular compound from its formula.

STEP 1	Look at the formula of the molecular compound: CO_2. Use the periodic table to name the first element.	C = carbon
STEP 2	Choose the correct prefix for the number of atoms of the element.	**carbon** There is only one atom of carbon, so the correct prefix is "mono." But "mono" is not included for the first element.
STEP 3	Use the periodic table to name the second element.	O = oxygen
STEP 4	Change the ending of the second element to "ide."	oxygen → oxide
STEP 5	Choose the correct prefix for the number of atoms of the element.	**2 = di → dioxide** There are two atoms of oxygen, so the correct prefix is "di."
STEP 6	Combine the two parts of the name.	carbon dioxide

▲ **Figure 2.12** Follow these steps to write the name of a molecular compound from its chemical formula. Carbon dioxide, CO_2, is used as an example.

Table 2.6 Numerical Prefixes Used for Molecular Compounds

Numerical Prefix	Number It Represents
mono-	1
di-	2
tri-	3
tetra-	4
penta-	5
hexa-	6
hepta-	7
octa-	8

Note: The prefix "mono" is used only for the second element in the name.

Note: When a prefix ending with a vowel ("o" or "a") is used with oxygen, the vowel is dropped. For example, use "monoxide" not "monooxide" and "tetroxide" not "tetraoxide."

It is important to note that these rules for naming do not apply to a large group of molecular compounds called organic compounds. Organic compounds consist of mostly carbon and hydrogen. They might also contain oxygen, sulfur, and a few other elements. Organic compounds have a naming system of their own. If you take more chemistry courses, you will learn about organic compounds.

LEARNING CHECK

1. Explain how molecular compounds are named.
2. Name these molecular compounds:
   a) SO_2 **b)** SO_3 **c)** CCl_4 **d)** PCl_5 **e)** CO

continued on the next page...

... continued from previous page

Writing the Chemical Formula of a Molecular Compound from Its Name

Now that you have learned how to write names for molecular compounds from their formulas, you can probably figure out how to write the formulas from the names. First, you look at the name to find the elements in the compound. Then, if you do not remember the symbols for those elements, you refer to a periodic table, such as the one on page 450, to find the symbols. Next, you look at the prefixes to determine the number of atoms of each element in the compound. If you do not remember the numbers represented by those prefixes, go to **Table 2.6** to find the number. Finally, you write the number of atoms of each element as a subscript on the symbol. **Figure 2.13** summarizes this process and provides an example that shows how to write the chemical formula of a molecular compound from its name.

STEP 1	Look at the name of the molecular compound: dinitrogen tetroxide. Use the periodic table to find the symbols for the elements.	nitrogen = N oxide = oxygen = O
STEP 2	Compare the prefixes in the name to those in **Table 2.6** on page 131 to determine the number of atoms of each element.	di = 2 two nitrogen = 2N tetra = 4 four oxygen = 4O
STEP 3	Write in the subscripts, and write the chemical formula.	N_2O_4

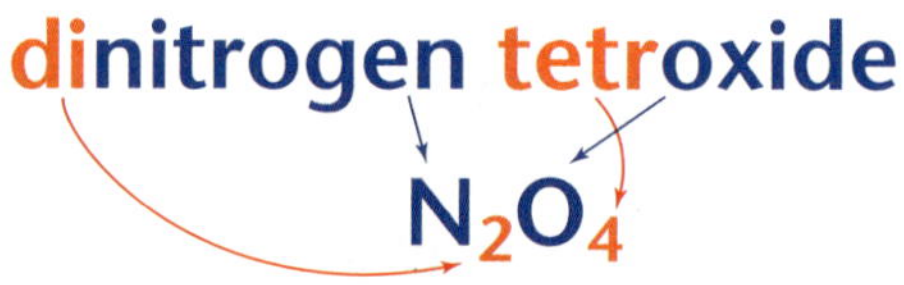

▸ **Figure 2.13** Follow these steps to write the chemical formula of a molecular compound from its name. Dinitrogen tetroxide, N_2O_4, is used as an example.

LEARNING CHECK

1. What feature of the name of a molecular compound tells you the number of atoms of each element in the compound?
2. Write the chemical formula for the following molecular compounds.
   - **a)** sulfur difluoride
   - **b)** nitrogen monoxide
   - **c)** disulfur trioxide
   - **d)** disulfur difluoride
   - **e)** silicon tetrachloride
   - **f)** diphosphorus pentoxide
   - **g)** carbon disulfide
   - **h)** carbon tetraiodide
   - **i)** dinitrogen tetrasulfide

Inquiry focus

Activity 2.7

BUILDING MODELS OF MOLECULAR COMPOUNDS

In this activity, you will build and name a number of molecular compounds.

What You Need

- materials to build molecular compounds

What to Do

1. Make a table in your notebook like the one below. Leave space in the last column to sketch your models.
2. Fill in the first four columns of the table. Refer to the information on pages 130 to 132 to help you.
3. Using the information in the first four columns of your table, build a model for each molecule. Hint: Start with the element in bold type in the table, and add the other elements around it.
4. Sketch your models in the fifth column of the table.

Building and Naming Molecular Compounds

Element 1 and Number	Element 2 and Number	Chemical Formula	Chemical Name	Sketch of Model
1 **C**	2 S			
		CO		
			nitrogen dioxide	
1 **B**	3 Cl			
		N_2O		
			phosphorus trifluoride	

continued on the next page...

... continued from previous page

A flowchart can be used to simplify the process of naming chemical compounds.

Go to **scienceontario** to find out more

The fist step in naming or determining the formula of a compound is deciding whether the compound is an ionic compound or a molecular compound. Use the flowchart in **Figure 2.14** to help you name chemical compounds. Use the flowchart in **Figure 2.15** on the next page to help you write chemical formulas.

Figure 2.14
How to name a chemical compound

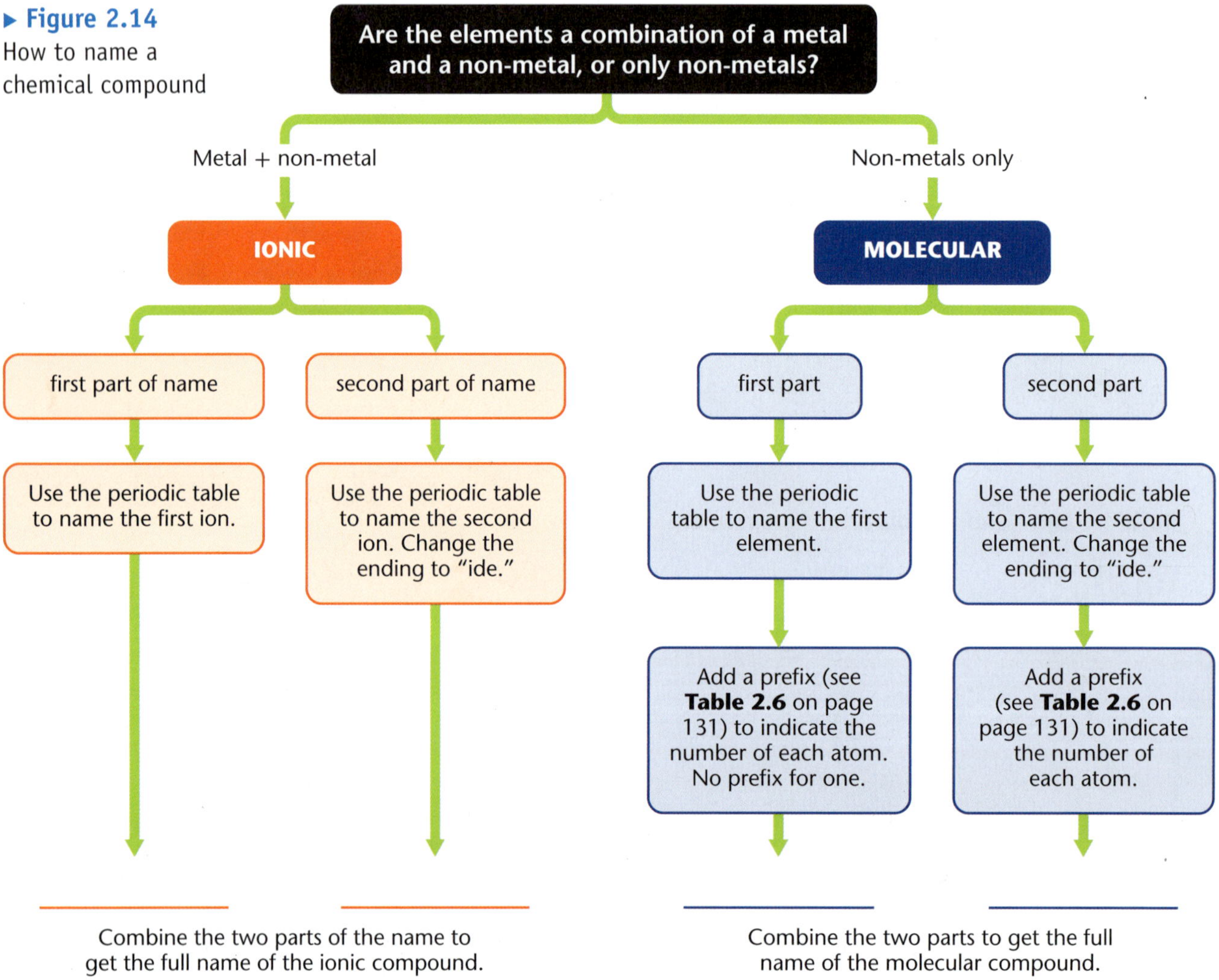

LEARNING CHECK

1. What is the first step in naming a compound from its chemical formula?
2. Identify the following compounds as ionic or molecular and name the compounds.

   a) KCl **b)** As_2O_5 **c)** $MgBr_2$ **d)** PCl_3 **e)** SeF_6 **f)** Mg_3P_2

▶ **Figure 2.15** How to write a chemical formula

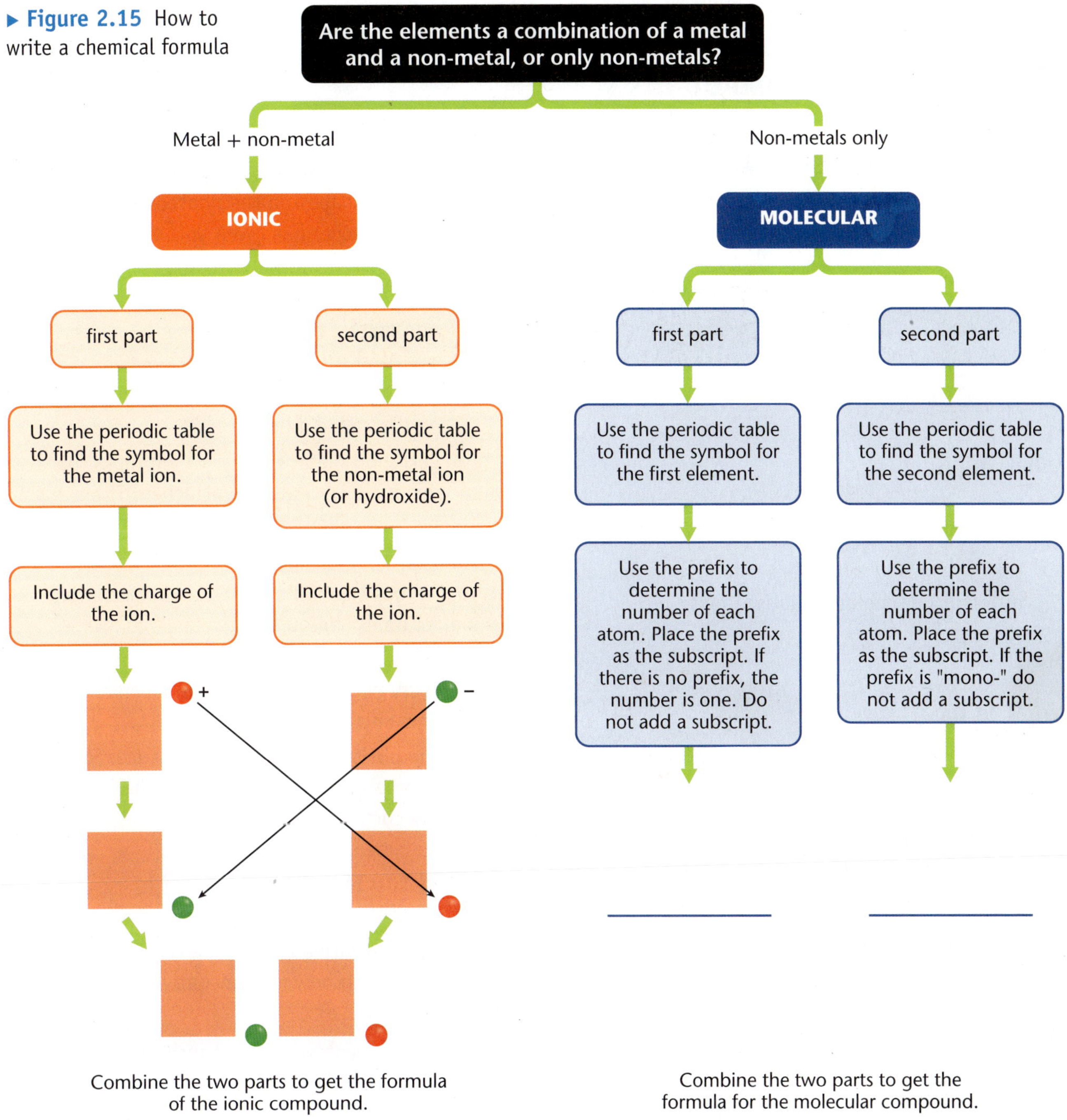

LEARNING CHECK

1. What is the first step in writing the chemical formula from a name?
2. Identify the following compounds as ionic or molecular and write the chemical formula.
   a) calcium oxide
   b) dinitrogen triiodide
   c) sodium phosphide
   d) iodine trichloride
   e) phosphorus pentabromide
   f) aluminum phosphide

Inquiry Focus

Activity 2.8

MODELLING IONIC COMPOUNDS

In this activity, you will use different shapes to represent metal ions and non-metal ions. These shapes can be combined in a way that closely matches the way that real ions combine during a chemical reaction. The patterns that you will discover here will help you write the names and formulas of ionic compounds.

Safety

What You Need

- set of shapes in one colour, representing different metal (positive) ions
- set of shapes in a different colour, representing different non-metal (negative) ions
- scissors

What To Do

1. Make a table like the one below to record your answers.

Building and Naming Ionic Compounds

Metal Ion (Positive)	Non-metal Ion (Negative)	Compound Name	Compound Formula
K^{+}	I^{-}		
Al^{3+}	P^{3-}		
Mg^{2+}	F^{-}		
Na^{+}	O^{2-}		
Ba^{2+}	Cl^{-}		
Ga^{3+}	F^{-}		
Ca^{2+}	N^{3-}		

2. Work with a partner to build the ionic compounds.
3. Cut out the shapes on the photocopied sheets that your teacher has given you. Keep these facts in mind:
   - Each shape represents a single metal or non-metal ion.
   - Each metal (positive) ion looks like a rectangle with a piece cut out. The cut-out part is called a hole.
   - Each non-metal (negative) ion looks like a rectangle with a piece attached. The extra piece is called a peg.
4. For each ionic compound, you will need one kind of positive ion and one kind of negative ion. You must follow these rules:
   - Every hole must be filled with a peg, and every peg must be in a hole. Keep adding ions until this happens.
   - The positive and negative ions must alternate as much as possible throughout the compound.

What Did You Find Out?

1. When the ionic compound model is complete, how many positive charges (holes) do you have, compared with how many negative charges (pegs) you have?
2. An unknown compound that includes the bromide ion (Br^{-}) has the chemical formula XBr_2. Use your models to find the charge on the ion that is represented by X in this chemical formula.

Activity 2-9

KITCHEN CHEMISTRY

Natural foods (such as apples) and processed foods (such as fruit leather) contain chemicals. However, only processed foods are labelled to show their chemical make-up. The ingredients on a label are listed in order of decreasing amount. For example, the label for table salt might read "salt (sodium chloride), calcium silicate, potassium iodide." This means that there is less potassium iodide in the product than any other ingredient. Sodium chloride is the main ingredient.

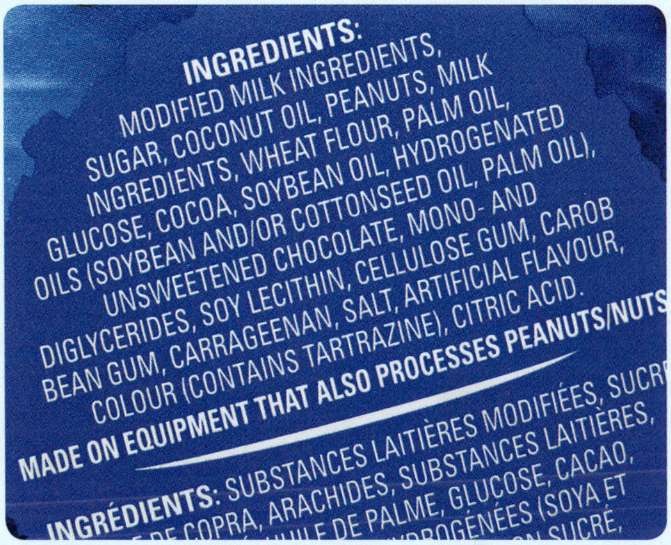

What To Do

1. Select one processed food product in your home, and answer the following questions.
   a) Name the product.
   b) List the ingredients in the same order that they are listed on the label.
2. Make a table like the one below. Select any three of the ingredients for which you can provide the information required by the table. Then complete your table. You may need to use the Internet or other resources to find the chemical formulas.
3. Research the properties of one of the ingredients in your table. Explain why this chemical substance is added to the processed food.

The Ingredients in a Processed Food

	Ingredient 1	Ingredient 2	Ingredient 3
Name			
Formula			
Elements It Contains			
Ionic or Molecular?			

Investigation 2A

Skills

initiating and planning

✓ **performing and recording**

✓ **analyzing and interpreting**

✓ **communicating**

Safety

- Do NOT taste any samples.

What You Need

- 250 mL beaker
- scoop
- stirring rod
- conductivity tester
- distilled water
- Epsom salts
- isopropyl alcohol (rubbing alcohol)
- washing soda
- sugar
- vegetable oil

Ionic or Molecular?

Like detectives searching for clues, chemists classify substances by matching their observations against theories about ionic and molecular compounds. In this activity, you will determine whether some common household substances are ionic or molecular by observing their properties.

What To Do

1. Make a table like the one below to record your data.

Ionic or Molecular?

Substance	State at Room Temperature (Is it a solid, liquid, or gas?)	Solubility in Water (Does it dissolve?)	Conductivity as a Liquid or Dissolved in Water
distilled water		n/a	
Epsom salts			
rubbing alcohol			
washing soda			
sugar			
vegetable oil			

2. Examine each of the five substances. Record whether it is a solid, liquid, or gas at room temperature.
3. Add approximately 100 mL of distilled water to a beaker. Use the conductivity tester, as demonstrated by your teacher, to determine whether the distilled water conducts electricity. Record your data.
4. Use the scoop to add a small amount of Epsom salts to the water. Stir with the stirring rod to try to dissolve the Epsom salts. Record the solubility of the Epsom salts in water. (Do they dissolve?)
5. Use the conductivity tester to test the solution of Epsom salts and water. Record the conductivity of the Epsom salts. (Do they conduct electricity?)
6. Clean your beaker, stirring rod, and conductivity apparatus.
7. Repeat steps 4 to 6 for the remaining substances. If a substance is a liquid at room temperature, test the conductivity of the liquid, not when it is mixed with water. Record your data, and clean up when you are done.

What Did You Find Out?

1. Use the information on pages 126 and 127 to classify the substances as ionic or molecular compounds.

Topic 2.2 Review

Key Concept Summary

- Chemical compounds are formed from elements in the periodic table.
- Chemical compounds are represented using chemical names and chemical formulas.
- Reactive elements can become more stable when they form compounds.
- Chemical compounds are described as either ionic or molecular.
- Ionic compounds are named with the metal ion first, and then the non metal ion ending in "ide."
- Molecular compounds are named using numerical prefixes.

Review the Key Concepts

1. K/U Answer the question that is the title of this topic. Copy and complete the graphic organizer below in your notebook. Fill in four examples from the topic using key terms as well as your own words.

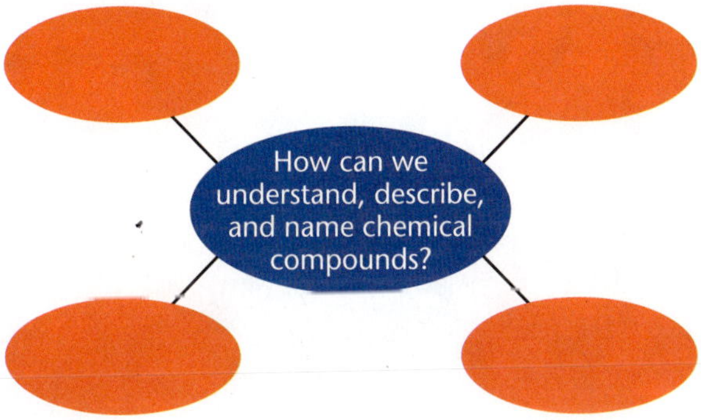

2. K/U **a)** Provide the name and symbol for a metallic element.

b) Which group of non-metals is the most reactive? Why?

c) Which metal is the most reactive? Why?

3. T/I Write the chemical formula for each of the following compounds given the number of each type of element present:

a) 2 atoms nitrogen, 2 atoms hydrogen

b) 1 atom calcium, 1 atom carbon, 3 atoms oxygen

c) 3 atoms calcium, 2 atoms phosphorus

d) 2 atoms sodium, 2 atoms sulfur, 3 atoms oxygen

4. T/I Classify the following compounds as ionic or molecular:

a) $MgCl_2$ **c)** $C_{25}H_{52}$ **e)** Ca_3N_2

b) $AlBr_3$ **d)** SiO_2

5. T/I For each of the following, state either the name or the chemical formula.

a) CsBr **d)** potassium chloride

b) BaO **e)** aluminum bromide

c) Ca_3P_2 **f)** potassium oxide

6. For each of the following, state either the name or the chemical formula.

a) P_2O_5 **d)** dinitrogen tetrafluoride

b) CF_4 **e)** sulfur hexachloride

c) PH_3 **g)** sulfur dibromide

7. T/I Which of the following ionic compounds is represented in the diagram? Explain your answer.

a) NaCl **b)** Na_2O **c)** Na_3P

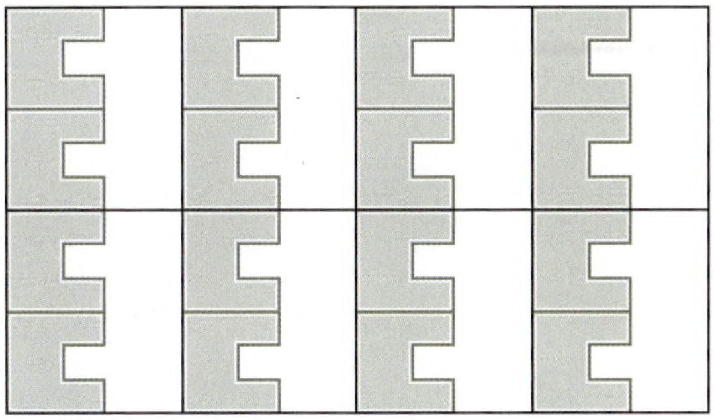

8. C Use the example calcium nitride to explain the steps in determining the chemical formula of a compound from its name.

Topic 2.3

What happens during a chemical reaction, and how can it be described?

Key Concepts

- During a chemical reaction, chemical compounds are changed into different compounds with different properties.
- The four types of chemical reactions can be described using word equations.
- Chemical reactions can be described using chemical equations.
- Atoms and mass are conserved during a chemical reaction.

Key Skills

- Inquiry

Key Terms

synthesis reaction
decomposition reaction
single displacement
double displacement
word equation
chemical equation
balanced chemical equation
law of conservation of mass

A	B	C	D	K
Ordinary Combustibles	**Flammable Liquids**	**Electrical Equipment**	**Combustible Metals**	**Cooking Oils**
For ordinary combustibles such as wood or paper	For flammable liquids such as oil, grease, or gasoline	For electrical fires	For flammable metals such as lithium, magnesium, sodium, and potassium	For kitchen fires such as cooking oil or fats catching fire in a frying pan

"FIRE! Get the fire extinguisher!"
"What kind of fire extinguisher?"
"Huh?"
"What kind of fire is it?"
"Huh?"
Did you know that there are five classes of fire extinguishers for different types of fires? The labels above can be found on the five different classes of fire extinguishers.

Starting Point Activity

Many types of materials are used in fire extinguishers. A few of these are described below. For each type of material, figure out what type (or types) of fire extinguisher might use this material. Discuss your ideas with the class. Then do research to find out if your conclusions were correct.

1. Water, under pressure, is used in some fire extinguishers. When it hits the burning substance, it cools the substance to below the temperature at which a fire can burn.
2. Carbon dioxide gas, under pressure, is used in some fire extinguishers. When it escapes from the fire extinguisher, it is very cold. It pushes the air (oxygen) away from the burning materials.
3. Non-flammable, dry materials are used in some fire extinguishers. When they reach the burning substance, they form a layer of dry material over the substance and prevent oxygen from reaching it. They also remove some heat.

The heat and light from a fire are forms of energy that are released during chemical reactions. A fire needs three things in order to continue burning—fuel, oxygen, and heat. If you remove any one of the three, the fire will go out.

Water can remove heat but it can cause other problems. For example, oil and grease will float on water and continue to burn. Water also can conduct electrical current. If there are any live wires in the fire, and you pour water on them, you could get a very serious shock. Also, water reacts violently with some metals such as sodium and potassium.

During a chemical reaction, chemical compounds are changed into different compounds with different properties.

The products of a chemical reaction are always new substances with properties that are different from those of the reactants. But it is not always easy to tell if new substances have formed. **Table 2.7** lists the evidence that can help you decide if a chemical reaction has occurred. When a chemical reaction has occurred, one or more of these pieces of evidence may be observed.

Table 2.7 Evidence of Chemical Reactions

Evidence	Description	Example
There is a change in energy.	All chemical reactions involve a change in energy, although it is not always possible to detect it. A change in energy may be • a temperature change (increase or decrease) • light produced • electrical energy produced	
There is a change in colour.	In some chemical reactions, the colour of the products is different from the colour of the reactants.	
A gas is formed.	Gases are formed in some chemical reactions. You would observe • bubbles in a liquid, or • odour (smell)	 
A solid substance (a precipitate) is formed.	In some reactions, when two clear solutions are mixed, the product is a solid that appears in the beaker. The solid that appears is called a precipitate.	

Inquiry Focus

Activity 2.10

EVIDENCE OF CHEMICAL REACTIONS

Read the steps for the three reactions below. Design a table to record the properties of the reactants, the properties of the products, and any evidence that a chemical reaction has occurred.

Safety

- Handle all the liquids very carefully.
- Clean up any spills immediately.
- Tie back loose hair.

What You Need

- candle
- candle holder
- water
- ice cubes
- 250 mL beaker
- matches
- tongs
- dilute hydrochloric acid
- zinc metal
- 2 test tubes
- test-tube rack
- vinegar
- bromothymol blue indicator
- baking soda
- scoop

What To Do

Observe as your teacher performs Reactions 1 and 2. A volunteer group can perform Reaction 3.

1. **Reaction 1: Candle Burning**
   - **a)** Observe the properties of the candle wax, including its colour, state, and texture. Record these properties in your table.
   - **b)** Watch as your teacher adds water and ice to the beaker and uses tongs to hold the bottom of the beaker over the lit candle.
   - **c)** Observe and record the properties of the substances that form at the bottom of the *outside* of the beaker.
   - **d)** Record any evidence that a chemical reaction has occurred.
2. **Reaction 2: Hydrochloric Acid and Zinc**
   - **a)** Observe the properties of the hydrochloric acid (HCl) and the zinc. Record these properties in your table.
   - **b)** Watch as your teacher adds the zinc to a small amount of HCl in a test tube.
   - **c)** Record your observations of the products of the reaction, as well as any evidence that a reaction has occurred.
3. **Reaction 3: Baking Soda and Vinegar (with Bromothymol Blue)**
   - **a)** Pour vinegar into a test tube to a depth of 1 cm. Add three drops of bromothymol blue.
   - **b)** Observe and record the properties of the vinegar-bromothymol blue mixture.
   - **c)** Observe and record the properties of the baking soda. Use a scoop to add a tiny amount of baking soda to the test tube.
   - **d)** Record your observations of the products of the reaction, as well as any evidence that a reaction has occurred.

What Did You Find Out?

1. Explain how you know that a chemical reaction occurred in each case.

LEARNING CHECK

1. Use a main idea web to summarize the evidence of a chemical reaction.
2. Burning gasoline in an engine uses oxygen and produces carbon dioxide and water vapour. Name the two reactants and the two products, and explain why this is a chemical reaction.

The four types of chemical reactions can be described using word equations.

synthesis reaction: two or more reactants combine to produce a new product

decomposition reaction: one compound breaks down into two or more simpler compounds or elements

single displacement reaction: one element takes the place of another element in a compound

double displacement reaction: the metal ions of two different compounds exchange places

word equation: uses words instead of chemical formulas to describe what happens to reactants and products during a chemical reaction

It simplifies the study of chemical reactions to separate them into categories. **Table 2.8** lists and describes four main types of chemical reactions. These are **synthesis reactions**, **decomposition reactions**, **single displacement reactions**, and **double displacement reactions**.

One way to describe what is happening during any type of chemical reaction is to use a word equation. A **word equation** uses words, instead of chemical formulas, to describe what happens to the reactants and products during a chemical reaction. Figure 2.16 shows the basic form of a word equation.

name of reactant 1 + **name of reactant 2** → **name of product 3** + **name of product 4**

▲ Figure 2.16 This is the general form of a word equation. The number of reactants on the left side of the arrow and the number of products on the right side of the arrow will depend on the chemical reaction that the word equation describes.

A word equation in chemistry is like an equation in math, except that there are words instead of numbers and an arrow instead of an equal sign. All the reactants are listed before the arrow, and all the products are listed after the arrow. You read a word equation just like you read a sentence. Figure 2.17 shows how you would read the word equation in Figure 2.16.

Go to **scienceontario** to find out more

name of reactant 1 and **name of reactant 2** react to produce **name of product 3** and **name of product 4**

▲ Figure 2.17 When you read a word equation, replace all the + signs with the word "and." Replace the arrow with the words "react to produce." (If there is only one reactant, you replace the arrow with the words "reacts to produce.")

Table 2.8 The Four Main Types of Chemical Reactions

Type of Reaction	Representation of the Reaction	Example
Synthesis reaction • Two or more reactants combine to produce a new product.	A + B → AB  hydrogen + oxygen ⟶ water	 Hydrogen gas is used as a fuel in rockets.
Decomposition reaction • One compound breaks down into two or more simpler compounds or elements.	AB → A + B  water ⟶ hydrogen + oxygen	 Oxygen gas is collecting at the top of the left tube and hydrogen gas is collecting at top of the right test tube.
Single displacement reaction • One element takes the place of another element in a compound.	A + BC → AC + B 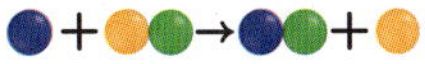 D + BC → BD + C 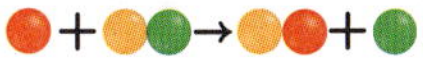 copper + silver nitrate ⟶ copper(II) nitrate + silver	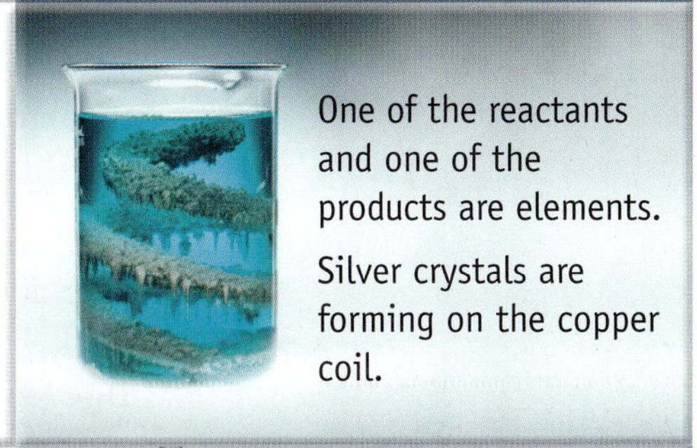 One of the reactants and one of the products are elements. Silver crystals are forming on the copper coil.
Double displacement reaction • The metal ions of two different compounds exchange places.	AB + CD → AD + CB  silver nitrate + potassium chromate ⟶ silver chromate + potassium nitrate	 A precipitate is often produced in a double-displacement reaction. The silver chromate forms the red precipitate.

LEARNING CHECK

1. When you read a word equation, what do the symbols + and ⟶ mean?
2. Use a drawing to show that a decomposition reaction is the reverse of a synthesis reaction.
3. Use a Venn diagram to compare the similarities and differences between a single displacement reaction and a double displacement reaction.

ACTIVITY LINK

Activity 2.13, on page 152

Chemical reactions can be described using chemical equations.

chemical equation: an equation that uses chemical symbols to represent reactants and products in a chemical reaction

Many chemical reactions involve several reactants and products. As well, the names of compounds are different in different languages. For these reasons, chemical equations are much more convenient than word equations to represent chemical reactions. A **chemical equation** uses chemical symbols to represent the reactants and products in a chemical reaction.

How To Write a Chemical Equation from a Word Equation

To write a chemical equation from a word equation, work with each reactant and product separately. Use the rules on pages 129 and 132, as well as the periodic table on page 450, to write the formulas of the reactant compounds and product compounds. Then replace each chemical name with a chemical formula. **Figure 2.18** shows how to convert a word equation into a chemical equation. The following word equation is used as an example:

barium chloride + sodium hydroxide → barium hydroxide + sodium chloride

This example also introduces you to a new type of negative ion. It is called a hydroxide ion. It consists of one oxygen atom and one hydrogen atom and it has one negative charge. The hydroxide ion is symbolized, OH^-. The two atoms remain attached during many chemical reactions. They behave very much like the non-metal ions that you have learned about. If there is more than one hydroxide ion in a compound, you put brackets around the symbols to show that the two atoms remain together. The subscript is written outside of the brackets. For example, calcium hydroxide is written, $Ca(OH)_2$.

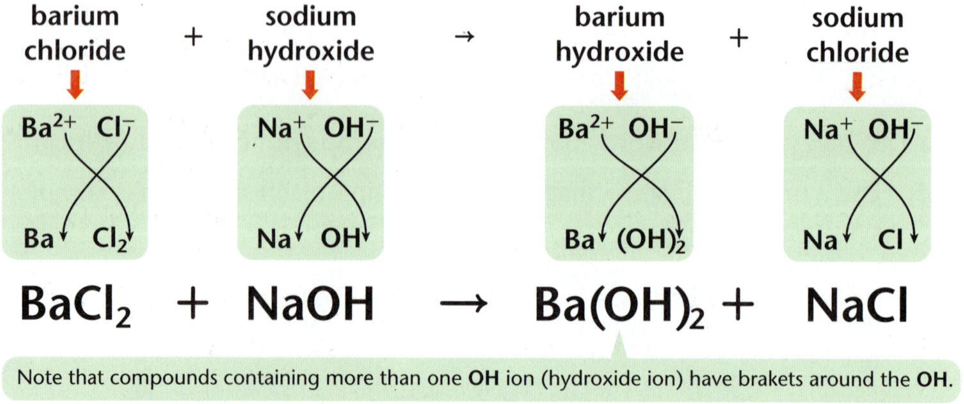

▸ **Figure 2.18** Writing a chemical equation from a word equation

Writing a Chemical Equation for Word Equations That Include Elements

The chemical formulas of most elements are the same as the elements' chemical formulas in the periodic table. However, some non-metal elements are found as a molecule that contains more than one atom of the element. All the non-metal elements that contain more than one atom of the element are shown in **Table 2.9.** When writing a chemical equation for a word equation that includes elements, use **Table 2.9** to determine whether or not each element contains more than one atom. If the element is not in **Table 2.9**, its chemical formula is the same as its symbol in the periodic table. Use **Figure 2.19** to see how this works.

Table 2.9 Elements That Contain More Than One Atom of the Element

Non-metal Element	Found in Nature as	Non-metal Element	Found in Nature as
hydrogen, H	H_2	sulfur, S	S_8
nitrogen, N	N_2	chlorine, Cl	Cl_2
oxygen, O	O_2	selenium, S	Se_8
fluorine, F	F_2	bromine, Br	Br_2
phosphorus, P	P_4	iodine, I	I_2

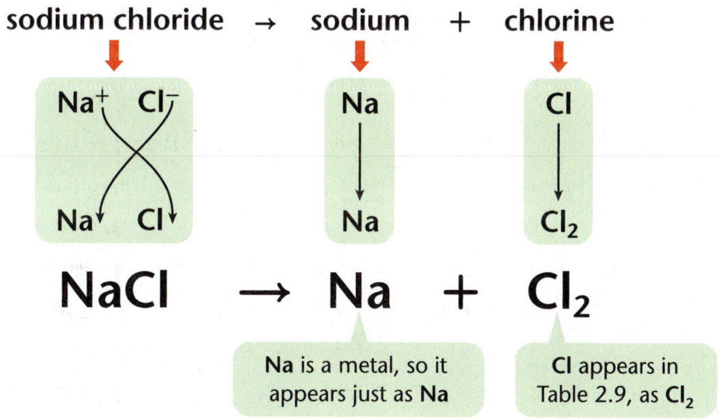

◀ **Figure 2.19** Some elements, such as chlorine, exist in nature as molecules containing more than one atom. These need to be accurately represented when writing a chemical equation from a word equation.

LEARNING CHECK

1. Explain the difference between a word equation and a chemical equation.
2. Provide symbols or formulas for the following elements and compounds:
   a) sodium **b)** dihydrogen monoxide **c)** sodium hydroxide **d)** hydrogen
3. Using your formulas from question 2, write a chemical equation for this word equation:
   sodium + dihydrogen monoxide → sodium hydroxide + hydrogen
4. Write a chemical equation for the word equation:
   calcium oxide + dihydrogen monoxide → calcium hydroxide

Atoms and mass are conserved during a chemical reaction.

balanced chemical equation: represents a chemical reaction using coefficients (numbers in front of the reactants and products) that tell you how much of the reactants are used and how much of the products are made

A chemical equation is like a food recipe. It has a list of ingredients (the reactants) and tells you what you will get at the end (the products). What is missing? A recipe tells you how much of each ingredient you will need and how much of the product you will be able to make.

A **balanced chemical equation** is more precise than a recipe. It represents a chemical reaction using numbers in front of the reactants and products. The numbers tell you how much of the reactants are used and how much of the products are made. The numbers in front of the reactants and products are called *coefficients*. Figure 2.20 shows an example of a balanced chemical equation.

$$2Na + 2H_2O \rightarrow 2NaOH + H_2$$

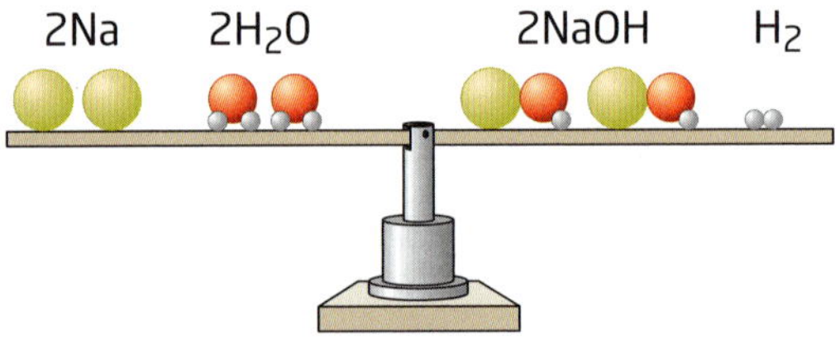

▶ Figure 2.20 A balanced chemical equation tells you how much of each reactant is used and how much of each product is made in a chemical reaction. You can count the number of sodium, hydrogen, and oxygen atoms on the two sides of the balance to see that they are the same.

The Law of Conservation of Mass

law of conservation of mass: during a chemical reaction, the total mass and number of atoms of the reactants equal the total mass and number of atoms of the products.

During a chemical reaction, atoms are not created and atoms are not destroyed. Instead, atoms of the reactants are rearranged to form the new product substances. This fact is summarized by a scientific law called the **law of conservation of mass.**

The law of conservation of mass
During a chemical reaction, the total mass and number of atoms of the reactants equals the total mass and number of atoms of the products.

INVESTIGATION LINK
Investigation 2B, on page 153.

The law of conservation of mass is the reason that chemical equations must be balanced. The quantity or mass of the reactants must always equal the quantity or mass of the products.

If a chemical equation is balanced, the number of each type of atom on the reactant side is equal to the number of each type of atom on the product side. You can see this in Figure 2.21.

$$2\,Na + 2\,H_2O \rightarrow 2\,NaOH + H_2$$

The 2 in front of **Na** means two atoms of **Na** or **Na Na**

The 2 in front of **H_2O** means 2 sets of **H_2O** $2 \times H_2 =$ **H H H H** $2 \times O =$ **O O**

The 2 in front of **NaOH** means 2 sets of **NaOH** $2 \times Na =$ **Na Na** $2 \times O =$ **O O** $2 \times H =$ **H H**

If there is no coefficient, it means a 1, so 1 set of **H_2** = **H H**

◂ **Figure 2.21** You can see that this equation is balanced because there are 2Na, 4H, and 2O in both the reactants (on the left) and the products (on the right).

Inquiry Focus

Activity 2.11

BALANCING CHEMICAL EQUATIONS

In this activity, you will build models of the reactants and products from the word equations you wrote in Activity 2.13 on page 152. Then you will use your models to balance the chemical equations.

What You Need

- materials to build models of reactants and products

What To Do

1. Make a table like the one below to record your data for each of the four reactions. Leave enough space to write the reactions and draw diagrams of the models you build.

Reaction	Chemical Equation and Diagrams of Models
1	→

2. Convert the first word equation from Activity 2.13 to a chemical equation and write it in the first row of your table.
3. Use the materials provided by your teacher to build each reactant and product in the first chemical reaction.
4. Ensure that the quantity of reactants used is equal to the quantity of products made. You may need to make more models so you can count the number of each reactant atom and each product atom.
5. Use coefficients in front of the reactants and products to show how many of each you had to build to make sure that mass was conserved.
6. Draw diagrams of your models below the chemical equation. Your diagrams and chemical equation should both be balanced for each type of atom.
7. Repeat steps 2 to 6 for the other three word equations.

What Did You Find Out?

1. Compare your results with those of your classmates. Explain and solve any differences.
2. Explain how the law of conservation of mass relates to the models you built for the chemical reactions.
3. How do you know when chemical equations are balanced?

LEARNING CHECK

1. What is the law of conservation of mass?
2. How does the law of conservation of mass apply to balancing chemical equations?

continued on the next page…

Balancing Chemical Equations

To balance a chemical equation, follow the steps below.

Go to **scienceontario** to find out more

Step 1 Make a table with the reactants and products. Count and record how many of each type of atom are on each side of the equation.

$Na + CuCl_2 \rightarrow Cu + NaCl$

Reactants	Products
1 Na	1 Na
1 Cu	1 Cu
2 Cl	1 Cl

Chlorine is unbalanced. Since there are only 2 Cl atoms on the product side, place the coefficient 2 in front of NaCl. (This means that you multiply NaCl by 2.) The coefficient must go in front of the whole compound, because it applies to the Na atoms and the Cl atoms in the whole compound.

Step 2 Identify an unbalanced atom. *Multiply* the compound on the other side of the equation, which contains that atom, by a coefficient to balance this atom in the reaction. Change the numbers in your table to indicate the change.

$Na + CuCl_2 \rightarrow Cu + 2\ NaCl$

Reactants	Products
1 Na	**2** Na
1 Cu	1 Cu
2 Cl	**2** Cl

Now sodium is unbalanced. Since there are now 2 Na on the product side and there is only 1 Na on the reactant side, place the coefficient 2 in front of Na on the reactant side. (Multiply Na by 2.)

Step 3 Repeat what you did in step 2 for any other unbalanced atoms, until all the atoms balance.

$2\ Na + CuCl_2 \rightarrow Cu + 2\ NaCl$

Reactants	Products
2 Na	**2** Na
1 Cu	1 Cu
2 Cl	**2** Cl

Step 4 Count the atoms on each side of the chemical equation to make sure that they are all balanced.

LEARNING CHECK

1. Balance the following chemical equations using the steps described on these pages.
   a) $Na + O_2 \rightarrow Na_2O$
   b) $SnO_2 + H_2 \rightarrow Sn + H_2O$
   c) $SeCl_6 + O_2 \rightarrow SeO_2 + Cl_2$
   d) $Fe + O_2 \rightarrow Fe_2O_3$ (HINT: Start with Fe)
   e) $Cu + S_8 \rightarrow Cu_2S$ (HINT: Start with S)
2. How can you be sure that you have balanced a chemical equation correctly?

Inquiry Focus

Activity 2.12

WORD EQUATIONS, CHEMICAL EQUATIONS, AND BALANCING

Now that you've had some practice with equations and balancing, you can put everything together in this activity.

Safety

- Tie back loose hair.
- Secure burner to a retort stand.

What You Need

- Bunsen burner
- spark lighter
- splint
- 3 test tubes
- test tube rack
- scoop
- test-tube clamp dropper bottles (for each solution)
- calcium oxide
- water
- pH paper
- calcium carbonate
- zinc metal
- silver nitrate solution
- barium hydroxide solution
- zinc nitrate solution
- Activity Cards supplied by your teacher
- materials to build models of reactants and products

What To Do

1. Make a table like the one below to record your data. Leave enough space to write the reactions and draw diagrams of the models you will build.

Part A: Observing or Performing Reactions

2. At each station, observe the demonstration or perform the reaction described.
3. Record any evidence of a chemical reaction.
4. Clean up as directed by your teacher.

Part B: Writing Reactions, Building Models, and Balancing Equations

5. Use the Activity Cards to make a word equation for the first reaction. Record the word equation in your table.
6. Write a chemical equation for the word equation using the rules on page 146. Record the chemical equation in your table.
7. Use the materials from your teacher to build each reactant and product in the first reaction.
8. Use the rules for balancing chemical reactions, and the models you built, to balance the chemical equation. **Hint:** Make more models of each reactant and product as you need them.
9. Place the correct coefficients in the chemical equation you have written.
10. Draw diagrams of your models under the chemical formulas. Your diagrams and chemical equations should both be balanced for each type of atom.
11. Use **Table 2.8** to identify the type of chemical reaction. Record the reaction type in your table.
12. Repeat steps 5 to 11 for the other three reactions.

Reaction	Evidence of Chemical Reaction	Word Equation, Balanced Chemical Equation, Diagrams of Models, and Reaction Type
1		calcium oxide + water →
2		calcium carbonate →
3		zinc + silver nitrate →
4		barium hydroxide + zinc nitrate →

Inquiry Focus

Activity 2.13

WRITING WORD EQUATIONS

Writing a word equation is often easier when you can see the evidence of a chemical reaction. At each lab station in this activity, you will observe a chemical reaction and write a word equation based on your observations.

Safety

- Tie back loose hair.
- Secure burner to a retort stand.

What You Need

- Hoffman apparatus
- 4 test tubes
- medicine droppers
- steel wool
- water
- aluminum metal
- copper(II) chloride solution
- dilute sodium hydroxide solution
- calcium nitrate solution
- magnesium ribbon
- Bunsen burner
- tongs
- wooden splint
- activity cards
- reaction type cards

What To Do

1. Make a table like the one below to record your observations.
2. At each station, record the properties of the reactants. Then either observe the demonstration or perform the reaction described.
3. Record the properties of the products and any evidence of a chemical reaction.
4. Clean up as directed by your teacher.

What Did You Find Out?

1. Using the activity cards, write a word equation for each reaction.
2. Using the information from **Table 2.8** and your word equation, classify each reaction using the reaction type cards.
3. Compare your results with your classmates' results.

Evidence of Chemical Reactions

Lab Station and Reaction	Properties of Reactants	Properties of Products	Evidence of Reaction
1. hydrogen gas + oxygen gas (using Hoffman apparatus)			
2. aluminum + copper(II) chloride			
3. sodium hydroxide + calcium nitrate			
4. magnesium + oxygen			

Investigation 2B

The Law of Conservation of Mass

In this investigation, you will compare the masses of reactants and products in a chemical reaction to see if they support the law of conservation of mass.

Skill Check

initiating and planning

✓ **performing and recording**

✓ **analyzing and interpreting**

✓ **communicating**

Safety

- Rinse any spills with plenty of water, and report them to your teacher immediately.
- Sodium hydroxide can cause blindness.

What You Need

- graduated cylinder
- dilute sodium hydroxide solution
- 200 mL Erlenmeyer flask
- dilute iron(III) nitrate solution
- small test tube
- stopper
- balance

What To Do

1. Read the steps of the investigation. Then design a table to record the measurements and the observations you will be making.
2. Use a graduated cylinder to measure 20 mL of sodium hydroxide solution. Pour the solution into the Erlenmeyer flask.
3. Pour iron(III) nitrate solution into the small test tube until it is about half full.
4. Tilt the flask and carefully let the test tube slide down inside. Do not let the solutions mix. Seal the flask with the stopper. Refer to the photo.
5. Measure the mass of the flask and its contents. Record the mass in your table. Also record the appearance of the contents of the flask.
6. Tip the flask so the solutions can mix.
7. Measure the mass of the flask and its contents. Record the mass in your table. Also record the appearance of the contents of the flask.
8. Follow your teacher's instructions to safely dispose of the materials and clean up your work area.

What Did You Find Out?

1. How did the mass of the reactants, flask, test tube, and stopper before the reaction compare with their mass after the reaction?
2. Do your results support the law of conservation of mass? Explain why or why not.

Inquire Further

3. The word equation for the chemical reaction in this investigation is:

   iron(III) nitrate + sodium hydroxide →
   sodium nitrate + iron(III) hydroxide

   The chemical formulas for these compounds are:

   iron(III) nitrate: $Fe(NO_3)_3$
   sodium hydroxide: NaOH
   sodium nitrate: $NaNO_3$
   iron(III) hydroxide: $Fe(OH)_3$

   Write a balanced chemical equation for this chemical reaction.

Strange Tales of Science

Crime Scene Chemistry

Solving a crime is all about logic and reasoning, right? Not quite, Inspector Clouseau! If you've ever watched a crime scene TV show, you know that solving a crime is also about chemistry. Check out the following tale of murder and mayhem to find out what chemical reactions tell investigators about the nature of a crime.

So... What do you think?

1. You are a detective investigating a crime scene in a field a year after the crime was committed. Do you think luminol could still detect the presence of blood in the soil? Explain your reasoning.
2. Work with a partner or in a small group. Write a script for a 10 minute scene in a crime scene investigation television show. Include at least two chemical reactions in your script. Present your scene to your class.
3. Chemical reactions are also used to identify illegal drugs. Choose one illegal drug. Use library or computer resources to learn more about a chemical reaction used to identify it.

Making a DIFFERENCE

Simon Pickup became interested in the explosive possibilities of hydrogen when he was in Grade 4. Simon built a mini-hydrogen electrolyser for a science project. A hydrogen electrolyser splits water into hydrogen and oxygen and creates energy. "At the time, I thought it would be the coolest thing to blow something up," he says. "But as I learned more about hydrogen, I became less interested in blowing hydrogen up for the sake of an explosion and more interested in blowing it up in our cars."

As Simon learned more about hydrogen's potential as a clean, renewable energy source, he asked himself, "Why don't we live in a hydrogen-powered world yet?" With this question in mind, Simon founded Youth Hydrogen in 2004. The organization is dedicated to clean energy and the development of the world's first hydrogen-based city.

How could you find out more about a topic that is important to you?

When Sergio Morales and Andrew Hanna saw a newscast about the number of people who die each year from heart attacks or strokes, they decided to do a science project on heart attacks. They discovered research that suggests daily doses of Aspirin™ can reduce the risk of heart attacks, and a single dose taken during a heart attack can increase the chances of survival.

Aspirin™ dissolves in hydrochloric acid in the stomach. It thins the blood and can break down clots. Sergio and Andrew found that Aspirin™, crushed to increase its surface area and taken with carbonated lemonade, dissolves the quickest in hydrochloric acid.

They created a website to educate people about their results, and a "Heart Attack Kit," which can be used to quickly create a mixture of Aspirin™ in lemonade to increase the chance of survival from heart attack or stroke.

Is there a news story you have seen that you could investigate further in a science project?

Topic 2.3 Review

Key Concepts

- During a chemical reaction, chemical compounds are changed into different compounds with different properties.
- The four types of chemical reactions can be described using word equations.
- Chemical reactions can be described using chemical equations.
- Atoms and mass are conserved during a chemical reaction.

Review the Key Concepts

1. K/U Answer the question that is the title of this topic. Copy and complete the graphic organizer below in your notebook. Fill in four examples from the topic using key terms as well as your own words.

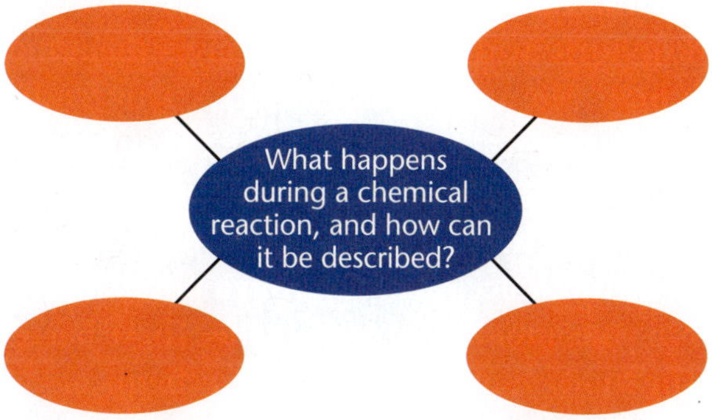

2. C Use an organizer such as a word web or a flowchart to summarize the types of evidence that can help you decide if a chemical reaction has occurred.

3. K/U Classify the following reactions as one of synthesis, decomposition, single-displacement, or double-displacement:

a) $2\ Na + CaCl_2 \rightarrow 2\ NaCl + Ca$

b) $BaCl_2 + 2\ AgNO_3 \rightarrow Ba(NO_3)_2 + 2\ AgCl$

c) $N_2 + 2\ O_2 \rightarrow 2\ NO_2$

d) $2\ Al_2O_3 \rightarrow 4\ Al + 3\ O_2$

4. T/I Write word equations for the reactions in question 3.

5. T/I Write a chemical equation from each of the following word equations.

a) water reacts to produce oxygen and hydrogen

b) lithium and water react to produce lithium hydroxide and hydrogen

c) zinc and hydrogen chloride react to produce zinc chloride and hydrogen

d) potassium iodide and silver nitrate react to produce potassium nitrate and silver iodide (HINT: nitrate is NO_3^-. Similar to OH^-, it acts as a unit.)

e) sulfur and oxygen react to produce sulfur dioxide

6. A During a chemical reaction, your measurements show that the mass of the products is greater than the mass of the reactants that you started with. Is this possible? Explain what probably happened.

7. T/I Balance the following chemical reactions.

a) $2\ C + O_2 \rightarrow CO$

b) $Cl_2 + NaBr \rightarrow Br_2 + NaCl$

c) $NH_3 \rightarrow N_2 + H_2$

d) $Na + H_2O \rightarrow NaOH + H_2$ (HINT: Water can also be written as HOH.)

e) $NaOH + H_2S \rightarrow Na_2S + H_2O$

8. A Propane, the fuel used in many gas barbeques, has the chemical formula C_3H_8. When propane burns in oxygen, it produces carbon dioxide and water.

a) Write the chemical formula for the reactants and products in this reaction.

b) Write a chemical equation for the reaction.

c) Balance the chemical equation. (HINT: Balance the oxygen last.)

Topic 2.4

What are acids and bases, and how do they react?

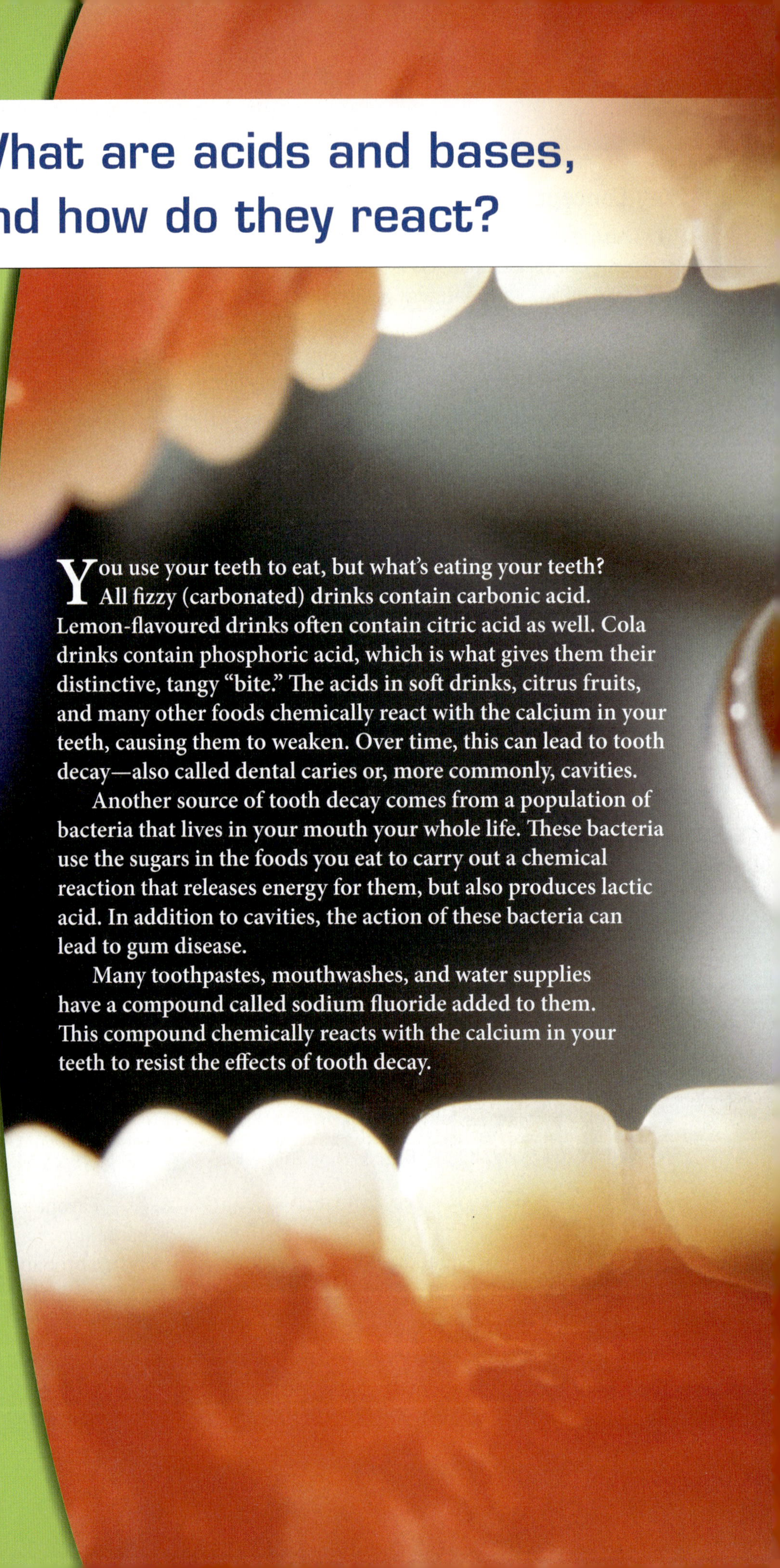

Key Concepts

- Acids and bases are compounds with specific properties.
- An acid and a base react in a neutralization reaction to produce a salt and water.
- Chemical reactions involving acids, bases, and other compounds require safe handling to minimize hazards.

Key Skills

Inquiry
Research

Key Terms

acid
base
acid-base indicator
pH scale
neutralization reaction
antacid

You use your teeth to eat, but what's eating your teeth? All fizzy (carbonated) drinks contain carbonic acid. Lemon-flavoured drinks often contain citric acid as well. Cola drinks contain phosphoric acid, which is what gives them their distinctive, tangy "bite." The acids in soft drinks, citrus fruits, and many other foods chemically react with the calcium in your teeth, causing them to weaken. Over time, this can lead to tooth decay—also called dental caries or, more commonly, cavities.

Another source of tooth decay comes from a population of bacteria that lives in your mouth your whole life. These bacteria use the sugars in the foods you eat to carry out a chemical reaction that releases energy for them, but also produces lactic acid. In addition to cavities, the action of these bacteria can lead to gum disease.

Many toothpastes, mouthwashes, and water supplies have a compound called sodium fluoride added to them. This compound chemically reacts with the calcium in your teeth to resist the effects of tooth decay.

Starting Point Activity

You can model the effects of acid on your teeth. All you need is white vinegar, a jar with a lid, and a clean, cooked chicken bone. (The chicken bone contains the same calcium compound that your teeth do.)

First, predict what you think you will observe after the bone has been left in the acidic vinegar for several days. Then test your prediction. As an alternative, observe the acid-treated bone that your teacher may have prepared in advance.

CAUTION: Wash your hands each time you handle the chicken bone. Do not taste the vinegar.

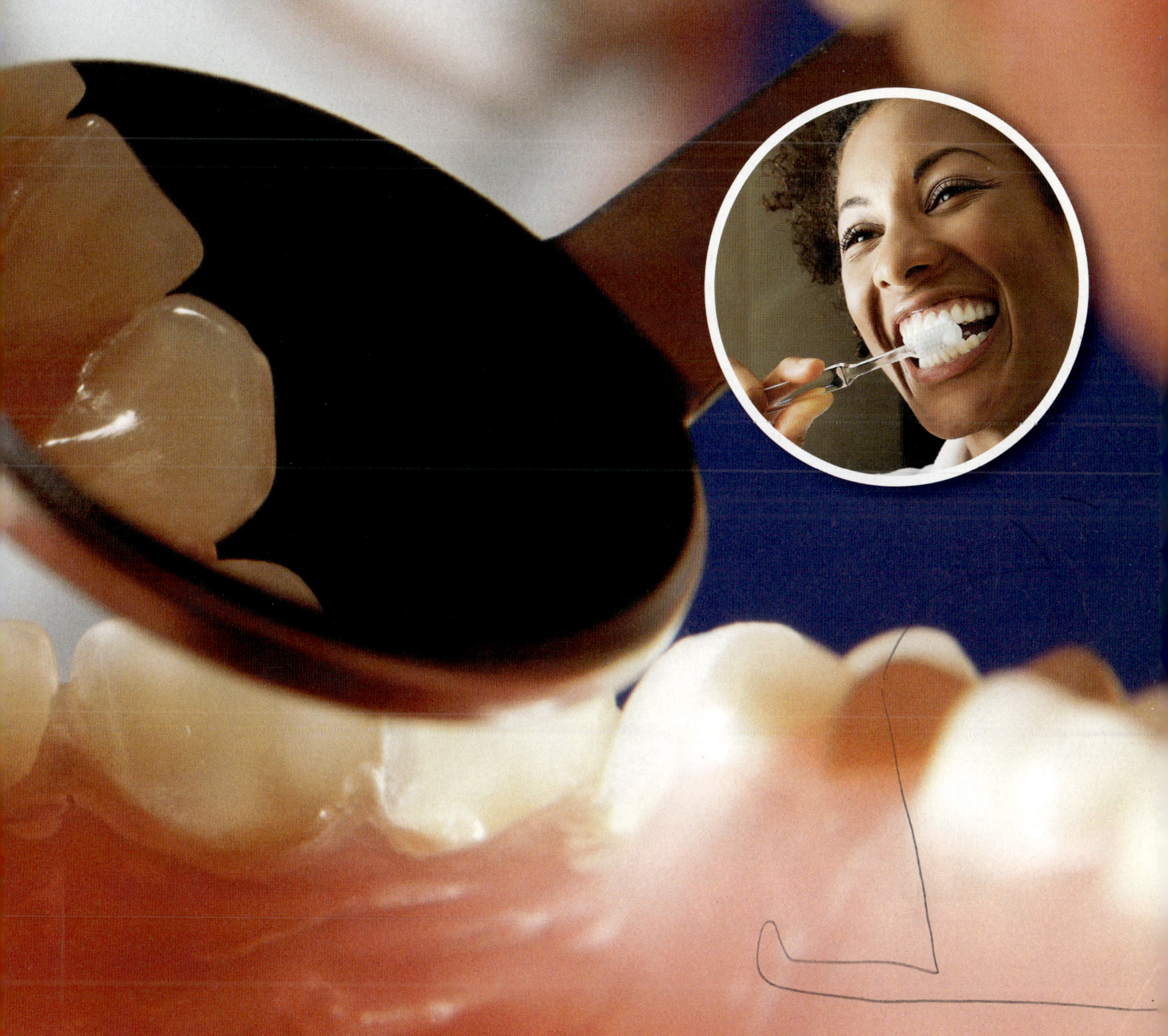

Acids and bases are compounds with specific properties.

acid: a compound that tastes sour, corrodes metals and tissue, and turns blue litmus paper red

base: a compound that tastes bitter, has a slippery texture, corrodes tissue, and turns red litmus paper blue

You experience **acids** and **bases**, and their properties, on a daily basis. Acids and bases are in many of the foods you eat, the soil that grows your food, the fluids in your body, the products you clean with, and the colours of the clothing you wear.

Common Examples of Acids and Their Properties

Common examples of foods that contain acids include lemons, grapefruits, vinegar, apples, and yogurt. These foods have a sour taste. Sourness is one of the properties of acids.

Having a sour taste doesn't mean that it is safe to use the property of taste to identify acids. In fact, many acids are dangerous. They can cause severe burns to the skin and other body tissues because of another property of acids: corrosion. *Corrosion* refers to a chemical reaction in which one substance (such as an acid) "eats away at" or "breaks down" the surface of another substance. Many metals are easily corroded by acids.

As you can see in Figure 2.22, there are many other examples of acids in the world around you. **Table 2.10** lists some properties that are used to identify acids and compares them with properties that are used to identify bases.

▾ **Figure 2.22** Acids are a part of foods, medicines, batteries, cleaning products, and dyes for fabrics and clothing. **CAUTION:** Many acids are dangerous. They can cause severe burns, which can lead to disfigurement and sometimes death. Never touch or taste an unknown acid, or mix an acid with a base or any other substance, without the instruction of a qualified person.

Common Examples of Bases and Their Properties

Common examples of foods that contain bases include eggplant, unsweetened chocolate, bitter melon, and tonic water. These foods have a bitter taste. Bitterness is one of the properties of bases.

The fact that bases have a bitter taste doesn't mean that it is safe to use the property of taste to identify a base. Like acids, many bases are dangerous because they are corrosive. They can corrode skin and other living or once-living tissue. This is one reason why bases are common in oven-cleaning and drain-clearing products. However, bases do not corrode metals, which is another reason why bases are common in oven-cleaning and drain-clearing products.

As you can see in **Figure 2.23**, there are many other examples of bases in the world around you. **Table 2.10** lists some properties that are used to identify bases and compares them with properties that are used to identify acids.

Table 2.10 Comparing Properties Used To Identify Acids and Bases

Property	Acids	Bases
Taste	taste sour	taste bitter
Texture (feel)	have no characteristic texture	have a slippery texture
Conductivity	conduct electric current when dissolved in water	conduct electric current when dissolved in water
Corrosion	corrode living and once-living tissue, as well as metals	corrode living and once-living tissue
Chemical reaction with metals	are reactive with metals	are not reactive with metals
*Chemical reaction with litmus paper	turn blue litmus paper red	turn red litmus paper blue
*Chemical reaction with each other	lose many of their properties when they react with bases	lose many of their properties when they react with acids

*Properties marked with an asterisk (*) are described in more detail on pages 162 to 163 and pages 164 to 165.

▲ **Figure 2.23** Bases are a part of foods, medicines, batteries, cleaning products, and dyes for fabrics and clothing. **CAUTION:** Many bases are dangerous. They can cause severe burns, which can lead to disfigurement and sometimes death. Never touch or taste an unknown base, or mix a base with an acid or any other substance, without the instruction of a qualified person.

LEARNING CHECK

1. Convert **Table 2.10** into a Venn diagram that compares the properties of acids and bases.
2. Name three acids and three bases that you either have or probably have in your home.
3. Explain why people who work with acids and bases should treat these compounds with care and with proper regard to safety.

continued on the next page...

... continued from previous page

Acid-Base Indicators and the pH Scale

acid-base indicator: a substance that changes colour when added to an acid or a base

One way to identify acids and bases is to use an acid-base indicator. An **acid-base indicator** is a substance that changes colour when it is added to an acid or a base, or when an acid or a base is added to it. Figure 2.24 shows litmus paper, which is one of the most commonly used acid-base indicators.

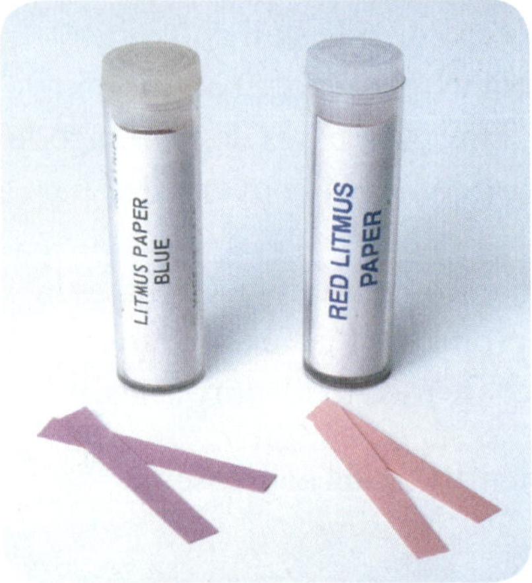

◂ **Figure 2.24** Litmus paper often comes in two colours—red and blue. Acids turn blue litmus paper red. Bases turn red litmus paper blue.

Another way to identify acids and bases is to use numbers. Not all acids are the same, and neither are all bases. For instance, some acids are more sour, more corrosive, or more reactive than others. Likewise, some bases are more bitter, more corrosive, or more reactive than others. Scientists use the pH scale, like the one in Figure 2.25, to give a numerical value to a substance. The **pH scale** is a sequence of numbers from 0 to 14 that describes how acidic or how basic a substance is. The lower the pH number, the more acidic a substance is. The higher the pH number, the more basic a substance is. When the pH number changes by one, the strength of the acid or base changes by ten times. For example, pH 3 is ten times more acidic than pH 4. Also, pH 9 is ten times more basic than pH 8.

pH scale: a scale from 0 to 14 that describes how acidic or basic a substance is

▴ **Figure 2.25** Acids have a pH less than 7. Bases have a pH greater than 7. Substances with a pH of 7 are neutral, which means that they are neither an acid nor a base.

LEARNING CHECK

1. A substance is tested with red and blue litmus paper. The red litmus paper turns blue, the blue litmus paper stays blue. Identify the substance as an acid or a base.
2. Identify the following as acidic, basic, or neutral: **a)** egg white (pH 7.8); **b)** coffee (pH 5.0); **c)** urine (pH 6.0); **d)** bleach (pH 12.4).
3. Sort the items in question 2 from most basic to most acidic.

Inquiry Focus

Activity 2.14

USING INDICATORS TO IDENTIFY ACIDS AND BASES

In this activity, you will use two acid-base indicators to identify samples of acids and bases. Litmus paper is one of the indicators you will use. Cabbage juice is the other.

Safety

What You Need

- spot plates (10 wells needed per group)
- paper towels
- solutions with pH values from 3 to 11
- tweezers
- litmus paper cut into small squares
- coloured pencils or markers
- medicine dropper
- cabbage juice indicator (prepared in advance)

What To Do

1. Make a table like the one below to record your data.

Indicator Colour in Various Solutions with Different pH Values

pH	3	4	5	6	7	8	9	10	11
Litmus									
Cabbage juice									

2. Number the wells of the spot plate from 3 to 11.
3. Place a paper towel beside the spot plate.
4. Add five drops of the solution with a pH of 3 to the well marked 3.
5. Add five drops of the solution with a pH of 4 to the well marked 4.
6. Continue adding five drops of the pH solutions to the wells with matching numbers.
7. Use tweezers to pick up one piece of litmus paper. Dip the litmus paper into the solution with a pH of 3. Place the damp litmus paper on the paper towel.
8. Use coloured pencils or markers to duplicate the colour of the litmus paper in your table.
9. Use a dropper to add five drops of cabbage juice indicator to the solution with a pH of 3.
10. Use the coloured pencils or crayons to duplicate the colour of the cabbage juice in your table.
11. Repeat steps 7 to 10 for the other solutions in the wells.
12. Clean up as directed by your teacher.

What Did You Find Out?

1. List the solutions you tested from most acidic to most basic.
2. Which indicator is better for identifying acids and bases? Explain.

An acid and a base react in a neutralization reaction to produce a salt and water.

The chemical reaction between an acid and a base is a double displacement reaction. In many cases, the products of a double displacement reaction are an ionic compound and water. This happens because acids contain hydrogen (H) and bases contain hydroxide (OH). When an acid and a base take part in a chemical reaction, the H in the acid combines with the OH in the base to form water: HOH, or H_2O. The other elements in the acid and base combine to form an ionic compound, as shown in Figure 2.26. The ionic compound is called a salt. There are many other salts in addition to table salt, which is sodium chloride.

▶ **Figure 2.26** An acid and a base react in a double displacement reaction to form an ionic compound (a salt) and often water.

$$HA + B\text{-}OH \rightarrow AB + H_2O\ (HOH)$$

Acids have a hydrogen (H)

Bases have hydroxide (OH)

The other parts of the acid and base combine to make a salt

The hydrogen **(H)** and the hydroxide **(OH)** often combine to make water **(H_2O or HOH)**

Neutralization Reactions

neutralization reaction: a reaction between an acid and a base that "neutralizes" their acidic and basic properties

The double displacement reaction between an acid and a base is also called a **neutralization reaction.** It is called a neutralization reaction because the acidic and basic properties cancel each other out. They are neutralized. Study the example in Figure 2.27.

▶ **Figure 2.27** The properties of the acid and base are neutralized when the acid and base react.

$$HCl + NaOH \rightarrow NaCl + H_2O\ (HOH)$$

pH < 7 turns blue litmus red

pH > 7 turns red litmus blue

pH = 7 (neutral) no change to litmus paper

LEARNING CHECK

1. Explain what happens during a chemical reaction that involves an acid and a base.
2. You could think of an acid and a base as being the chemical opposites of each other. Explain how the concept of a neutralization reaction supports this.
3. Look at the chemical equation shown in Figure 2.28. Is this a balanced chemical equation? Explain why or why not.

INVESTIGATION LINK

Investigation 2C, on page 172

Examples of Neutralization Reactions

One example of a neutralization reaction takes place in your body when you eat. Your stomach produces a powerful acid to kill germs that might be in food. This acid is neutralized by a base in your small intestine. If your stomach produces too much acid, you may feel pain around the area of your chest and throat. This is called acid reflux, but you may have heard it called heartburn. **Antacids** are stomach-acid neutralizers. They are made of non-toxic bases. They relieve the pain of excess stomach acid by neutralizing some of the acid. Antacids should only be used to relieve occasional heartburn. Prescription medication should be used if you have heartburn regularly.

Figure 2.28 shows another example of a neutralization reaction. Sulfuric acid is important for manufacturing many substances and products that are used around the world. However, sulfuric acid is often transported by rail, and accidents sometimes occur. When 150 000 L of sulfuric acid accidentally spilled into the Blanche River in the Temiskaming region of northeastern Ontario, clean-up efforts included the use of a base called lime to neutralize the acid.

ACTIVITY LINK

Activity 2.16, on page 170

antacid: non-toxic base that is used to neutralize stomach acid

INVESTIGATION LINK

Investigation 2D, on page 173

▼ **Figure 2.28** People working to clean up the spill of sulfuric acid into the Blanche River used lime to neutralize the acid. The chemical name for lime is calcium hydroxide, and its chemical formula is $Ca(OH)_2$. The word equation and chemical equation for the neutralization reaction are shown on top of the photo.

sulfuric acid + calcium hydroxide → calcium sulfate + water

$$H_2SO_4 + Ca(OH)_2 \rightarrow CaSO_4 + 2H_2O$$

Chemical reactions involving acids, bases, and other compounds require safe handling to minimize hazards.

Go to **scienceontario** to find out more

Acids, bases, and other compounds that are used or produced during chemical reactions can be hazardous to peoples' safety, to the environment, or to both. But with proper precautions, the risks can be minimized. The photos and captions on the next page show examples of professionals who must have specialized knowledge to handle chemical compounds and chemical reactions at their work sites.

LEARNING CHECK

1. Name one hazard experienced by
   a) auto body technicians **b)** food preparation workers
2. What precautions should be taken by the following workers before doing their job?
   a) hair stylist **b)** welder

Research Focus

Activity 2-15

MINIMIZING THE RISKS

Work in small groups. Divide up the professions shown on page 167 so that each group has one profession to explore further. Other professions can be added as necessary.

With your group, do research to find examples so that you can fill in a table like the one shown below. Combine the information in your table with other groups to create a single summary table. Your summary table should include information about:

- professions that use chemical compounds and chemical reactions
- ways that risks and hazards are minimized in these professions.

Be sure to consult WHMIS and MSDS regulations when you are doing your research.

Profession	Benefits of Chemical Reactions (what compounds are used, and how are they used?)	Ways To Minimize Risks to Personal Safety from Compounds and Chemical Reactions	Ways To Minimize Risks to the Environment from Compounds and Chemical Reactions

Hair stylist If you read the warnings on hair products from a drugstore, you know how dangerous these products can be if they are not used properly. The products stylists use in a hair salon are more concentrated and must be handled even more carefully. Stylists wear gloves to protect their hands and aprons to protect their clothes.

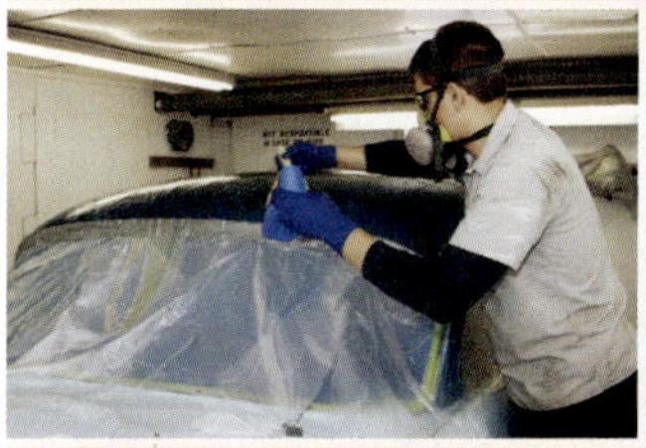

Auto body technician The chemicals used in car paint make the paint durable enough to withstand winter road conditions, but they can cause severe damage to skin, eyes, and lungs. Auto body technicians must wear a full-face air-purifying respirator to protect their face and lungs from exposure.

Nail technician Nail technicians are exposed to the chemicals in polish, solvents (nail polish remover), adhesives (for gel and acrylic nails), and the dust formed from polishing. The chemicals that make nails look great can cause both skin irritation and respiratory problems from exposure.

Custodian Some people think the "best" cleaning products are the ones with the most hazard symbols on them! More and more schools and office buildings are switching to "green" cleaning products that not only reduce the environmental impact of cleaning products, but also protect custodians from exposure to dangerous compounds that can harm skin and other body tissues if they are not handled safely.

Food preparation We use a variety of compounds to sanitize surfaces to protect us from food-borne illnesses caused by bacteria and other microbes. But the same compounds that are toxic to microorganisms are also toxic to us. People who work in food preparation must take care to ensure that their skin doesn't come in contact with the chemicals, that they don't breathe in the fumes, and that all traces are washed away before any food comes into contact with these surfaces after cleaning.

Welder You may have noticed that welders wear eye protection to protect their vision against ultraviolet radiation. Other risks that welders face include exposure to metal fumes and the possibility of an explosion. A balloon filled with acetylene, a common welding fuel, has the explosive power of 20 sticks of dynamite!

Firefighter Firefighters not only fight fires, but also battle spills from industrial and automobile accidents. The compounds spilled may be any combination of toxic, flammable, or hazardous—including acids and bases. They must be prepared to protect themselves, the people nearby, and the environment, from the hazardous effects. They wear heat and chemical-resistant clothing, and have breathing apparatus if needed. When possible, they will use other chemical products to help neutralize or clean up the spill.

Case Study Investigation: Acid Rain—Still an Ongoing Concern

What's the Issue

With climate change in the headlines so often, it's easy to forget that there are other serious environmental issues. One of those is acid deposition, often referred to more simply as acid rain.

Normal rain water is naturally acidic because carbon dioxide in air interacts with rain water to form carbonic acid. The resulting acidic rain has a pH of about 5.6. But pollutant gases such as sulfur dioxide and nitrogen oxides also interact with rain water, causing the pH to drop even further. Eastern Canada especially has suffered, and continues to suffer, great damage due to the ongoing formation of acid rain.

The Science behind the Issue

Acid rain is destroying forests in Canada and around the world.

Acidic rain, snow, and ice causes damage to ecosystems on land, in oceans, and even in our towns and cities.

Aquatic Ecosystems

Organisms that are adapted to living in lakes and ponds are very sensitive to the acidity of their watery homes. Some, such as eel and brook trout, can survive in water with a pH as low as 4.5. But others, such as perch and pike, die when the pH falls below 5.0. The pH of the water isn't the only factor that causes harm. Acid rain reacts with soil and rock materials, releasing poisonous metals that can drain into aquatic ecosystems.

Terrestrial Ecosystems

Plants are very sensitive to acidic soil. Many cannot grow in acidic conditions. In natural terrestrial ecosystems such as forests, acidic rain and snow damages the leaves of trees. This makes trees less healthy, interfering with their ability to withstand cold and fight off disease and insects. Acidic rain and snow also deplete the soil of nutrients that plants need to grow and thrive. Canadian scientists predict that unless acid deposition is reduced, half of the conifers in eastern Canada may be harmed.

The boat in this photo is adding lime (calcium carbonate) to a lake affected by acid rain. The calcium reacts with the acid in a neutralization reaction. This solution is a temporary fix, however.

Human Ecosystems

Stone buildings and statues are damaged as the acid in acidic rain and snow eats away at their surfaces. Regional economies can also suffer. For example, income from commercial fishing, sports fishing, and recreation are affected when lakes and forests that towns and cities depend on are damaged by acid rain.

In Ontario, the Sudbury area has been severely affected by acid deposition due to sulfur dioxide emissions from nearby smelter—factories that extract metal from ore. Lakes were hit especially hard. Loss of fishing-related jobs and income was heavy as sports fish levels declined in acidified water. Fortunately, the story of Sudbury has a relatively happy ending. Once smelter emissions were reduced in the area, ecosystem health soon began to improve. However, not all sources of acid rain are local—the United States is a huge contributor to the problems experienced in Canada.

This photo shows a statue after it has been exposed to acid deposition.

Over to You

1. Read the caption for the photo showing a boat adding lime to a lake. Infer why this solution is only a temporary fix to the problem.
2. Why does acid rain affect eastern Canada more severely than western Canada? Do research to find out.
3. Do research to find out why solutions to the problem of acid rain in Canada involve the cooperation of the United States as well.
4. Killarney, Ontario was severely affected by acid rain in the 1970s. Find out why, and find out what people have been doing ever since to help their area recover.

Inquiry Focus

Activity 2.16

NEUTRALIZATION REACTIONS

In this activity, you will use an acid-base indicator to determine when a neutralization reaction is complete. The acid-base indicator you will use is called bromothymol blue. It is blue in a base, yellow in an acid, and green when neutral.

Safety

- Hydrochloric acid and sodium hydroxide are corrosive. Work with them carefully.
- Sodium hydroxide can cause blindness.

What You Need

- graduated cylinder
- dilute hydrochloric acid
- small test tube
- test-tube rack
- dropper with dropper bottles (for each solution)
- bromothymol blue indicator
- dilute sodium hydroxide

What To Do

1. Make a table like the one below to record your data.

Volume of Acid (mL)	Number of Drops Needed to Neutralize Acid
5.0	
2.0	
3.0	

2. Use the graduated cylinder to measure 5.0 mL of the acid. Pour the acid into the test tube.
3. Add two drops of bromothymol blue indicator. Gently swirl the test tube to mix the indicator and the acid. The colour should be yellow.
4. Add one drop of the base to the test tube, and gently swirl to mix. Add a drop at a time until you see the colour change to green.
5. When the colour changes to green, the reaction is complete. The acid is neutralized. Record the number of drops of base you added to neutralize the acid.
6. Rinse the test tube, and repeat steps 2 to 5 using 2.0 mL of acid.
7. Rinse the test tube, and repeat steps 2 to 5 using 3.0 mL of acid.
8. Clean up as directed by your teacher.

What Did You Find Out?

1. What is the pH when the base has neutralized the acid? How do you know?
2. What is the link between the volume of base that is needed to neutralize the acid and the volume of the acid? Explain.
3. You used very small volumes of acid and base in this activity. Yet you did not use acids with a pH of 1 and 2 or bases with a pH of 12, 13, or 14. What does this tell you about the strength of acids and bases with these pH values?

Inquiry Focus

Activity 2.17

THE pH OF COMMON SUBSTANCES IN THE HOME

In this activity, you will use pH paper to determine the pH of some common substances in the home. pH paper is another type of acid-base indicator. It has a different colour for each pH.

Safety

What You Need

- variety of common substances (including cleaners used in the home, fruit juices, and soft drinks)
- distilled water
- small beakers
- pH paper cut into small pieces
- spot plate
- dropper with dropper bottles (for each solution)

What To Do

1. Make a table like the one below to record your data. Leave enough space for the number of substances you will be testing.
2. In the first column, write the name of each substance you will be testing.
3. Predict whether each substance is an acid, a base, or neutral. Write your prediction in the "Prediction" column.

Substance	Prediction (Acid, Base, or Neutral)	Colour of pH Paper	pH	Acid, Base, or Neutral?

4. If any substance is a solid or thick paste, mix a small amount of the substance with distilled water in a beaker to form a solution.
5. Place a small square of pH paper in a well of a spot plate.
6. Use the medicine dropper to place two drops of the first substance being tested on the pH paper. Record your results.
7. Repeat steps 5 and 6 for the remaining substances.
8. Clean up as directed by your teacher.
9. Complete the data table using the colour key for the pH paper.

What Did You Find Out?

1. How did your predictions compare with your results? Explain.
2. Describe the pH of cleaners used in the home. Why do you think these cleaners have this pH in common?
3. Draw and label a pH scale from 3 to 11. On your scale, label the pH of each substance you tested.

Investigation 2C

Skills

- ✓ **initiating and planning**
- ✓ **performing and recording**
- ✓ **analyzing and interpreting**
- communicating

Safety

- Clean up any spills immediately.
- Sodium hydroxide can cause blindness.

What You Need

- dilute hydrochloric acid
- dilute sodium hydroxide solution
- other materials, as determined by your procedure

Acid-Base Neutralization Reactions

You have learned that an acid and a base react to form a salt and water. The water is pure water, with a pH of 7 (neutral). How can you determine that a salt is produced? After all, many salts dissolve in water, so they would not be visible. In this investigation, you will design and carry out a procedure to neutralize an acid with a base and then demonstrate that a salt is produced.

What To Do

1. Work in small groups.
2. Design a procedure to neutralize an acid with a base and separate the salt that is produced. Consider safety precautions, as well as proper clean-up and disposal, in your procedure. Make sure that you have your teacher approve your procedure before you begin.
   Hints:
   - See Activity 2.16 on page 170 for help designing your procedure to neutralize an acid with a base.
   - You can separate the salt that is produced by removing all the water from the neutralized solution. Think about how salts are left behind on glasses and kettles.
   - Make a list of the equipment and materials you will need as you design your procedure.
3. Create a table to record your observations.
4. Follow your procedure, and record your results.
5. Clean up, and put away all the equipment. Wash your hands.

What Did You Find Out?

1. What is the pH of the solution that is produced when an acid is neutralized by a base?
2. How do you know that a salt is also produced in the neutralization of an acid with a base?
3. What is the common name of the salt that was produced in this chemical reaction? (**Hint:** Write the chemical formula for the acid and the base. Note that hydrochloric acid is hydrogen chloride gas dissolved in water. Then write a chemical equation for the reaction.)